THE PALACES OF
CRETE

THE
PALACES
OF
CRETE

BY

James Walter Graham

PRINCETON, NEW JERSEY

PRINCETON
UNIVERSITY PRESS

1962

To Ariadne

PREFACE

THE STORY OF Minoan Crete is as new as the twentieth century. Much of importance doubtless remains to be discovered, and much that archaeologists have unearthed they have as yet failed to publish fully in scientific reports. It is not surprising therefore that students of Minoan architecture have hesitated to attempt to present a comprehensive account of the dwellings of the Bronze Age Cretans.

Yet the attempt cannot be postponed indefinitely. And surely the efforts of two generations of such outstanding scholars as Evans, Pernier, Hazzidakis, Chapouthier, Miss Hawes, and their successors, should make it possible, by a careful comparison of similar features wherever they occur, to determine with considerable clarity what is truly typical in Minoan architecture. Likewise by combining every clue which the large number of excavated ruins now makes available, we may endeavor to go a little further in reconstructing in imagination even those important parts of the palaces of which there exist little or no actual remains; but we must constantly remember that for the stability even of "castles in the air," firm foundations are an essential requirement.

In this volume, which it is hoped will prove of interest to the layman and prospective visitor to Crete, as well as to the scholar, footnotes and other scholarly paraphernalia have been kept to a minimum. This has been facilitated by publishing the more complex problems in a series of fully detailed and documented discussions in the *American Journal of Archaeology* (which I have been permitted to draw upon freely) between 1956 and 1961 (see Bibliography), and to these the specialist reader is referred for further information.

The viewpoint of the study is architectural. The first chapter is intended as an introduction for the general reader, and whatever the individual specialist may think of the views of the chronology and history of the Minoan civilization there outlined (a very controversial subject at the moment), these have very little bearing on the conclusions reached in the following chapters. It is on the form of the houses and palaces presented in their final, pre-destruction, phase that I have concentrated; we are not, I think, ready at present to attempt to trace the evolution of Minoan architecture and to relate it closely to the political or social history of the period.[1] Nor are we yet in a position, I believe, to assess the influence of foreign architectures on the development of the Cretan palace, in spite of the confident assertions recently made by several distinguished archaeologists.

With but one or two exceptions all the photographs reproduced in this volume were taken by the author during visits to the island in 1955 and 1959. These trips were made possible by grants from the American Philosophical Society and the University of Toronto, together with a senior fellowship awarded by the Canada Council; to these institutions I express my sincere thanks.

The many individuals to whom I am grateful for assistance in various ways include Professors John L. Caskey and Henry Robinson, the former and the present director of the American School of Classical Studies at Athens, Eugene Vanderpool of the same institution, Nikolaos Platon, the ephor of Cretan Antiquities, and Stylianos Alexiou, now the ephor for Western Crete; and many others connected with the Cretan Antiquities Service, especially Emmanuelis Phigetakis of Siteia, Alexandros Venetikos at Phaistos, Manolis Katsoulis at Mallia, and Eleutherios Synadinakis at Arkhanes. Officials of the British, French, and Italian Schools have also been most helpful, particularly Misses Luisa Banti and Carla Gerra, and Messrs. Hood, Piet de Jong,

[1] Ludwika Press has shown what can be done along this line in two articles cited under his name in the Bibliography.

viii

Levi, Courbin, Daux, Demargne, and Dessenne; and I am grateful for the permission to photograph and to measure freely at the various sites controlled by these Schools, and to draw on their published plans and illustrations for publication. My indebtedness for particular figures is listed at the end of the book, but I am especially glad to be able to reproduce, I believe for the first time, though unfortunately not in the original colors, two of the excellent restorations recently done by Piet de Jong in cooperation with Platon, and now exhibited in the Herakleion Museum (Figs. 44, 45). I am also greatly indebted to the interest of Prof. Hugo-Brunt of the Division of Town-Planning in the University of Toronto, which led him to make for me the axonometric restoration of the Palace of Phaistos, Fig. 55. Miss Frances Brittain, of the staff of the Royal Ontario Museum, has taken great pains in doing the final versions of three of the restored drawings: the perspective of the Palace of Mallia (Fig. 58), that of House Da at Mallia (Fig. 21), and the west entrance of the Palace of Phaistos (Fig. 48). I am likewise grateful to my wife, my daughter Margaret, and my son Robertson for their assistance during the six pleasant weeks we toured the far corners of Crete in our "Volvo" station-wagon in the spring of 1959, and especially to my wife for her criticisms and helpfulness at all stages of my work. The Princeton University Press and particularly Miss Harriet Anderson have always been most encouraging, and Mrs. E. B. Smith, through whose capable hands have passed first the *AJA* articles, and afterwards, as copy editor, the text of this book, has suggested many improvements in the style. To include all these in my thanks is not to incriminate them for the shortcomings that remain.

Prof. Spyridon Marinatos' recent book, *Crete and Mycenae*, with its magnificent plates by Prof. Max Hirmer, only became available to me in the last stages of my work. Most of the translations from Homer are from Lang, Leaf, and Myers' *Iliad*, and Butcher and Lang's *Odyssey*; a few (so marked) are from Rieu's translation in the Pelican Series.

L. R. Palmer's *Mycenaeans and Minoans*, so important for the history and chronology of the Late Bronze Age, appeared when my book was already in proof (Nov. 1961), and I have made no changes in the text of Chapter I. His views, which are based on first-hand knowledge only in the philological field (though he has been careful to consult archaeological authority), do not alter my conviction (1) that there is no significant relationship between the supposedly Luvian palace at Beycesultan and the Minoan palaces, and (2) that architecturally the Palace of Minos remained essentially Minoan (not Mycenaean) down to its last days. Whether there is any valid evidence for the presence of Greeks at Knossos in the half century before 1400—an idea largely (but not wholly) based on the assumption that the Linear B tablets found there were LM II—should be carefully reconsidered (see Chapter I, note 16); I agree with Prof. Palmer that historically it would be much simpler to suppose that the Greeks first invaded Crete about 1400 B.C.

For reasons largely of economy, references within the book are made by chapter and section rather than by page; more exact references can usually be found by consulting the full index. Except for a few well-Anglicized forms like Athens and Mycenae, Greek names have been transliterated directly; the *delta* of modern place-names has, however, been represented by "dh" (pronounced like "th" in "there").

It should be noted, especially by those who use the book at the sites, that detailed descriptions of special rooms or architectural features (such as the "Grand Staircase" at Knossos) may appear in chapters other than those presenting the general description of the building (Chs. ii, iii). Such descriptions can be located through the Index.

J.W.G.

University of Toronto

CONTENTS

CONTENTS

CONTENTS

THE PALACES OF
CRETE

THE LAND, THE PEOPLE, AND THE HISTORY OF MINOAN CRETE

There is a land called Crete in the midst of the wine-dark sea, a fair land and a rich, begirt with water, and therein are many men innumerable, and ninety cities.—(ODYSSEY, 19, 172-174)

SUCH was Crete when Homer sang, nearly three thousand years ago, when the island was still heavily forested with cypress, and when the fertile earth still supported a teeming population.

But even by Homer's day the memory had already grown dim of a time, little more than half a millennium earlier, when Crete had enjoyed a prosperity eclipsing anything in the Aegean area, and could boast a civilization rivaling that of its contemporary, New Kingdom Egypt. Today, the forests have vanished through most of the island, the fertility of the valleys has diminished, and the ninety "cities" have mostly shrunk to small towns.[1] Yet the island is still beautiful. Along its hundreds of miles of rocky shores and gleaming sand beaches the clear blue waters of the Mediterranean still break in white surf, and never is one far from sight or sound of the sea (Figs. 35, 63), for the island is nowhere more than thirty-six miles (58 km.) in width (Fig. 1).

Rugged mountains stretch almost continuously from east to west the entire 160 miles (250 km.) of its length, and allow no room even for a road along much of the nearly harborless south coast. The White Mountains in the west (Fig. 34), traversed by spectacular gorges, leave scant space for man except for a

[1] Paul Faure, "La Crète aux cent villes," *Kret. Chron.*, 13 (1959), pp. 171-217.

3

few small plains along the north coast where the present capital, Khanea, is located; and somewhere in its neighborhood, still undiscovered, lay the important Minoan city of Kydonia with its palace. The range of Ida reaches heights of over 8000 feet (2500 m.) in the center of the island (Fig. 51); but since Crete is wider here, room is left for a considerable plain on the north, where lies Herakleion (Fig. 36), the largest city, with a population of about 40,000, and for a much larger and more fertile valley in the south, the Messara (Fig. 46). It is no accident that in Minoan times Crete's greatest cities, Knossos and Phaistos, were situated in these two plains. East of Ida the range of Dikte, over 7000 feet (2150 m.), encloses the high plain of Lasithi, possibly the site, at Plati, of a Minoan palace (Fig. 30); today it is famous for its potatoes and for the ten thousand windmills that pump water to the thirsty fields in summer. In a coastal plain to the north lies the third largest known palace, that of Mallia (Fig. 56). Across the low isthmus of Hierapetra the mountains stage one final grand upheaval before they slip down steeply into the sea at the east end of the island. The coastal road from Hagios Nikolaos on the Gulf of Mirabello, at the north end of the isthmus, to Siteia near the northeast tip of the island, is perhaps the most spectacular in Crete. Far below, for much of the way, the two tiny islets of Mochlos and Pseira, where the American archaeologist Seager dug early in the century, rise from a sea of unbelievable blues and greens. The absence of palaces in the east is explained by the smallness of the plains; the plain of Siteia is but one thirty-fourth the size of the Messara.[2]

In addition to abundant timber—especially the cypress, highly valued in ancient days for building ships and palaces— the mountains furnished plenty of limestone of good quality and, while little of the fine marble for which the mainland of Greece is famous was available, gypsum quarries supplied a

[2] Wroncka, *BCH*, 83 (1959), p. 538. A bibliography of Cretan geography is given by Philippson, *Die griechischen Landschaften, IV, Das aegäische Meer und seine Inseln* (Frankfurt am Main, 1959), pp. 353-354; but unfortunately no account of Cretan geography is given in this otherwise comprehensive survey of Greece.

handsome and easily worked stone particularly prized for decorative purposes (Fig. 125).

On the highest mountains snow lingers through much of the year (Fig. 51), but in general it is rarely very cold in winter; the latitude, 35° north, is about that of Memphis, Tennessee. In summer the sun's blazing heat, felt especially on the south side facing Africa, is usually relieved by tempering breezes from the surrounding sea. In the west there is a fair annual rainfall, but this tapers off badly toward the east and, thanks to the progressive deforestation, there is little running water during the long summer months. Spring is the botanist's paradise; even the rocky hillsides are carpeted with an amazing variety of wildflowers, many of them of diminutive size.

Though less than half the size of Lake Ontario (Fig. 1, inset) and but two-thirds that of the state of Connecticut, Crete is much the largest of the hundreds of islands that compose the Aegean archipelago, and as the nearest considerable land-mass of Europe to the ancient civilizations of Egypt and the Near East—a half-way house, as it were, between three continents— it is not surprising that it cradled the first European civilization. This historical fact is mirrored mythologically in the quaint tale of the princess of Phoenicia, bearing the significant name of Europa, who was ferried in miraculous fashion from her Asiatic homeland on the back of a handsome white bull—Zeus in bovine disguise according to Greek legend—to Crete, where she became by courtesy of the god the mother of three famous Cretan dynasts, Minos, Rhadamanthys, and Sarpedon.[3]

As early as the Neolithic Period the island was inhabited by a scattered population living partly in caves, but also concentrated at Knossos in one of the largest Neolithic settlements in the eastern Mediterranean area. Little is known of the origins of these first settlers, but the associations suggested by the pottery and other artifacts are with Anatolia and possibly Egypt rather than with the Greek mainland; considerable reinforcements seem to have arrived perhaps from the same areas about

[3] Marinatos, *RA*, 34 (1949), pp. 5-18.

the beginning of the Bronze Age, that is sometime after 3000 B.C. A recent study of place-names suggests that a considerable element in the Cretan population was related to the Luvians who, at any rate in the Middle and Late Bronze Ages, were established in Asia Minor southwest of the Hittites, where one of their cities, at Beycesultan, is currently being excavated by British archaeologists (Fig. 1, inset).[4]

Cultural development through the third millennium (3000-2000 B.C.) was "accelerando" and the population increased and spread throughout the island in this Early Bronze or Early "Minoan" period. Sir Arthur Evans, who more than anyone else is responsible for the recovery of this forgotten civilization, devised a system of chronology into which to fit his discoveries which is still generally followed, though many have grave doubts about certain details such as the date of the beginning of Early Minoan. Here in round numbers, adequate for our purposes, is the scheme, named of course from the famous legendary king of Knossos:

Early Minoan (E.M.)   3000-2000 B.C.
Middle Minoan (M.M.)   2000-1600 B.C.
Late Minoan (L.M.)   1600-1200 B.C.

These three divisions correspond roughly to, and in fact were suggested by, Old Kingdom, Middle Kingdom, and New Kingdom Egypt, and the tentative dates are largely dependent upon lists of pharaohs and their regnal years as recorded by the Egyptians.

Little is yet known of the architecture of Crete during the Early Minoan period (Fig. 33), still less of its history, government, and religion, matters which the material remains unearthed by the archaeologist can only dimly and very imperfectly illumine.[5] The consistent improvement of pottery in quality,

---

[4] Mellaart, *AJA*, 62 (1958), pp. 9-33; cf. Palmer, *Mycenaeans and Minoans* (London, 1961), chap. VII, 3.

[5] On the basis of his recent excavations at Phaistos Doro Levi would practically eliminate the Early Minoan period since the "Neolithic" (rightly so called?) pottery seems directly to underlie Middle Minoan at that site and elsewhere, *Nuova Antologia*, 467 (1956), pp. 221-240; cf. *PdP*, 71 (1960), p. 116.

shape, and decoration throughout the period, however, is an index of the general cultural progress. Quantities of handsome vessels in a variety of shapes were made from beautifully veined and colored stones—a craft long practised by the Egyptians; and gold jewelry and ornaments found in E.M. graves exhibit remarkably advanced craftsmanship both in design and execution.

The significant but unspectacular developments of this "prepalatial" period may be compared to the heat which builds up unseen within a great stack of hay until it explodes spontaneously into a brilliant burst of flame. About 2000 B.C. such a "cultural explosion"—not without parallel in the history of other civilizations—occurred. At the very beginning of the Middle Minoan period fairly large and substantial palaces spring into being, and a system of writing appears. No doubt the latter was triggered by developments in Egypt where an intricate system had been in use for a millennium; yet the Cretan shows little resemblance in the form of the characters to the Egyptian and develops quite on its own into a reasonably efficient syllabic method of writing known to the archaeologist as Linear A.

But nothing, so far as the available archaeological record goes, is so eloquent of the new progress as pottery. The most significant variety is called Kamares Ware, named from a cave sanctuary on the south slopes of Mt. Ida facing Phaistos (Fig. 51), where quantities of this pottery were dedicated. The love of color and movement, so characteristic of Cretan art, is brilliantly illustrated. A common shape is a bridge-spouted, two-handled jar with a strongly swelling profile, painted in white, red, and orange against a black background (Fig. 153, A). Though resembling vegetable or animal forms, often in swirling patterns which suggest the vitality of nature, the designs are strongly formalized and excellently suited to the shape of the vase. This happy union of nature and convention is typical of Cretan art at its best, though at times the feeling becomes much more informal, and architecture is always predominantly informal.

Our knowledge of the history of the Middle Minoan period is almost as meager as that of the preceding period. Of material and artistic progress and of the growth of population there can be no doubt, and the brilliant development of the palaces and the mansions of the rich by the end of the age bears witness to a level of civilization reached by the aristocracy comparable to that found in contemporary Egypt and Mesopotamia. Such finds as Kamares pottery discovered in association with the monuments of Middle Kingdom pharaohs, a statue of an Egyptian merchant[5a] of the twelfth or thirteenth dynasty found in the Palace of Minos, a Babylonian sealstone about the time of Hammurabi in a Cretan tomb, and objects of Cretan style in the Shaft Graves of Mycenae around 1600 B.C., show that Crete was in contact with her neighbors on all sides, and incidentally provide badly needed clues for dating the development of Minoan civilization.

Cretan ships were probably responsible for most of the transferal of such goods as these to and from Crete. The scarcity of identifiable fortifications or of other signs of martial activity on the island is usually interpreted, especially in the following period (L.M.), as meaning that Crete possessed a fleet of warships with which she fended off her enemies; yet this picture of Crete as the first Mediterranean sea power, supported though it is by ancient Greek historians, is far from proven.[6] In any case it may be doubted whether Egypt or any other of the Near Eastern nations during the period 2000 to 1400 B.C. ever had the power, the opportunity, and the incentive to mount an organized naval expedition against an island so well removed from their shores as Crete.

[5a] Hardly an official, as Evans thought; see Ward, *Orientalia*, 30 (1961), pp. 28-29. On the date of the statue see Pendlebury in *Studies presented to D. M. Robinson* (ed. G. E. Mylonas, St. Louis, 1951), I, p. 189.

[6] Starr, "The Myth of the Minoan Thalassocracy," *Historia*, 3 (1954-1955), pp. 282-291, and *Origins of Greek Civilization* (New York, 1961), p. 38. However, Lionel Casson holds to the traditional view, largely on the grounds of the lack of fortifications, *The Ancient Mariners* (New York, 1959), p. 31; he also reviews the general question of Cretan relations with her neighbors (pp. 21-24). As for the lack of fortifications see Lawrence, *Gr. Arch.*, p. 24; and Marinatos, *Crete and Mycenae*, New York, 1960, p. 28. But cf. Press, *Archeologia*, 10 (1958), p. 61.

But another growing power was closer at hand. On a clear day the mountains of western Crete can actually be seen from the southeastern tip of the Greek mainland (Fig. 1, inset), and since about 2000 B.C. the dominant element of the mainland population had been a Greek speaking people. Their descendants, the Greeks of the Classical period (first millennium B.C.), however brilliant they may have been, can scarcely be accused of having been a peaceful folk. Nor were their Bronze Age ancestors, from the first bands who conquered new homes with fire and sword at the beginning of the Middle Bronze Age to those who toward the end of the Late Bronze (thirteenth century B.C.) sacked and burned the citadel of Troy.

It is therefore not an unlikely hypothesis that a destruction of the Palace of Minos which occurred toward the end of the M.M. period, that is sometime in the early seventeenth century, was due to a piratical, sea-borne raid by the "Mycenaean" Greeks of the mainland, or, since Crete was subject to periodic devastating earthquakes, that the Greek raiders followed in the track of a severe quake which had left the Cretan cities temporarily defenceless. On this hypothesis some of the masses of gold and other treasure found by Schliemann in the royal Shaft Graves inside the citadel of Mycenae, the leading city of the mainland, would represent part of the loot. Indeed a recent ingenious theory, for which there is some evidence at the Egyptian end, goes further and suggests that the temporary shift in the balance of power between Crete and the Greek mainland was partly responsible for the expulsion of the Asiatic Hyksos from Lower Egypt where they had ruled for a century, and for the consequent founding of a new Egyptian dynasty (the eighteenth) initiating the New Kingdom. According to this theory the Hyksos had been favored by Crete (the lid of an Egyptian alabaster vessel bearing the cartouche of the Hyksos king Khyan was discovered in the ruins of the Palace of Minos), whereas the native Egyptians were now aided by the Greeks who, like the Classical Greeks a millennium later, served as mercenaries in the Egyptian army. This would also help to explain the numerous traces of Egyptian (as well as Cretan) influence in the Mycenaean Shaft Grave burials.[7]

The last and the most brilliant, if not the most prosperous, phase of the Minoan civilization is that of the Late Minoan period, about 1600-1200 B.C. Extensive excavations, thousands of inscribed tablets, and numerous traditions preserved by the Classical Greeks, combine to throw a flood of light (comparatively speaking) on this period. In spite of this it is impossible at the present time even to outline with any confidence the history of the final glory, decline, and fall of the Minoan civilization, for recent happenings have thrown all the ideas about this period that seemed to be safely established back into the melting pot for reinterpretation. The following sketch, therefore, is offered with the full realization that much of it may shortly be contradicted by evidence not yet available to the writer.

Expressive of the level of refinement and culture attained in the first century of the Late Minoan period, following the rebuilding of the palaces on lines more splendid than before and the appearance of many handsome new mansions throughout the island,[8] are the beautiful naturalistic pottery styles known as the Floral (L.M. Ia) and the Marine (L.M. Ib). A magnificent example of the latter is the Octopus Vase discovered in the ruins of the modest little town of Gournia (Fig. 153, B): the Cretan potter with his Midas touch has transformed the repulsive creature of the deep into a thing of beauty, into a living pattern whose eight tentacles surround and confine the globular vase as naturally as its skin envelopes an orange. A Mycenaean Greek rendering of the same subject already displays the Classical Greek preference for symmetry and geometric form (Fig. 153, C). Both representations are beautiful, but in quite different ways.

[7] Cf. Schachermeyr, *Archiv Orientálni*, 17[2] (1949), pp. 331-350.

[8] Marinatos suggests that many of these mansions, often spaced 7 to 10 miles apart, were centers of local administration, *C. and M.*, pp. 18, 66.

For all its brilliance this first phase of the new epoch was also, for most of the important centers except Knossos, virtually their final stage as well. That these flourishing cities and towns were suddenly destroyed is clear from their remains, but the cause of such a general catastrophe is less obvious. The eminent Greek archaeologist and explorer of many Cretan sites, Professor Spyridon Marinatos, has recently put forward the attractive hypothesis that it was the result of a violent explosion on the island of Thera (modern Santorini) in the Aegean Sea directly north of Crete.[9] The evidence for a cataclysmic eruption in which the major part of the island disappeared in one or more gigantic blasts is clear from the excavations on Thera made by the Germans in the 1890's, and has been dated to approximately 1500 B.C. Like the catastrophic eruption of Krakatoa in the Dutch East Indies in 1883 tremendous "tidal waves" must have been generated, which Marinatos believes would have been far greater in the case of the eruption of Thera. The entire north coast of Crete, hardly more than thirty miles away, was exposed to the full force of these titanic waves.

In the Villa at Amnisos, only a few yards from the sea (Fig. 76), massive blocks of the stone foundations were found by Marinatos to have been shifted out of place, and quantities of volcanic pumice, carried in by the flood, mantled the ruins. The waves must have traveled far inland over the lower parts of the island, overwhelming many other sites including Mallia, Gournia, Nirou Khani, and Palaikastro.

Such a terrific onslaught of nature would have at least temporarily crippled the social, economic, and political life of Crete. How many tens of thousands of its inhabitants may have perished we shall never know. Since coastal communities would have been the hardest hit we may suppose that for a time Cretan contacts with its neighbors were abruptly severed. Is this the long sought origin of the Lost Island of Atlantis? According to the tale told by the Egyptians a millennium later to the

[9] *Antiquity*, 13 (1939), pp. 425-439; *C. and M.*, pp. 20, 22; *Kret. Chron.*, 4 (1950), pp. 195-213.

Greek sage, Solon, Atlantis, though a large, populous, and powerful island, in the course of a single dreadful day and night and after a series of calamitous earthquakes and inundations, disappeared forever beneath the sea.[10]

But what of the fact that other Cretan sites, surely high above the reach of the ravaging waves, were also destroyed at a perhaps slightly later date or dates, including Sklavokambos, Tylissos, and Hagia Triadha. Even the great palace at Phaistos, on its hilltop site, was destroyed sometime in the fifteenth century and never rebuilt. Was this due to the earthquakes which often follow such eruptions? Or was it the result of the Mycenaean Greeks' seizing the opportunity to invade the island when Cretan defences were down, especially if, as ancient tradition claims,[6] she depended on a navy for her protection.

The Palace of Minos, too, three miles from the sea and enclosed by high hills, seems to have been seriously damaged somewhat later still, about the year 1400 B.C.[11] Perhaps the damage to the palace at this time was not nearly so extensive, however, as its excavators have thought, and Sir Arthur Evans himself was constrained to admit that the building had been reoccupied to some extent, though in his opinion this was but a degenerate "squatter" occupation. Professor L. R. Palmer of Oxford University has lately challenged this opinion.[12] He suggests that the palace was inhabited throughout the closing centuries of the Bronze Age by a dynasty of Mycenaean Greek rulers who adapted the Minoan system of writing to suit (rather badly) their own language, and continued to keep administrative

[10] The equation Atlantis = Crete was made long ago; see Frost, *JHS*, 33 (1913), pp. 189-206. But it still seems reasonable; see Marinatos, *Kret. Chron.*, 4 (1950), pp. 195-213.

[11] The relative dating of the destruction of the various sites is a much disputed point; see Levi, *Boll. d'Arte*, 44 (1959), pp. 253-264.

[12] Orally, in the public press, and in multigraphed statements circulated privately; a definitive expression of his views will perhaps not be published until certain manuscript notebooks of Sir Arthur Evans and possibly others, relative to the excavations at Knossos, are published; cf. Hood, *Antiquity*, 35 (1961), pp. 80-81, for a contrary view and for bibliography. See now Palmer, *Mycenaeans and Minoans*, especially chap. VI.

records as the native Cretan kings had done before them—a practice which spread to the Greek rulers of the mainland.

Signs of the inevitable change in spirit at Knossos, due to the installation of this foreign and warlike Mycenaean dynasty, did not go entirely unobserved by Evans and others, though they interpreted them differently. Pendlebury referred to the L.M. II "Palace Style" pottery, conspicuous for its grandiose character and pompous monumentality, as the "pottery of empire";[13] significantly, this pottery has rarely been found in Crete except at Knossos, though it is common on the Greek mainland. Evans noticed similar changes in the wall paintings of the L.M. II period, illustrated for example in the stiff, symmetrical composition of the Griffin Fresco in the Knossos Throne Room (Fig. 130), which has since been found at Pylos on the mainland. "As compared with the great artistic traditions, such as characterized the preceding Palace stage . . . ," he remarks, "the new work takes a severely regulated shape. Lost is the free spirit that had given birth to the finely modelled forms of the athletes in the East Hall groups and to the charging bull of the North Portico. Vanished is the power of individual characterization and of instantaneous portraiture that we recognize in the lively Miniature groups of the Court Ladies. Departed, too, is the strong sympathy with wild Nature. . . . A sacral and conventional style now prevails . . . grandiose conceptions . . . the wholesale adoption . . . of the processional scheme. . . ."[14] The aesthetic feeling in the murals and pottery is indeed so distinct that a close student of the development of Cretan pottery styles, Arne Furumark, commented on the "colossal change in mentality that had taken place during one or two generations."[15]

Recognized also was a *volte-face* in the previous peaceful character of the Minoan civilization. The appearance of "warrior tombs," of military elements in the wall paintings, of clay tablets recording military equipment, all sound a new militaristic note

[13] *A. of C.*, p. 208.
[14] *Knossos*, IV, p. 880.
[15] *Op. Arch.*, 6 (1950), p. 258.

which Evans sought to explain as due to a sudden wave of imperialism infecting the Lords of Knossos: the appearance of a new and aggressive dynasty which proceeded to conquer and destroy the other Minoan palaces and to develop a great maritime empire.[16]

The Greek historian, Thucydides, writing in the fifth century B.C., remarked that the navy of Minos was the first to control the seas.[17] But Thucydides is likely to have been wrong, unless we interpret this as meaning a Greek "Minos." At any rate the navy that dominated the East Mediterranean in the Late Bronze Age was surely that of the Mycenaean confederacy; and the discovery, thanks to Ventris' brilliant decipherment of "Linear B" in 1952,[18] that thousands of the tablets found at Knossos were written in Mycenaean Greek, makes it certain that the "new and aggressive dynasty" was not native Cretan but composed of invaders from the mainland—a conclusion diametrically opposed to Evans' tenaciously held conviction that the mainland had been colonized and ruled by the Minoans.

The picture, then, which seems to be emerging of Crete in the latter part of the Late Minoan period is that it was dominated by Greek-speaking rulers ruling from a single center, namely Knossos; and that there occurred a gradual spread of Mycenaean Greek influence throughout the island, accompanied by a weakening of the native Cretan culture. The loss of population from the tidal catastrophe of 1500 seems to have been more than made good.

It is not surprising, therefore, that when Agamemnon summoned his vassal kings to join him in the war against Troy,

[16] *Knossos*, IV, pp. 884-888. However, some of the signs of change I have mentioned above should perhaps be attributed to the LM III rather than to the LM II period; and if Palmer (*Mycenaeans and Minoans*, especially pp. 210-215) is correct the seizure of Knossos by the Greeks from the mainland occurred about 1400 (marked by a partial destruction of the palace) rather than about 1450. According to Palmer (p. 214), agreeing with Furumark, the "peaceful and fruitful coexistence (of Crete and the mainland) degenerated (about 1450) into rivalry and conflict, resulting in the victory of the mainland *c.* 1400" (the parentheses are mine). The more military aspect of Knossos during this half century could then be due to an attempt to prepare to meet the threat from the mainland.
[17] I, 4.   [18] Ventris and Chadwick, *JHS*, 73 (1953), pp. 84-103.

sometime after the middle of the thirteenth century, Homer represents Idomeneus, "grandson of Minos," as joining him: "And of the Cretans Idomeneus the famous spearman was leader, even of them that possessed Knossos and Gortys of the great walls, Lyktos and Miletos and chalky Lykastos and Phaistos and Rhytion, stablished cities all; and of all others that dwelt in Crete of the hundred cities. . . . With these followed eighty black ships."[19]

Not many years after the return of the Greek leaders from Troy, that is about 1200 B.C., Knossos shared the fate of Mycenae, Tiryns, Pylos, and many another "stablished city": to be sacked and burned by the invading Dorian Greeks. But the blaze that destroyed the palaces at Knossos and Pylos also baked thousands of the clay tablets containing the records of royal administration, and so they were preserved for the archaeologist to find and painfully but eagerly decipher more than three thousand years later.

If this interpretation of Cretan history from about 1600-1200 B.C. proves to be near the truth it naturally follows that the architectural stage presented by the ruins of the Palace of Minos is not exactly comparable to that presented by the other palaces, since these were destroyed some two centuries earlier. Indeed we might expect to observe certain Mycenaean Greek architectural features in the ruins at Knossos, and something of a case could perhaps be made out in favor of such a view. Details which, in the present state of our knowledge (or ignorance), are common to Knossos and the mainland palaces, but are elsewhere unknown in Crete, include fluted column shafts and the triglyph half-rosette frieze (Fig. 136, A,B), as well as mural decorations such as the Shield Fresco, and the Griffin Fresco which "guards" the throne both at Knossos and Pylos. Some would even add the Knossos Throne Room plan as a whole. Surely, however, its resemblance to the Mycenaean "megaron" is very slight,[20] in spite of the fact that if the Mycenaean dynasts

---

[19] *Iliad*, 2, 645-652.
[20] Reusch in *Minoica*, pp. 334-358; but cf. Blegen, *ibid.*, p. 66.

of Knossos did any extensive remodeling or repairing of the Palace of Minos, as a result of a destruction about 1400, we might well expect them to have introduced the megaron, so indispensable a feature of their own palaces (Fig. 150).[21] Its conspicuous absence reassures us, in my opinion, that we are right in treating the Palace of Minos as essentially a Minoan palace; and I find it highly unlikely that even such features as the fluting of columns or the carving of the triglyph half-rosette frieze were introduced into Crete from Mycenaean architecture.

If we can accept the hypothesis of an occupation of Crete by Mycenaean Greeks for a period of more than two centuries during the Late Bronze Age this will have to be considered as a factor of considerable significance in the development of western civilization. Contact with Crete had undoubtedly been largely responsible for the first beginnings of culture amongst the rude Greek-speaking folk who began to enter the peninsula of Greece sometime about 2000 B.C., and for the development of a rudimentary civilization there by the end of the Middle Bronze Age, the time of the famous Shaft Graves of Mycenae. But the infinitely closer contacts arising from a prolonged residence of Mycenaeans of the ruling class in Crete itself would result in a far more intensive and extensive transference of Cretan ways of life to the less cultured Greeks. The more obvious effects of this would appear in architecture, wall painting, pottery, gem engraving, etc., and, we should add, in the art of writing. But in the less directly provable fields of thought and behavior, the influence is also likely to have been great: in religion and law, for example, and probably in oral (and written?) literature—how much may the Homeric epic owe to a succession of nameless Minoan predecessors?[22]

Something of the rich Minoan heritage perhaps continued to affect the development of Greek culture down to early Classical times; but eventually Crete became little more than a back-

---

[21] See Mylonas, *Ancient Mycenae*, pp. 51-59.
[22] Severyns, *Grèce et Proche-Orient avant Homère*, Brussels, 1960, pp. 99-100, 171, 204. On the date of the coming of the Greeks see Palmer, *Mycenaeans and Minoans*, chap. VII; he would put it about 1600 B.C.

water of Hellenism, though some of the "true" Cretans (the "Eteocretans") lived on in the eastern part of the island and continued to speak a non-Greek tongue. Through the Roman and later periods Crete in general shared the fate of the Greek mainland, though it was not until 1896 and after many bloody revolts that it was freed from foreign domination; in 1912 it finally became part of the modern Greek nation.

Today Greek archaeologists from both the mainland and from Crete itself are busily engaged in recovering the long and varied history of the island. British, French, and Italian excavators have resumed the investigations interrupted by the last war, and the magnificent treasures of Minoan art are worthily displayed in a new museum at Herakleion under the capable direction of Nikolaos Platon.

We have spoken of the land and the history of Crete, but what sort of people were the Minoan Cretans who dwelt in the palaces and houses we shall visit in the following pages? Perhaps this is a question which should not be asked in a book which seeks to maintain an architectural point of view and does not pretend to be a social study. Perhaps it is a question which should not be asked at all since the Minoans cannot speak directly to us through a written literature—if they produced one—and since even the Greeks of Pericles' day knew of the Minoan civilization only what a meager stream of oral tradition had passed on to them, for the art of writing was lost in the "Dark Ages" that separated the Bronze Age culture from the Classical. Yet to rebuild in imagination these homes of 3500 years ago, only to leave them desolate and deserted, seems so unsatisfying that we can scarcely do other than grasp at whatever clues may be available.

A Greek historian of the time of Julius Caesar, Diodorus Siculus, repeats the tradition that the days of Minos coincided with the Golden Age of Cronus, father of the sky-god Zeus (the Roman Jupiter) who, it was said, was born in Crete. And since Diodorus remarks that "all the subjects of the rule of

Cronus lived a life of blessedness, in the unhindered enjoyment of every pleasure," this has given rise to an impression that the Minoans were an enervated and decadent race of hedonists.[23] Yet their "life of pleasure" (a modern would consider it simple indeed) is pictured by Diodorus as a reward of virtue: "because of the exceptional obedience to laws no injustice was committed by any one at any time."[24] Surely the tradition is not to be interpreted as meaning that the Cretans because of their virtue were privileged henceforth to lead a life of depravity!

The law-abiding character of the Cretans is also attested by the tradition that Minos "established not a few laws for the Cretans, claiming (Moses-like) that he had received them from his father Zeus when conversing with him in a certain cave."[25] The probity of Minos and of his brother Rhadamanthys (king of Phaistos?)[26] was posthumously recognized by making them perpetual judges in the Greek afterworld. It is also significant that the earliest known Classical Greek law code (ca. 500 B.C.) was found at Gortyn, a site where a large Minoan farmhouse has recently been excavated.

It should also be set down to the credit of the Minoans that, in the words of Sir Arthur Evans, their ever valiant and doughty champion, "from the beginning to the end of Minoan Art (there is) . . . not one single example . . . of any subject of an indecorous nature."[27]

Whether or not the Cretans were a highly religious people is difficult to decide on material evidence alone. On the one hand the entire absence of temples and of statues of gods is strikingly at variance with the situation in contemporary Egypt and Mesopotamia; on the other hand we seem scarcely able to move in the Palace of Minos, at least under the guidance of Sir Arthur, without running into small shrines or small representations of deities or their symbols: lustral chambers, pillar crypts, columnar shrines, temple repositories, incurved altars, sacral horns, double-axes, libation tables, baetylic stones, sacral

[23] 5, 66, 6.   [24] *loc. cit.*   [25] Diod. Sic. 5, 78, 3.
[26] See note 3, above.   [27] *Knossos*, II, p. 279.

knots, etc., not to mention representations of sacred birds, trees, bulls, and snakes. Religious scenes are common on gems and other forms of Minoan art (Figs. 100, 101). Possibly the fact that the Cretans built no great temples and carved no large statues of their deities merely indicates that they stood in no immoderate awe of the supernatural.

We have already referred to the fact that the Cretans seem to have been a remarkably peaceful people. The apparently exceptional change in spirit that took place in Late Minoan II or III merely proves the rule for, as we have seen, the military, imperialist character which Evans thought had led to a forceful conquest of the Greek mainland, was on the contrary apparently due to the Mycenaean invaders' having established themselves at Knossos.

This peaceful character is as strange in the world of the Bronze Age Egyptians, Babylonians, Assyrians, Mycenaean Greeks, Hittites, and, we may add, Hebrews, as in the world of the Classical Greeks and Romans, or in the distracted world of today—so strange indeed that it has encouraged the charge that the Minoans were decadent and enervated. Alas for more such "decadence"! Perhaps it was due in part to the isolated position of Crete and to the lack of any excessive pressure of population, but more I think to the homogeneity of the Minoan people. No doubt they came ultimately from a variety of racial stocks, but the continuity of the archaeological strata from earliest times suggests that the bulk of the population had lived on the island long enough to have become essentially homogeneous in language and in customs;[27a] one important illustration of this is the remarkable similarity in architectural forms throughout Crete but especially among the three major palaces. The peaceful co-existence of the two kingdoms of Phaistos and Knossos, hardly over twenty-five miles (40 km.) apart as the crow flies, may be compared to the century and a half of peaceful

[27a] A striking illustration of the close interconnections between the different Minoan centers is the finding of impressions from identical seal-stones at Sklavo-kambos, H. Triadha, Gournia, and Zakros (see Fig. 1), *DMG*, p. 110.

relations that have, for the same reasons, prevailed between Canada and its neighbor to the south.[28]

It is often possible to judge something of the character of an individual or of a people from their dress. The typical Cretan costume of the court class, an elaborately patterned short kilt for the men (Fig. 131, B), and a long elaborately flounced garment for the women which covered the legs entirely but left the breasts bare (Fig. 43), presents a rather odd medley of primitive and sophisticated elements, and this is probably also true of their general outlook, religious and social. They were obviously a brilliant, gifted people living in a physically beautiful and stimulating environment, but the transition from a condition of simple peasantry to a relatively complex urban society, at least in the upper levels of the social scale, was rapid and recent. The transformation was naturally not complete.

The considerable degree of urbane elegance reached by this society is revealed in their domestic architecture. From the spacious and commodious design of the living quarters of the palaces and better houses, often adorned with alabaster veneering and plaster walls painted with scenes from nature or court ceremonial (Figs. 131-134), provided with bathrooms and toilets and with ingenious devices to secure adequate lighting and ventilation, and looking out through columned porticoes upon terraced and beautiful landscapes, it is clear that the Cretans aimed at comfortable living. The great suites of state reception halls and banquet halls, which must be left largely to our imagination to picture, for they were on the lost upper floors,

[28] Yet A. W. Lawrence writes, "It is incredible that there can have been three separate independent states so close together in central Crete"; he suggests that Phaistos was the winter residence for the dynasty that reigned at Knossos in summer. (*Gk. Arch.*, pp. 24-25). To me it seems more incredible that the same dynasty should have possessed two or even three palaces, so similar in plan "that their functions must have been almost identical" (Lawrence). What a biennial moving day that must have been when the whole court transferred itself bag and baggage across the 2000 foot pass of Mt. Ida from Knossos to Phaistos and vice versa!—and when did they trek to Mallia? On the other hand the H. Triadha villa, so near Phaistos and surely of royal character, is a distinctly different type of structure and might well have served as a pleasant occasional retreat from the official residence.

would tell the same story. But this can hardly be called luxuriant debauchery.

They were not a soft, lazy people, however much they may contrast with the vigorous and bellicose Mycenaean Greeks. Fat bellies, as common in Egyptian officialdom, to judge from their art, as in America today, are rarely seen in Cretan art. Characteristically the Cretans are shown with shoulders carried far back, with slim limbs, and a waist so small that some suspect the Minoans of practising artificial constriction (Fig. 131, B). Boxing, dancing, acrobatics, and bull-leaping we know from direct representations were popular, while the traditions of the great athletic festivals of Classical Greek times perhaps point to Crete as their ultimate place of origin. Many think that Homer has the Cretans in mind when he draws his delightful picture of the mythical Phaeacians in the *Odyssey*. They boast that they "excel all men in boxing, and wrestling, and leaping, and speed of foot," though it is true that after viewing Odysseus' prowess they tone down their claims somewhat, "for we are no perfect boxers, nor wrestlers, but speedy runners, and the best of seamen; and dear to us ever is the banquet, and the harp, and the dance, and changes of raiment, and the warm bath, and love, and sleep."[29]

Finally it may be noted that women played an important part in Cretan society. Goddesses seem to have had the dominant role in Cretan religion, and their ministrants were as predominantly priestesses (Figs. 100, 101); female likewise were the sacred dancers. Even in the dangerous bull games lady toreadors took part, while in the audience women mingled with the men, and the special "boxes" were reserved for ladies of the court (Fig. 133). The elaborate costumes of the female aristocracy likewise indicate the importance of women (Figs. 100, 101, 131, A). The assured place which they held in Mycenaean society, to judge from the Homeric epics, probably owed much to the example of the polished culture of the Minoan courts.

[29] *Odyssey*, 8, 102-103, 246-249.

A strong hint of this is found in one of the scenes on the famous Shield of Achilles, as described in the *Iliad*, which is actually placed at Knossos itself: "Also did the glorious lame god (Hephaistos) devise a dancing-place like unto that which once in wide Knossos Daidalos wrought for Ariadne of the lovely tresses. There were youths dancing and maidens of costly wooing, their hands upon one another's wrists. Fine linen the maidens had on, and the youths well-woven doublets faintly glistening with oil. Fair wreaths had the maidens, and the youths daggers of gold hanging from silver baldrics. And now would they run round with deft feet exceeding lightly . . . and now anon they would run in lines to meet each other. And a great company stood round the lovely dance in joy; and among them a divine minstrel was making music on his lyre (Fig. 100), and through the midst of them, leading the measure, two tumblers whirled."[30]

[30] *Iliad*, 18, 590-606.

CHAPTER II

THE MAJOR PALACES

1. THE PALACE OF MINOS AT KNOSSOS

The mighty city of Knossos wherein Minos ruled in nine-year periods, he who held converse with mighty Zeus.—(ODYSSEY, 19, 178-179)

AT ATHENS with its wealth of remains of Classical Greece the traveler can board a plane and in less than two hours find himself a thousand years back in time at the court of King Minos of Crete. To fly to the island of Daedalus and Icarus has a certain appropriateness. It also affords splendid panoramas of sea and islands en route, and for many miles the view to the south embraces the whole length of the island of Crete with the three great mountain masses of Dikte, Ida, and the White Mountains standing out high above all else.

A more intimate and leisurely first look at Crete is provided by a comfortable Greek steamer which will bring one in the early morning light, after an overnight trip from Athens, to Soudha Bay near the west end of the island (Fig. 1). Then, after several hours sail along the north coast, the harborage of Retimo is reached, and toward noon the northern slopes of Mt. Ida loom in the distance. Bare hills dip steeply down into a sea of indigo blue through which the ship ploughs a wake of white foam; and shortly before Herakleion is reached the isolated mountain of Iuktas, conspicuous also from Knossos, takes on the profile of a gigantic recumbent human face—according to the Classical Greeks, that of Zeus himself.

23

Gliding into the harbor through a narrow gap in the break-water, the ship berths beside Venetian walls from which the Lion of St. Mark still looks down. Though hard hit in the last war Herakleion is now largely rebuilt and well supplied with small hotels. At a restaurant west of the harbor one can eat to the music of the pounding surf, or on the main square enjoy a meal in the open beside a quaint old Venetian fountain appropriately carved with Nereids and other beings of the sea.

The chief attraction of Herakleion to most visitors is the newly built, well lighted, and attractively arranged Archae-ological Museum with its fabulous treasures of Minoan art. An Historical Museum also provides interesting displays representing the Venetian, Turkish, and modern periods, while extensive Venetian fortifications are still to be seen.

The site of the Minoan city of Knossos, whose population in its heyday might be more conservatively estimated at about half the 80,000 generously accorded it by Sir Arthur Evans,[1] lies some three miles (5 km.) inland, and can be reached in a few minutes by car or public bus. The palace was far from spectacularly situated on a low hill which slopes off fairly steeply on the east and south to the small stream known as the Kairetos. For even a glimpse of the sea or of Mt. Ida one must climb one of the bare hills that now rise bleakly on all sides (Fig. 36). A scattering of small houses, a guardroom and pavilion for visitors, a grove of pine trees that have grown up since the excavations and through which the winds blow gratefully in the summer heat: that is all (Fig. 37).

Inevitably one wonders why such a site should have been thickly populated from Neolithic times. However, there is a considerable amount of good agricultural land in the vicinity (better watered in antiquity); also it enjoyed a position conveniently near the bay at the mouth of the Kairetos which supplied the best outlet for central Crete on the Aegean side, and

---

[1] *Knossos*, II, pp. 563-564; cf. Faure, *Kret. Chron.*, 13 (1959), p. 210, who estimates 30,000.

commanded the cross-island road which ran from this port to Phaistos in the Messara plain and on to the southern beaches that looked toward distant Africa.

It is certain, at any rate, that Homer's "mighty city" was the outstanding city of Crete in Minoan times. To the Greeks its semi-mythical founder and ruler, Minos, was the son of their principal deity, Zeus, and enjoyed his confidence. Indeed most of the familiar mythical tales associated with Crete center about Knossos: Glaukos who was drowned in a jar of honey (one of his father's giant "pithoi"?—Fig. 93); Daedalus, builder of the Labyrinth to house the Minotaur and father of Icarus who flew too near the sun; and Theseus, the Athenian hero, who slew the Minotaur with the help of Minos' daughter, "Ariadne of the lovely tresses."

No wonder then that the name of Knossos is well known, and that many visitors are content to see its legend-haunted ruins and look no farther. Sir Arthur Evans, who spent the last forty years of his life and a large fortune in excavating, preserving, and sumptuously publishing the site, has contributed no little to its fame through his own colorful career, which lack of space prevents us from recounting here.[2] Since Sir Arthur throve on controversy it is not surprising that much of what he wrote and did here has provoked dissension. The present study will not infrequently disagree with his pronouncements. The four-volume (in six), three thousand page publication, *The Palace of Minos at Knossos*, is both magnificent and exasperating[3]; it is at once an encyclopedia covering the whole range of Minoan antiquities, and at the same time it often omits details essential to the understanding of the Palace of Minos itself. It provides no plan of the building adequate for serious study, and the architectural description is distributed throughout the six books in a fashion which without the Ariadne's clew furnished

[2] See the recent biography by his half-sister, Joan Evans, *Time and Chance*, London, 1943.
[3] Cf. Levi, *PdP*, 71 (1960), p. 95.

by a seventh *Index Volume* would leave the user almost as lost in labyrinthine meanderings as the youths and maidens of the ancient tale.

Much of the criticism has been leveled at his restorations or, as he preferred to term them, "reconstitutions." They have been called unnecessary, ugly, and downright wrong, and occasionally perhaps they are all three. Yet after considerable study both of the actual ruins and of Evans' writings I cannot help but agree on the whole with the judgment of Georg Karo,[4] the distinguished former director of the German Archaeological Institute, of whom Nilsson says, "no living scholar knows the course of excavations in Crete so well."[5] Karo caustically comments that many of the most vocal critics are "unencumbered by knowledge of the facts," and that he himself is perhaps the only living scholar who knows what brain-racking (*Kopfzerbrechung*) each new phase of the excavations brought because of the extremely perishable nature of the remains. Without restoration, he declares, the site would be little today but a heap of ruins. "If one will examine the immense remains carefully to see how many restorations were essential and mandatory he will find surprisingly little that was unnecessary." Certainly it cannot be doubted that the restorations add much to the interest of the ordinary visitor; if he is occasionally misled this will be outweighed by what he is helped to comprehend correctly. Unrestored buildings are often, in their way, quite as misleading as over-restored.

However, to return to an examination of the site. The general map shows that crowding around the palace itself were many large mansions or villas, the abode, we may suppose, of Minos' prime officials. These we must visit later. The finest of them vied with the palace itself in splendor though they were far

---

[4] *Greifen am Thron*, especially pp. 18, 24-26; Platon agrees with Karo, in a review of his book, *Kret. Chron.*, 13 (1959), p. 233. Marinatos, *C. and M.*, p. 126, and Levi, *PdP*, 71 (1960), pp. 112-114, express similar views. Evans explained and defended his reconstitutions in *Antiquaries Journal*, 7 (1927), pp. 258-267.

[5] In a review of Karo's book, *AJA*, 64 (1960), p. 198.

outranked in size, for the Palace of Minos in its final period sprawled over an area of about three acres (Fig. 2).[6]

And sprawl it did, for the Cretan palace was not laid out within definite exterior limits, rectangular or square, like a Classical Greek temple. Instead it grew, or was planned, from the inside out, rather like a tree (Ch. XIII, 1). The "heart" was the great Central Court around which the different units of the building centered and which formed the focus of the system of circulation and intercommunication (Ch. IV).

It is not quite accurate to say, however, that the palace *faced* on the Central Court, or at least that it faced exclusively inward like the Classical Greek house, for in all three of the major palaces (and Gournia too) the west exterior façade was given special architectural treatment and fronted on a broad area paved with slabs of stone. At Knossos slightly raised walks or "causeways" crossed this West Court in various directions, one leading directly to the West Porch (Figs. 2, 128). The lower part of the wall of the west façade was massively constructed of a high course of smoothly dressed blocks of stone, the ortho-states ("standers"), resting on a low sill course, the euthynteria ("leveling" course). As in the other palaces this west wall is not straight but advances and retreats in a curious series of bays and projections the reason for which we will perhaps discover later (Ch. XIII, 3); in addition the wall is interrupted at intervals by shallow breaks or recesses that are peculiarly characteristic of the west palace façades.

North of the West Court lies a small flagged area flanked by banks of low steps on the east and south and enclosing a kind of elevated "box" at the junction (Fig. 41). The "Theatral Area," as Evans dubbed it, was evidently designed for some kind of spectacle or performance, though hardly of a dramatic nature

[6] The "over six acres" mentioned by Evans, and frequently repeated, includes a generous amount of the surrounding courts and houses (*Knossos*, I, p. 206); my estimate is for the building itself with its Central Court. The dimensions assigned to the palace (inadvertently credited to the Central Court by the omission of a comma) by Miss Vaughan, 600 by 400 ft., are also based on this inclusive method of reckoning, *The House of the Double Axe*, New York, 1959, p. 39.

as the name might suggest. Inevitably one thinks of Homer's description of the "dancing-place that in wide Knossos Daedalus wrought for Ariadne of the lovely tresses."[7]

The ordinary visitor to the site, whether he uses a plan or not, can scarcely fail to find the layout of the building bewildering. This is in part due to the numerous alterations and modifications that were introduced in the course of the successive partial rebuildings which followed severe earthquakes or other forces of destruction. But a more adequate explanation is that most of what we see merely constitutes the service rooms: storage rooms, workrooms, small cult rooms, etc. Many of the more important rooms, with the exception of the main floor of the residential quarters, were located in the upper storeys, an arrangement also found in the other palaces. In fact it is from the Palace of Minos that we get our word "labyrinth," for like some other words with this ending that we still use, such as hyacinth, plinth, and turpentine (from *terebinthos*), it is a Cretan word in origin. The "labrys," that is, double-axe, occurs innumerable times carved on the stone blocks of the palace walls, or on sacred pillars, or represented on objects found within the palace; recently too the cult title, "Our Lady of the Labyrinth," has been read on a tablet from the palace.[8] The palace, then, was the Labyrinth itself, the "House of the Double-Axe," where the Minotaur was housed, in other words where, in the Central Court, the bull games were performed (Ch. IV). After the destruction of the building the term gradually came to be understood as referring to the "labyrinthine" character of the ruins, and with this new meaning the word passed on to the Greeks and Romans.

A magnificent entranceway in the form of a stepped and columned portico led up from the river-crossing to the southwest corner of the palace in its earlier days, but before the Late Minoan period this had disappeared and the palace seems to have had but two main entrances, a northern and a western.

[7] *Iliad*, 18, 590-592.
[8] *DMG*, p. 310, no. 205.

The north entry was reached, as at Mallia (Fig. 6), by a well-paved road from the west; passing a large pillared hall of uncertain use[9] (Fig. 40) it continued south as a narrow passage sloping sharply upward to the north end of the Central Court. The west entry was clearly the ceremonial one. Causeways from the north, west, and south, led the visitor into the West Court where rose the impressive façade whose upper storeys housed the main reception rooms of the palace (Fig. 128 and Ch. VI, 1). The great stone orthostates that form the base of the walls are still smoke-blackened from the furious fire that destroyed this part of the building. At the southeast corner of the court a columned porch, once decorated with scenes from the bull ring, led past a guardroom into the narrow "Corridor of the Procession" which, when excavated, retained traces of brightly painted rows of processional figures. In Egypt such figures would represent foreigners bringing tribute to Pharaoh and kneeling humbly at his feet; here they seem to be Minoan subjects of Minos bringing presents or offerings to him, or possibly to "Our Lady of the Labyrinth." We can imagine the colorful procession passing along the narrow corridor which, after turning twice at right angles, reached the foot of a broad staircase leading up to the "Piano Nobile," or principal floor, where the king was waiting to receive it. On the restored west wall of the formal porch or "South Propylon" preceding the stairs several of these processional figures, including the best preserved, the famous "Cupbearer" (Figs. 42, 131, B), have been replaced in replica.

The floor of some of the great public halls of the Piano Nobile has been restored, partly as a protective measure for the rooms below (Fig. 116); and although the plan is conjectural in detail it is clear that these upper halls were spacious and that they were handsomely decorated with wall paintings of which

---

[9] "It is improbable that the north hypostyle hall served as an agora (so Karo on p. 30) or as a custom's house (so Evans); rather it would have been a waiting-room for those coming by the harbor road," writes Platon in a review of Karo, *Greifen am Thron*, *Kret. Chron.*, 13 (1959), p. 238. Its form and size were perhaps largely determined by the room above it; see Ch. VI, 2.

scanty fragments were found in the fill. We shall have something to say of their plan at a later point (Ch. vi, 1).

On the ground floor, beneath the western series of rooms of the Piano Nobile a long row of storage magazines opens off a common corridor running north to south, parallel to the Central Court (Fig. 93). Huge clay jars (pithoi), perhaps once numbering over four hundred and capable of holding, altogether, some 16,000 American gallons (over 60,000 liters) of olive oil, line their walls. The wealth of the Cretan kings is further tantalizingly suggested by the shreds of gold found in rows of pits down the center of the rooms beneath the floor (Ch. vii, 1).

Between the Corridor of the Magazines and the Central Court, and south of another monumental stairway leading from the court to the Piano Nobile, lies a group of small rooms used for religious purposes. Their front on the Central Court apparently took the form of a "Tripartite Columnar Shrine" whose appearance may be conjectured from a detail of the so-called Grandstand Fresco (Figs. 44, 133). Two of the inner rooms have stone pillars marked twenty-nine times with the sacred symbol of the *labrys* or double-axe, and in another room are large cists for the storage of sacred apparatus or sacerdotal treasure (Ch. vii, 2). In fact in excavating these a wealth of objects in clay, faïence, and crystal was discovered: two-handled jars, decorative pieces, snake-goddess figurines, libation tables, shells, and two beautiful relief plaques, one representing a goat suckling its kids, the other a cow with its calf.

North of these cult rooms and the stairway to the Piano Nobile lies a group of rooms including the famous "Throne Room," where a formal stone chair was found by the excavators in its original position against the north wall (Fig. 130). To preserve the room the upper walls were rebuilt and the whole roofed over with a clerestory chamber above, whose walls are now hung with reproductions of restored Minoan wall paintings from this palace and elsewhere. From the Central Court four openings between piers lead (Figs. 37, 44), by way of a broad flight of four steps, down to an anteroom with low benches of stone against the walls, and in a gap between them a wooden replica of the throne in the inner room. In the center of the anteroom now stands a shallow stone basin, found nearby, perhaps intended for ablutions.

The walls of the main room are painted with restored scenes of griffins, one pair of which heraldically guards the throne, and are lined with stone benches as in the outer room. The "oldest throne in Europe" is a handsome piece of furniture with a high back of undulating outline, a comfortably hollowed seat, and an arched design of legs and cross-braces which plainly betrays its origin in a wooden chair (Fig. 139, D). Gypsum flagging frames a red-painted plaster panel in the center of the floor, and the remains of a number of decorated clay jars found here conjured up for the excavators a dramatic scene of Minos and his councillors performing some religious ceremony in this room just before the final catastrophe, perhaps with a view to averting the impending danger.[9a]

In any event the presence of a "lustral chamber," that is a stone-lined pit reached by a short flight of steps directly opposite the throne, does indicate that the room was used for certain ritual purposes (Ch. v, 3). That this low-ceilinged "basement" chamber constituted *the* Throne Room of the palace is most unlikely[10]; the important ceremonial rooms were surely in the upper storeys (Ch. vi, 1). In fact the view that Minos here performed certain ritual acts depends on the hypothesis that he was a priest-king; but Helga Reusch is probably nearer the truth in her recent suggestion that this "throne"—better, "cathedral chair"—was intended not for a king but for a high priestess who, sitting here amid her ministrants, represented the epiphany or divine apparition of the Minoan Goddess—the "Lady of the Labyrinth(?)."[11]

[9a] Pendlebury in *Studies presented to D. M. Robinson*, I, p. 195.
[10] Hugh Plommer also says of it, "surely not the only throne room," *Ancient and Classical Architecture*, p. 77.
[11] *Minoica*, pp. 334-358 (another gem showing the goddess guarded by two griffins has recently been found by Platon, *Praktika*, 1959, pl. 110c); Platon likewise considers it a cult room, *Kret. Chron.*, 5 (1951), pp. 392-394.

Miss Reusch has also made it clear that this complex of rooms, though not closely paralleled elsewhere in Crete, is essentially Minoan in nearly all details. The resemblance to the Mycenaean megaron in the position of the throne, to which some have called attention,[12] is confined to this feature alone; and even this point is weakened by its identification as a cathedra for the priestess.

The northeast quarter of the palace, that is the section lying north of the heavy east-west wall on the axis of the east side of the Central Court, was largely occupied, on the ground floor, by storerooms and by the royal workshops. Remains of unfinished products and of the raw materials used by the potters, lapidaries, metal workers, and so forth, were found in this area. The conspicuous rectangular block of heavy walls in the southern part of this quarter, with its west end facing on the Central Court, indicated to Evans that in the storey above there was a Great East Hall; and this view is strengthened by the finding of fragments of fine mural paintings and reliefs which had fallen into the rooms beneath. The discovery of bronze locks of hair, apparently from a colossal statue, further suggested to the excavator that the room had been a sanctuary for the Mother Goddess.[13]

The best preserved part of the Palace of Minos is the southeast quarter, termed by Evans the "Domestic Quarter," that is, the residence of the royal family (Fig. 12). In this area the hill sloped off rapidly to the east and south, and in the later history of the palace a great cutting or vertical scarp was made to a depth of nearly thirty feet (9 m.), providing space for the construction, below the level of the Central Court, of two storeys served by a handsome and ingeniously built stone stairway known as the "Grand Staircase" (Fig. 38). Thanks to the fact that this portion of the palace seems not to have collapsed

---

[12] Blegen in *Minoica*, p. 66; the use at Pylos of griffins on either side of the throne does not prove that the room at Knossos was a throne room—for one thing the theme may have been imitated without comprehension of its religious meaning. On the dating of the Throne Room see Palmer, *Mycenaeans and Minoans*, chap. VI, 5.

[13] *Knossos*, III, pp. 497-525.

till long after the ruin of the rest of the building, sufficient time elapsed for a great mass of debris from the floors above the level of the Central Court to fall into the lowest storeys, and thus to help maintain much of the walls and even much of the Grand Staircase in nearly their original positions. Evans' careful excavation, followed by a skilful replacement of the decayed wooden columns and of the flooring over the lowest storey, enables us to get an almost uncanny but essentially accurate impression of an entire suite of rooms much as they appeared in 1500 B.C. A detailed description will be given in connection with an account of similar suites in the other palaces (Ch. v, 1). For the present it will be enough to say that the lowest storey contained a great hall, the "Hall of the Double-Axes" (double-axe signs were cut on the walls of the light-well) opening on broad terraces (Figs. 39, 45); a smaller and more private chamber, the "Queen's Hall," with private bathroom, and a series of small rooms, reached by a long passage, including a toilet (Figs. 43, 81). The floors, walls, and ceilings of the halls were beautifully decorated with alabaster veneering or with painted designs and representations. South of the Residential Quarter a complex of small rooms including two bathrooms may have been designed for the reception of guests (Ch. v, 5).

The north, east, and south sides of the Central Court are too poorly preserved to determine whether they resembled the porticoed courts at Mallia and Phaistos. The west side, however, was certainly similar to the west side of the Phaistos Central Court, and the restored drawing in Fig. 44 probably gives a fairly correct impression: from right to left, the series of piers framing the doorways into the Throne Room; the broad stairway to the Piano Nobile with its intermediate column; the Tripartite Sanctuary; and a pillared portico perhaps continuing to the south end of the court. In the upper storeys open galleries probably formed a front for the halls of the Piano Nobile.

But before we attempt to ascend to these upper halls let us leave Knossos for the time being and cross the island to the plain of the Messara.

2. THE PALACE OF PHAISTOS

The amenities and excellencies of its design, with the advantage of a superb situation, admittedly make Phaistos the most attractive of the Cretan Palaces, if not one of the finest architectural achievements of the Bronze Age in the Near East. (SINCLAIR HOOD, *Director of the British School of Archaeology at Athens*)[14]

ALTHOUGH the drive from Herakleion to Phaistos is only thirty-five miles (56 km.) it takes considerably longer by car than might be expected, partly because the road winds up to a pass some 2000 feet (600 m.) above sea level and then zigzags down again with fine panoramas of the fertile Messara valley. The picturesquely situated citadel of Prinias, an important archaic Greek site, can be seen en route, and a stop is usually made at Gortyn, capital of Crete in the Roman period. Here a large Minoan farmhouse has recently been excavated by the Italian School of Archaeology, which has also been excavating at Phaistos and Hagia Triadha since 1900, the year in which Evans began at Knossos.

Leaving the main road, which continues on past H. Triadha to the south coast, we cross the Geropotamos, a small but constantly flowing stream, and wind up the steep motor road to the top of the ridge at the eastern end of which lies Phaistos, and at the western, H. Triadha. A small tourist pavilion just above the palace welcomes the many daily visitors to Phaistos and finds space for the few who wish to stay overnight.

If the visitor, instead of driving, walks up the hill from the main road a question will present itself rather forcibly: why did the Minoans build their palace on the top of this ridge more than two hundred feet (70 m.) above the plain? It is not likely that it was for defence, for although the edge of the hill on the north, east, and south of the palace drops off steeply, it continues to rise toward the west, reaching a height of nearly four

---

[14] *Gnomon*, 26 (1954), p. 375.

hundred feet (120 m.) above the palace in an eminence known as the Acropolis, and there are no traces of fortifications facing in this direction along the unprotected west front of the palace.

A possible explanation is that it was considered to be more healthful on the hill. Or it may be that the psychological value of setting the king's house above those of his "subjects" (literally "those placed beneath") was fully appreciated. But it is difficult to avoid the impression that the magnificence of the view exercised not a little influence on the rulers of Phaistos in selecting this site for their royal residence.

Forty miles (64 km.) to the east the bold profile of Mt. Dikte, best seen with the "rosy-fingered Dawn" behind it, marks the landward end of the valley. To the west one may catch a glimpse from the Central Court of the Bay of Messara; to the south a long ridge (Asterousia Mts.) shuts off the valley from the coast (Fig. 46). But it is to the north that the eye is drawn again and again. Here the long sheltering range of Ida culminates in the twin peaks of Mt. Ida itself, over 8000 feet (2500 m.) high (Fig. 51). From dawn to dusk the deeply creviced hills fluctuate in an everchanging pattern of light and shade, and the cloud masses which float over and sometimes partly envelop the rugged slopes are never alike two days in succession.

At night there are no urban lights to dim the brilliance of the sky, and standing among the shadowy ruins one starred night we looked down into the valley to discover, as it seemed, another starry heaven beneath us. Had some great flood, we wondered momentarily, converted the whole plain from hill to hill into a vast, still mirror? No, for these "stars" were moving uncertainly about and blinking in and out in most erratic fashion. They were, we presently realized, but the torches of nearby villagers gathering succulent snails for tomorrow's dinner.

A fine, almost bird's-eye, view of the palace may be gained from the roof of the Pavilion (Fig. 46). The ground plan is well preserved except along the south end and the southern half of the east side of the Central Court, where whatever rooms

35

there may have been have disappeared over the eroded edge of the hill (Fig. 4).[15]

Along the west side of the palace are two courts (not shown) connected by a stone staircase (Fig. 138). The lower, West Court, during the existence of the penultimate palace—and it is in this stage that the excavators have left it (Fig. 49)—had a flagged surface, and was bounded on the north by a long flight of steps terminating at the top in a blank retaining wall supporting the south side of the Upper Court. The West Court with its flight of steps, or seats, is referred to as a "Theatral Area." But when the last palace was built the level of the West Court was raised about four feet (1.30 m.), just high enough to cover the orthostates of the older palace façade (now visible in the middle of the court, Fig. 49) and all but four of the flight of northern steps, and was then surfaced with cement (Fig. 55); the court was also enlarged by moving the west face of the new building eastward about twenty-four feet (7.20 m.). In both stages the main entrance to the Central Court lay in the middle of its west side, and in the last palace the broad passage, 7, was controlled by double doors at both ends. The Central Court could also be reached at ground level by at least two other entrances: 41, in the center of the north end; and 62, at the northeast corner (Fig. 4).

North of the Central Court, and connected with it by Corridor 41, was a smaller paved court, 48; and at a higher level to the west of this was still another court enclosed by porticoes on all sides. This Peristyle Court, 74, with four columns on each side (Fig. 126), finds its only Minoan parallel, on a monumental scale, in the Little Palace at Knossos (Fig. 13).

But the Central Court, which is similar in size, proportions, and orientation to that at Knossos, is of course the principal court. The surface was paved in a fairly regular fashion with flagstones, and along probably the whole of both the long east and west sides ran continuous porticoes, no doubt with galleries

[15] Marinatos suggests that parts of the palace were never finished, *C. and M.*, pp. 60, 134.

along the east, if not also along the west, at the second storey level (Fig. 55). On the east, where a considerable stretch is preserved, the portico was fronted by an alternating succession of square pillars and round columns, a scheme popular in Minoan architecture.

On the west side of the Central Court near its northern end a central oval column of large size flanked by two pillars on either side—all rising, it would seem, to a height of two storeys (Fig. 50)—forms the imposing façade of Room 25, the largest room on the ground floor of the palace, about 31 by 28 ft. (9½ by 8½ m.). The importance of the room is further emphasized by the two oval column bases on its east-west axis, by the floor laid in a particularly careful pattern of gypsum slabs, and by the walls lined with a wainscotting of gypsum veneer surmounted by painted plaster and furnished with niches let into the walls on three sides. Surely the room served some function more important than merely to act as an anteroom to a series of magazines (27-38), though that is the view taken by the official Italian publication of the building; a suggestion of what that function may have been will be made later (Ch. IV).[16]

Along the north end of the Central Court occurs one of the most carefully designed schemes for which there is evidence in Minoan architecture (Fig. 51). Set almost precisely on the axis of the court, the broad doorway to Corridor 41 is framed on either side by a pair of half-columns of which only the bases are preserved (Fig. 53); next, symmetrically spaced to right and left, is a deep niche decorated with a distinctive pattern which will be discussed in another connection (Ch. IV); and finally, and again symmetrically on either side, a shallow recess of a type otherwise met only along the main façades of the palaces (Fig. 122). As shown in Fig. 145 the position of the individual elements was fixed by a predetermined plan based on whole numbers of Minoan feet, though the placing of each point was not always precisely adhered to in the actual process

---

[16] It is called a "vestibolo," *Festòs*, II, pp. 67, 79; note that there was at least another opening into the area of the magazines via Room 31 from Corridor 7, *Festòs*, II, pp. 44, 90.

of building. A reconstruction of the façade is presented in Fig. 50, with the half-columns extended up through two storeys and surmounted by a second pair of half-columns in the third storey half the height of those below, and with windows in the recesses at the level of the upper storeys. The scheme resembles, and perhaps is the ultimate inspiration of, the façades of the later royal tombs at Mycenae known as the Treasury of Atreus and the Tomb of Clytemnestra.[17]

The imposing character of this façade, the discovery of fragments of painted wall decoration fallen from above into the rooms behind, and the broad stairway, 42-43, guarded by a sentry box in Corridor 41 (see Ch. IV), is ample evidence that the rectangular block measuring some 75 by 50 ft. (ca. 23 by 15 m.) and lying between the Central Court and Court 48, contained rooms of outstanding importance (Fig. 87). The position of bases in the walls of the ground floor rooms 58-61 and 91-92, points to a large "East Hall" on the second floor, about 30 by 47 ft. (ca. 9 by 14½ m.), containing two rows of four columns each; while the narrowness of the partition walls separating Rooms 44-46 indicates a single large "West Hall" in the second storey, about 15 by 30 ft. (ca. 4½ by 9 m.), which is narrow enough to be roofed without internal supports. For various reasons it is clear that the area over Corridor 41 was unroofed except near its south end. A third storey above the level of the Central Court can be confidently postulated because of certain relationships between this block of rooms and the royal reception halls over the Magazine-Propylon block (see Ch. VI, 1). It will be suggested later that the dining halls of the palace were located in this block of rooms north of the Central Court, probably in the second-storey East Hall.[18] The small rooms on the ground floor would be suitable for the storage and preparation of food, and it is a fact that the excavators did discover quantities of pottery in a cupboard under the stairway 42-43, and that there are stone-lined niches in the walls

---

[17] But cf. *Festòs*, II, pp. 443-445.
[18] For a full discussion see *AJA*, 65 (1961), pp. 165-172.

of 45 and 46 (Fig. 99), similar to niches found recently in early stages of the Phaistos palace with pottery still in place in them as if on a pantry shelf.[19]

The rooms beneath the East Hall were in easy communication by way of Corridor 58 with the northeast quarter of the palace which, as at Knossos and Mallia, would seem to have been the service quarter (Fig. 4). This quarter was provided with a direct outside entrance, 53, a small room with doorways on the north, east, and west, and with benches against the walls. A few yards north of 53 a steep stairway descends to a loosely planned building which includes a number of storerooms, some of them "stock-piled" with domestic pottery. From this building the fields are easily reached by a gentle slope where the hill runs out in a long point toward the northeast.[20] All of this would suggest an obvious route for bringing the daily food supplies into the palace.

Court 90, with the remains of an oven or furnace in the middle, must have been designed for the use of the staff, and the series of rooms marked 54-55, for storage. Rooms 88 and 89 would also have been used for storage; the former, below ground level and entered by steps down, was considered by Pernier as a rather mysterious room possibly used for religious purposes (on the analogy of the "lustral chambers"), but it would seem more likely that it was simply a kind of "cold cellar."[21] North of 88 were several cisterns. Finally 49, which was almost certainly an unroofed area with a single door opening off another court, 48, can be reasonably explained in this general context as a pen for animals awaiting conversion into meat for the royal table or to provide a fresh supply of milk.[22]

The principal royal Residential Quarter was located at the north end of the palace, and reached by a long stairway descend-

[19] *Annuario*, 30-32 (1952-54), p. 457, figs. 94, 95; *Festòs*, II, fig. 156, shows pottery in the niche in Room 46.
[20] *Festòs*, II, p. 455.
[21] *Festòs*, II, pp. 203-208, 586; Banti rejects the religious hypothesis but leaves the purpose of the room unexplained.
[22] The responsibility for most of the ideas suggested in this paragraph is mine; the Italian publication presents the facts and avoids conjecture.

ing from the Peristyle Court (74). This court, together with the very large room, 93, opening on it through a six-bayed pier-and-door partition, should quite possibly be considered as forming a part of the private rather than of the public apartments of the palace, as some would regard them. Room 93 and the porticoes of Peristyle 74 were paved with gypsum flagstones, those of the former being of a unique rhomboidal shape; at least the west wall of 93 was gypsum faced and contained a niche like those in Room 25.

As at Knossos the Residential Quarter was built on an artificially leveled terrace at the edge of the hill, and much of it is quite well preserved. Since it enjoyed a northern exposure with a superb panorama of the range of Ida, it was probably used as the summer residence of the royal family. A smaller but similar suite east of the Central Court (63-64) would then have served as living quarters in colder weather. Both have a Main Hall (77-79 and 63), a Queen's Hall (81 and 63b), a bathroom off the latter (83 and 63d), and a porticoed terrace (85 and 64); they will be described in more detail later (Ch. v).

West of the Central Court Rooms 23 and 24 (Fig. 96), with wide openings on the west portico and furnished with gypsum benches, may have been used merely as comfortable and convenient "sitting rooms," like the Classical Greek "exedra," but it is quite possible that they were used for some cult purpose. Behind them and reached by a long corridor, 12-13, from the passage, 7, two suites of rooms each with a private bath (17, 18, 19 and 16, 20, 21) and with a "living room" shared in common (15), may have been Guest Apartments (Ch. v, 5).[23] Rooms 27-37 opening on either side of Corridor 26 must have served for storage or other service purposes, though they may have played a special role at the time of the bull games (Ch. iv).

The most conspicuous architectural feature of the Phaistos palace was the magnificent entranceway north of the Magazine

[23] I would agree with Miss Banti (*Festòs*, II, pp. 452-455) that there was no circuitous southwest entry to the palace similar to that at Knossos (Corridor of the Procession); the wall west of the guest rooms, shown in lighter hatching on the plan (Fig. 4), is only a retaining wall.

Block. It consisted of a splendid stairway, forty-five feet (over 13½ m.) broad with deep, low risers, which ascended to an imposing propylon in the form of a double porch, the outer opening of which (67) was supported by a massive central column of oval shape, while the inner (69) consisted of two large portals (without doors) on either side of a broad pier (Figs. 49, 137, 138). At the rear of these porticoes three oval columns supported the front of a very large light-well (69A). A door at the southeast corner of 69A connects by means of a stairway with Room 25 and the Central Court, and in the other direction with Peristyle 74.

From 69 three steps through a doorway ascend into Room 70 whose cement floor is about 7½ ft. (2.30 m.) above that of the magazines, 27-38; 70 may have been merely a guardroom, or it may have formed an anteroom to a suite of public rooms at this level (Ch. vi, 1). Another rather wider doorway at the opposite end of 69 opens on a broad two-flight stairway, 72-73, which led, we believe, via a corridor over 68-69, to a grand suite of State Apartments covering the entire area of the Magazine Block.[24]

Even in plan the great square block, about a hundred feet (30 m.) to a side, which includes the Grand Propylon and Magazine complex, is impressive. What a magnificently unified and harmoniously proportioned architectural composition the combination of monumental entranceway and massive three-storeyed block containing the State Reception Halls must have presented is faintly suggested by our restoration of it as seen from the West Court (Fig. 48)—a splendid setting for the pomp and pageantry of a Minoan court.

3. THE PALACE OF MALLIA

Knossos is visited by everyone who goes to Crete, partly because of its fame, partly because of its easy accessibility. Phaistos, often with nearby H. Triadha and Gortyn thrown in, is a day's excur-

[24] For full discussion see *AJA*, 60 (1956), pp. 151-157.

sion for those who have a little more time and who like to combine scenery with archaeology. Mallia, though only twenty-five miles (40 km.) by road east of Herakleion, is almost a preserve of the specialist.

It is true that Mallia lacks the antique fame and the mythological glamor of Knossos; indeed even its ancient name is uncertain. It also falls short of Phaistos in beauty of location, though in this respect it excels Knossos since it has a view of the sea, which, with an excellent beach, is but a few minutes walk from the palace (Fig. 56); in addition the site, though low-lying, has a fine background of towering hills (Fig. 57). Very picturesque is the nearby plain watered today by hundreds of white-sailed windmills.

It is also true that the Palace of Mallia is considerably smaller than that at Knossos, being about 1.8 acres (nearly 8000 sq. m.) or about the size of the Palace of Phaistos (Fig. 7); it is also less sumptuously decorated than its sister palaces. Yet the Mallia palace enjoys the distinction of having its ground plan virtually intact, for no later buildings were constructed on the site (Fig. 6). It was discovered by the Greek archaeologist Hazzidakis who commenced its excavation in 1915, but since 1922 the site has been excavated by the French School which has not yet published its final account of the palace nor made an accurate plan of the remains.[25]

The Central Court, which is almost identical with that at Phaistos in dimensions and orientation, is of special interest for its excellent preservation, particularly of the porticoes on the north and east, which supply valuable clues for solving the problem of where the bull games were staged (Ch. IV). The court also resembles the one at Phaistos in having a broad portico along its eastern side, consisting of alternating piers and columns spaced with great regularity. But it excels Phaistos in one particular: across the north end of the court there was also a portico of columns set on white stone bases (Fig. 57). Except

[25] Three fascicles of a preliminary report have appeared (see Bibliography), and a fourth is in preparation by Demargne and Dessenne.

between the last two columns at the west end, where there was an opening with double doors, the spaces between the columns seem to have been closed either with low screen walls or some kind of balustrade.

To the west of the Central Court a block of magazines and service rooms is served by a "Corridor of the Magazines" running north to south as at Knossos. These magazines are grouped into two distinct blocks, and in each of these, as in the group of magazines 6 to 10 at Knossos, the partition walls are thickened at the center into piers to receive the weight of columns in the halls of the Piano Nobile overhead.

Between the Corridor of the Magazines and the Central Court and facing on it for about the northern two-thirds of its length is a rectangular group of rooms, vi and vii (Figs. 5, 6), some or all of which probably were connected with the religious activities of the palace. The position is similar to that of the Tripartite Shrine and associated rooms in the Palace of Minos. In the center of the northern section, vi 1 opens on the court for its entire width of fourteen feet (over 4 m.), and a flight of four steps ascends on either side of a pier to the floor of the room where a low base appears to have been intended for an altar or table of offerings. Behind this a narrow stairway of four steps between two columns descends again to a series of rooms used, it seems, for storing the cult paraphernalia, for in vi 2 was discovered a cache of several evidently highly prized objects now in the Herakleion Museum: a bronze bracelet, a bronze dagger, a great bronze sword with a crystal hilt, and a votive hatchet in the form of a panther.[26] In the middle of the southern group of rooms is a large Pillar Crypt, vii 4, with a flagged floor and two stone pillars marked with double-axes, stars, and a trident (Figs. 95, 98). Sections vi and vii connect via a short passage at the foot of a stone stairway 10 ft. 5 in. (3.20 m.) wide and with nine steps still in position. On the analogy of similar shrines it would be natural to assume that they led to a Colum-

<hr>

[26] *Mallia*, I, p. 21; *Mon. Piot*, 28 (1925-1926), pp. 1-18.

nar Shrine and connected rooms on the next floor. The breadth of the stairway, however, raises the possibility that it opened on the corridor immediately above the Corridor of the Magazines and so served the great halls over the West Magazines.

Nevertheless another even broader flight of stairs with four steps in place over twenty-five feet (ca. 7½ m.) long, near the south end of the court on the same side, might incline one to conclude that this stairway, and not the one to the north, formed the regular approach to the public reception halls of the Piano Nobile.[27] A decision between the two stairways is bound up with the question of the formal entry to the palace. It is commonly assumed that this was the North Entrance which, with a well-paved roadway leading up to it from the west, resembles the one at Knossos. But the entrance itself is not particularly impressive, and it reaches the northwest corner of the Central Court by a rather devious route which passes through the area of the North Service Court (see below). On the other hand two short, broad passages lead directly into the Central Court near its southeast and southwest corners.[28] Both of these are conveniently situated with respect to the Grand Staircase near the south end of the court, and the latter in particular has a very carefully paved entrance passage eighteen feet (5.45 m.) wide, whose inner end is directly at the foot of the stairway.[29]

The Palace of Mallia is especially remarkable for the large number of storage rooms and small workrooms in all parts of the building, which give it almost the agrarian character of a great country villa. In addition, at the southwest corner of the palace are two rows of circular granaries (Figs. 58, 62 and Ch. VII, 1). Exactly what the irregular clusters of rooms to the southeast and southwest of the Central Court were used for is

[27] Marinatos regards the southern flight of stairs as a "theatral area" (C. and M., p. 137 and fig. 58); if so it was poorly located for a view of the Central Court.

[28] The excavators have been unable to find evidence of paving south of the palace (letter of M. Daux, Aug. 19, 1960).

[29] Marinatos calls this south entrance the main entrance of the palace, C. and M., p. 64.

not clear; little or nothing has been said about them in the preliminary reports on the excavations.[30]

To the east of the Central Court is an interestingly designed and well preserved complex of magazines (xi 1-7), now enclosed to protect them, which will be described later (Ch. VII, 1, and Figs. 57, 91). Another group of three storage rooms, xii, lies to the south of these, and still another distinct group of six at the extreme north end of the palace (xxvii), with other storage or workrooms to the south. The North Service Court, as we would call it, had short, roughly-paved porticoes on the north, east, and south, and here we can picture the domestic staff busily receiving, sorting, or preparing food supplies for the royal household.

Between the Central Court and the North Service Court is a number of long narrow rooms, two stairways, and a very large room containing six square bases in two rows, preceded by a long room with a single base (Figs 59, 88).[31] The evidence points to the existence of a large, second storey room (which we may call the "Northeast Hall") with two rows of columns, accessible from both stairways. In size, form, and position its resemblance to the "East Hall" we have restored in the second storey north of the Central Court at Phaistos (Ch. II, 2) is so close as to suggest that both rooms were used for the same purpose, and both will be further discussed in Chapter VI, 2, "The Banquet Hall."

Another feature which links the Palace of Mallia with the other two great palaces is the presence of a royal Residential Quarter, although this has only recently been recognized.[32] Located in the northwest corner of the building (iii) it resembles in position, and to a remarkable degree in arrangement, the

[30] They will be described in the fascicle shortly to appear.

[31] The room with the six bases has been much discussed, and supposed Egyptian analogies have caused it to be referred to as the Hypostyle Hall, Joly, *BCH*, 52 (1928), pp. 324-346; *Mallia*, II, pp. 1-5; Charbonneaux rejected these analogies, *BCH*, 54 (1930), pp. 352-366. In my opinion it is the room above this which may show Egyptian influence (see Ch. VI, 2).

[32] By Platon, *Kret. Chron.*, I (1947), pp. 635-636.

principal Residential Quarter at Phaistos. It includes a Main or Men's Hall (iii 7) with a light-well at its south end, a Queen's Hall (iii 1) with attached bathroom (iii 4) and probably a toilet (iii 2). Both Halls opened on a columned portico with a view toward the sea. Stairs at iii b led to upper rooms. On some of the walls are remains of painted and incised plaster, but there is no evidence of alabaster veneering; the bases for the pier-and-door partitions were not of stone but apparently of wood, as were three bases, recently discovered, for a double doorway into iii 7 from iv 6.

Thus the atmosphere at Mallia is much more modest than at Knossos or Phaistos, almost rustic in tone compared with their urban splendor. Yet the palace displays the same solidly constructed west façade with vigorously projecting and receding blocks of rooms further enlivened with shallow recesses (Fig. 58) and reared on a solid base of stone orthostates and projecting sill course.

A flagged area similar to that extending west of the palace to form the West Court seems to have extended to the east of the palace as well. Stone-paved streets appear to have radiated in various directions (Fig. 24), and a number of interesting houses have been excavated. These we shall visit later (Ch. iii, 13-17).[33]

[33] Recent excavations have shown that "the West Court is crossed from north to south by a slab-paved road, and in the southern half of the Court is an interesting system of secondary paths," Hellenic Society, *Archaeological Reports for 1960-61* (1961), p. 23.

CHAPTER III

MINOR PALACES, VILLAS,
AND HOUSES

1. THE PALACE OF GOURNIA

IN ADDITION to the three major palaces there are several smaller and incompletely preserved or incompletely excavated structures which may have been minor palaces. The best known of these, excavated by an expedition from the University of Pennsylvania in 1901-1904, is at a site today called Gournia, easily reached by road from the small town of Hagios Nikolaos (Fig. 1).

Gournia lies on the Gulf of Mirabello at the northern end of the seven-mile (11 km.) Hierapetra Isthmus, and today it is but a few minutes' drive over a fine level road, dominated by a magnificent mass of hills on the east, to Hierapetra on the south coast, the site of a small but interesting local museum. Cross-island traffic along this route must have been heavy in ancient times.

The American expedition led by three intrepid women archaeologists proceeded to uncover the little town systematically. Scores of small, irregularly planned houses were crowded together along narrow winding streets which clambered up the slopes of a small hill (Figs. 8, 63). Though excavated in the early years of this century the site is still in a surprisingly good state of preservation and provides the visitor to Crete with his only opportunity to sense what conditions of everyday life were for the ordinary Minoan. A surprising variety of the tools and objects of daily living were found in the houses, and provided the basis for an account which still makes interesting reading though the excavator wrote it in the first decade of Minoan archaeology.

On the top of the hill on which the town was built, and commanding a fine prospect over the gulf, were discovered the poorly preserved remains of a structure which in certain features resembles the major palaces, though it covers an area of less than a third of an acre, or about one-tenth that of the Palace of Minos (Fig. 9).

The resemblance is clearest along the west façade. This fronts on a passage paved with cobblestones which widens out toward its northern end in a diminutive piazza or "West Court." Part of the base of the wall of this west façade and around the corner on the south end of the palace is built of dressed limestone blocks of considerable size set on a low plinth, a style of masonry which, as we have seen, is characteristic of the west façades of the major palaces. The similarity is heightened by the fact that just south of the main west entrance, which is marked by a well dressed stone threshold, there occurs one of those recesses (twelve Minoan feet long) which are so typical of the west palace façades. Moreover portions of the façade alternately project and recede as in the larger palaces (though on a very modest scale), and one section measures sixty Minoan feet, a figure repeated at Phaistos and Mallia (Ch. xiii, 1).

A further point of likeness is the occurrence of a number of magazines of the usual elongated shape which are distributed in not too distinct groups along the west front, while above these, as the excavator conjectured, would have been the State Apartments reached by stairs of which there are slight traces just south of the west entrance.

The higher terraces to the east and north have been so denuded as to provide little further information about the plan of the building. Three long magazines (24) were surely covered by a single large room in the upper storey, and in the adjacent magazine (23) twelve clay jars were found in their original position around the walls. A small, cement-floored room (28) at the north end of the palace has been identified as a bathroom, though it does not have the familiar descending steps, this may provide a clue to the position of the Residential Quarter. Near the southeast corner of the palace is a small, open-fronted room with a low bench around its walls; in both these respects it resembles Rooms 23 and 24 west of the Central Court at Phaistos. This room faces west on what is surely a small court[1] bounded along its west side by a row of alternating pillars and columns, a common Minoan scheme (Ch. XI, I).

The small court just mentioned is of course very unlike the great central courts of Knossos, Phaistos, and Mallia; but immediately adjacent to the palace, on the south, is a large, open, cement-floored area called on the plan of the site a "Public Court." Though a little narrower and perhaps a little shorter than the courts of the three major palaces, it is similar in proportions and orientation, and this suggests that it too may have been designed with the bull games in mind (see Chapter IV). At its northern end is a low flight of steps forming an angle, quite reminiscent of the "Theatral Areas" at Knossos and Phaistos. Just south of this, opening along the west side of the court, is a short pillared portico with small rooms behind it which form a southward extension of the palace. Again we are reminded of the Tripartite Columnar Shrine at Knossos, Room 25 at Phaistos, and Room vil at Mallia. Fragments of stone "sacral horns" were found nearby, likewise a large flat block of stone pierced transversely with a hole. The possible meaning of this will be discussed in the following chapter (Ch. IV).

2. THE VILLA OF HAGIA TRIADHA

A forty minute walk along the northern foot of the ridge, on whose opposite extremities the two palaces of H. Triadha and Phaistos stand, leads through groves of citrus and gnarled old olive trees seen against the snowy peaks of Ida to one of

---

[1] The excavator felt uncertain on the point (*Gournia*, p. 26); but the spans would have been long (minimum 6.65 m. from east to west), and there is a capacious drain through the south stylobate (16 cm. wide by 17 cm. deep).

the loveliest Minoan sites in Crete. The oddly inappropriate name, "Holy Trinity," comes from a chapel and hamlet which once existed nearby.

It is commonly supposed that H. Triadha formed a sort of seasonal residence for the rulers of Phaistos. Its situation not only afforded a magnificent view of Ida (Fig. 65) but of the whole sand-fringed Bay of Messara with the mountains of western Crete in the background. Gypsum veneering was lavishly used throughout the palace, and the frescoes, so strangely absent at Phaistos, rank among the finest discovered in Crete. In addition to a hoard of nineteen bronze ingots together weighing over 1100 lbs. (over 500 kgs.), choice objects of Minoan art were discovered in the ruins, including steatite (soapstone) vases with scenes carved with the utmost skill and liveliness in low relief, one showing a festive procession of harvesters, another a presentation of sacrificial bulls' hides,[2] and a third, scenes of boxing and the bull game.[3]

The palace was excavated by the Italian School of Archaeology in the first decade of this century, but until the appearance of the promised final publication our information concerning this extraordinarily interesting building must remain very incomplete. In plan it forms a rather irregular L, the vertical stroke running west to east, the horizontal, north to south. The open area enclosed by the L was at least in part flagged, and lay on the crest of the ridge into whose slopes the ground floor rooms were terraced (Fig. 66).

Occupying most of the southern extremity of the building was a series of small rooms served by a common corridor (Fig. 10); the excavators suggest that these were used by the servants. A number of storerooms containing large clay jars are located in the middle of the north wing, and to the east of these is a suite of interconnecting Minoan Halls with many pier-and-door

[2] So Forsdyke, *Journal of the Warburg and Courtauld Institutes,* 15 (1952), pp. 13-19. Platon calls it the presentation of the spoils of the hunt, review of Karo, *Greifen am Thron, Kret. Chron.,* 13 (1959), p. 239.

[3] All three are well illustrated in Matz, *Kreta, Mykene, Troja,* Stuttgart, 1957, pls. 66, 67, 69.

partitions of the familiar pattern (Ch. v, 2). These rooms were well decorated with gypsum floors and walls lined with alabaster veneering; they were also liberally supplied with gypsum benches, and with windows and light-wells.[4] A substantial stairway led to obviously important rooms on the upper floor or floors. Clearly this constituted an important residential part of the palace but its exact purpose seems unknown.

A handsome suite of rooms in the northwest corner of the palace evidently formed the main Residential Quarter (Fig. 11). Its plan is similar to that of the major palaces and will be described in more detail later (Ch. v). The Men's Hall with connecting rooms (3, 12, 4) is as fine as anything at Knossos (Fig. 151), while one of the rooms (14) in the women's section (Fig. 68) contained the Cat and Bird Fresco and other beautiful mural paintings (Fig. 134). From the colonnaded court (11) the view is unsurpassed.

Although in many features the Villa of H. Triadha does resemble the major palaces it has no Central Court; its façades on the north and west, though built of ashlar masonry, lack the typical recesses; and there is no clear indication of a series of royal reception halls on the Piano Nobile. It seems reasonable then to regard it as a pleasure palace for the rulers of Phaistos, a Trianon to its Versailles, rather than as the administrative center of a separate realm.

3. THE LITTLE PALACE AT KNOSSOS

Some two hundred and fifty yards (230 m.) northwest of the Palace of Minos, and reached from it by way of the Minoan paved road running west from the North Entrance, Sir Arthur Evans excavated the remains of a building which he called the Little Palace (Figs. 3, 36, c).[5] Though it was far smaller than the great palaces, measuring only about one-fifth of an acre

---

[4] The *Enciclopedia Italiana, s.v.* Hagia Triada, says that the rooms were "decorate con affreschi, bagni, gabinetti"; I have been unable to see anything of these at the site.

[5] *Knossos*, II, pp. 513-544; *Handbook*, pp. 57-62.

(about 800 sq. m.), yet it contained a suite of connecting rooms which can help us gain some idea of the splendor of the vanished State Apartments in the Piano Nobile of the palaces at Knossos and Phaistos (Fig. 13).

The Main Hall at the north end of this suite is paved with gypsum and divided into two halves by a pier-and-door partition of four bays; another of six bays runs the whole length of the room and opens on a narrow columned portico or veranda which seems to have opened in turn on a terrace with a broad view to the east (Fig. 64). On the south the Hall opened through another four-bayed partition into a spacious square peristyle with three columns on each side; the only comparable peristyle known in Minoan architecture is the one in the Palace of Phaistos (74). Three steps extending the full width of the peristyle led down to an entrance hall, but the details of the actual approach have been lost.

In addition the Little Palace contained three Pillar Crypt rooms, a lavatory off the Main Hall, a "Lustral Chamber" of considerable architectural interest (Ch. v, 3), and a broad two-flight stairway to the second storey. There is, however, no clearly defined "women's quarter." The lower part of the outer walls was built of fine dressed masonry still standing on the west to a height of eight courses.

4. THE ROYAL VILLA, KNOSSOS

The "Royal Villa" was apparently reached by a short paved road running northeast from the palace (Fig. 3).[6] Built on an artificial terrace created by scarping back the hill, the Villa enjoyed a protected position and a pleasant view to the eastward over the valley (Fig. 36, b). Although of outstanding quality it was not particularly large, measuring only about sixty feet from north to south by about thirty-two, as preserved, from east to west (ca. 18 by 10 m.). The plan, except for the oblique

---

[6] *Knossos,* II, pp. 396-413; *Handbook,* pp. 62-64.

line of the northeast corner, is fairly compact and rectangular with only slight jogs on the west and south (Fig. 14); if restored correctly, an entrance on the ground floor level opened into the light-well of the Hall (C).

As the name implies this was no ordinary house. It will be noticed that even on the ground floor there are no storerooms. The entire east-west axis is occupied by the Hall, with the usual pier-and-door partition and two-columned light-well. The lower part of the walls was adorned with panels of gypsum veneer preserved to a height of over six feet (2 m.), and the floor of the main (inner) part of the Hall was surfaced with gypsum slabs laid in the usual system of a broad border about a central rectangle. Access to this part of the Hall could also be gained by a double door on the south near the foot of a stairway in the southwest corner of the house. But the most interesting feature of the room is the heavy stone balustrade, 32 in. (81 cm.) high at its west end, supporting columns on either side of an opening through which three steps led up to a narrow area behind the balustrade, 15 in. (38 cm.) higher than the floor of the Hall (Fig. 74). A handsome pedestaled lamp of purple stone was found standing on the steps, and in a niche on the axis of the room the remains of a formal stone seat were discovered in position.

Immediately adjacent to the balustrade a door opens to the north into a Pillar Crypt, almost as large as the main part of the Hall from which it is entered, and the finest and best preserved of cult rooms of this type (Ch. VII, 2). Its walls were of gypsum blocks in regularly coursed masonry, and the ceiling was supported by a system of huge split tree trunks resting on a central gypsum pillar and lodged in sockets in the masonry at the top of the walls (Fig. 97). In the gypsum floor were sunk a channel and two basins, evidently intended to catch liquid offerings poured before the sacred pillar.

It seems clear that the whole complex served some important

function of a religious nature, or at least with religious over-
tones. It is tempting to imagine that Minos, who "ruled wholly
in accordance with law and paid the greatest heed to justice,"[7]
sat in judgment on the recessed seat, accompanied by his ad-
visers, on the dais behind the balustrade. Here he was able to
communicate, unobserved, with his clerks or officials on the floor
above through the open well which, as Evans has shown, existed
over the area beyond the balustrade; they in turn could communicate with the functionaries in the Pillar Crypt by means of a
stairway at the west end of the room. The whole arrangement
is pregnant with suggestive possibilities of awesome religious
or political ceremonies, or of downright chicanery designed to
impress the lay audience in the Hall.

The southeast corner of the Villa was occupied by what
appears to be a private suite of rooms: a paved Hall (E) with
a closet (F) and a bath (?) opening off it (G), and a light-well
or little court (H). Was it intended for guest rooms, women's
quarters, or as rest rooms for His Worship during recesses in
the session?

The second storey seems to have had a Hall above, and
similar in plan to, the one (C) on the ground floor, and there
was no doubt an entrance from the terrace on the west.

The form of the stairway in the southwest corner of the
house is unique. The first flight, from the ground floor, runs
up to a wide landing from which a second flight ascends to the
second storey at each end, on either side of the well of the first
flight (Fig. 73). The upper flight to the east, with a door at
its head, served the Upper Hall and adjoining rooms; the
western one seems to have continued on up to a third storey.
Again the arrangement whereby the second floor rooms could
be secured against intrusion, while leaving the stairway to the
first and third storeys free, is suggestive of the special purposes
this edifice appears to have served.

[7] Diod. Sic., 5, 79, 2.

5. THE SOUTH HOUSE, KNOSSOS

Evans calls the South House the "best normal idea of a good burgher dwelling of the beginning of the New Era (L.M.) either at Knossos or elsewhere."[8] It was built on a scarped terrace encroaching on part of the early southwest approach to the palace (Fig. 3), and faced south over the ravine in the direction of the "Caravanserai." Slightly larger than the Royal Villa (62 by 38 ft.; 19 by 11½ m.) it was a little more regular in outline though not without the usual jogs corresponding to the arrangement of the rooms (Fig. 15).

Thanks to the slope of the hill remains of three storeys are preserved and have been supplemented by restoration (Fig. 71). The rear (north) wall stands to a height of eight courses of massive masonry (Fig. 72).

The lowest storey consists of a long narrow storeroom with three stone pillars on the axis, and a smaller room opening off it in which was found a number of bronze tools, including three saws and two double-axes. The peculiar way in which the doors of these rooms were secured will be described later (Ch. ix, 3). Platon considers these rooms shrines.

Twelve steps lead up from the basement to the main floor where is found the usual Hall with light-well, pier-and-door partitions, and gypsum-faced walls and floor, the center of the main part being occupied by a "mosaiko" pavement (Fig. 72); in the east wall was a window placed, when first built, in a bay. Other rooms include a lavatory (?), a toilet with drain through the wall, and a bathroom. In its original form the bathroom floor was at a lower level reached by a short flight of steps, and the walls seem to have been decorated with paintings of birds and flowers. In the northwest corner of the house a Pillar Crypt contained a single pillar flanked by a base for a double-axe and a stand for sacral objects (horns?). As in the Royal Villa

---

[8] *Knossos*, II, pp. 373-390 (quotation, p. 389); *Handbook*, pp. 65-66.

adjacent stairs led to a room above, from which appears to have fallen a "silver service," consisting of a pitcher and three bowls, one decorated with spirals. Whether for ceremonial or for household use they give evidence of the affluence of the owner of the South House.

6. THE HOUSE OF THE CHANCEL SCREEN, KNOSSOS

The House of the Chancel Screen, built at the southeast corner of the palace (Fig. 3), was about the size of the Royal Villa, about 55 by 42 ft. (17 by 13 m.), and was also generally rectangular with the usual jogs (Fig. 16).[9] On the ground floor, which alone is preserved, are three magazines (9, 12, 13), a Pillar Crypt with a single pillar (10), a bathroom (6) perhaps forming part of the Private Apartments, and an important complex of rooms in the northeast angle of the house.

This complex consists of a Hall (2) with pier-and-door partitions on three sides and the main house entrance on the fourth. This connects through a four-bayed partition on the north side with another large Hall whose floor was paved with irregular flagging, and which was lighted not from a light-well but, according to the excavator, by a large window in the east wall. On the opposite side of the room is a balustrade similar to the one in the Royal Villa. Beyond an opening in the center of this balustrade, framed by columns, two shallow steps lead up to a higher floor level. In the center of the rear wall of the balustraded area, which was much deeper than in the Royal Villa, traces were found of a raised dais supposedly for a formal seat. Here again, then, we seem to have some kind of formal audience chamber; but it will be noted that the Pillar Crypt is not in this instance so intimately associated.

7. THE SOUTHEAST HOUSE, KNOSSOS

The Southeast House lies next to the House of the Chancel Screen at the southeast corner of the palace (Fig. 3).[10] The

[9] *Knossos*, II, pp. 391-395; *Handbook*, p. 64.
[10] *Knossos*, I, pp. 425-430; *Handbook*, pp. 64-65.

Main Hall, K 1, in the southwest corner, has gypsum-faced walls and a floor of clay surrounded on the inner sides with a narrow, slightly raised border paved with gypsum (Fig. 17). The Hall opens east through a three-bayed pier-and-door partition on a small flagged court, about 8 by 6½ ft. (2½ by 2 m.), with three columns about an angle (Fig. 80), similar to one in House A at Tylissos (Fig. 19).

Room H 1, opening off the north portico of this court, presents a puzzle. Its walls on three sides are built of fine limestone masonry—unusual for interior walls—nine courses being preserved in one place, and faced with gypsum veneer. The fourth (east) side was also "faced" with the same thin gypsum "veneering," but without a solid backing of any kind, only a narrow space, G 1, with a door adjoining the one into H 1.

The Pillar Crypt, C 1, will be discussed later (Ch. VII, 2). Against the base of the single pillar, which was marked with three double-axe signs, was found a stone base for a double-axe, and nearby a "sacral knot" in ivory.

At the northwest corner of the house is a two-flight stairway with the ten gypsum steps of the first flight and two of the second in position; the total height of the stairway, and therefore of the first storey, must have been approximately 8½ ft. (2.60 m.). Remains of plaster painted with lilies were found in the narrow passage from the stairs, A 1.

8. THE HOUSE OF THE FRESCOES, KNOSSOS

The House of the Frescoes lies to the northwest of the palace and south of the "Royal Road" running west from its North Entrance (Fig. 3).[11] It was a small and simple house and much disturbed by later building. Little can be said of the individual rooms (Fig. 18). The principal room, H, in the southeast corner had a floor with a plaster border and an ironstone center; its walls bore remains of an interesting zoned decoration (Fig. 129, A).

The chief interest of the house, however, lies in the frescoes,

---

[11] *Knossos*, II, pp. 431-467; *Handbook*, p. 57.

which were found not on the walls nor even fallen from them, but neatly and evidently deliberately stacked in E, as if awaiting the archaeologist, in fragile sheets of stucco little more than an eighth of an inch (4 mm.) thick. As many as thirty-four layers could be counted, and the whole formed a pile some twelve feet long by five feet wide. "Eighty-four trays (2 × 2 ft.)," writes Evans, "were finally filled with the fragments, and the process of extraction and removal, mainly carried out by four expert workmen specially trained in this work, took over five weeks."[12] Among the fine paintings thus rescued were the Blue Monkeys and the Blue Bird Fresco.

9. THE HOUSE AT NIROU KHANI

One of the finest houses, if it really was a private house, outside of Knossos, was excavated in 1918-1919 by Xanthoudides at Nirou Khani, about eight miles (13 km.) east of Herakleion and only a few yards from the sea at a point where traces of Minoan harbor works have been found (Fig. 31).[13]

Like the Knossian villas the base of the outer walls in conspicuous positions is built of coursed and dressed masonry; there are remains of wall paintings; and a Hall of normal form (2a, 2) had a carefully paved gypsum floor and walls dadoed with gypsum panels (Fig. 75). Two other rooms, 5 and 12, have floors with a central rectangle of ironstone flagging within a border of gypsum, and 12 has a gypsum bench around the walls on two sides. A stone stairway (10, 10a), and remains of stone jamb bases and of gypsum flooring fallen from above indicate that there was a second storey of importance. The small room, 9, and the narrow passage, 8, leading to it, were both floored with gypsum flagging, and both were lighted by small windows in the exterior walls. Other features worthy of mention include a light-well providing light to Room 12, and, through a window, to Corridor 11; a large paved court to the east and

[12] *Knossos*, II, pp. 445-446.
[13] *Ephemeris*, 1922, pp. 1-25; *Knossos*, II, pp. 279-285.

a smaller paved area to the south, several storage rooms in the house itself (15-18), a number of magazines with pithoi (24, 25, 31), and a series of rectangular grain-bins (26-30) in a walled courtyard to the north.

The possibility that it may have been something other than a private dwelling is suggested mainly by the contents of certain rooms. Room 18 contained some forty to fifty clay altars neatly stacked in piles, and others were found in 16 and 17; in Room 14 were four large stone lamps; and in 7 were discovered four very big double-axes of thin bronze, one about four feet (1.20 m.) wide, intended obviously for ritual use. One fragment of wall painting bears a representation of a sacral knot; in the court to the east there were remains of sacral horns and a niche evidently designed to receive them, and nearby a kind of altar.

The Greek excavator and Evans have suggested that the building was the headquarters of a High Priest, indeed a kind of central bureau for the dissemination of the Faith. Architecturally, however, there is little or nothing to distinguish it as anything but a private house. Very unusual, if not unique, is the use of the smaller part of the Hall (2) as a sort of porch with two columns facing on to an open court rather than on a light-well. This superficially megaron-like scheme may have occurred also in the Royal Villa and in House Za at Mallia, but these are probably to be restored as true light-wells. The group of small rooms, 3-10, opening off the Hall may have formed the private living quarters, though there is no distinct bathroom (see Ch. v).

10. HOUSES AT TYLISSOS

In the heart of a little town, still known by its perhaps four thousand year old name of Tylissos, lie the remains of three very interesting Minoan buildings. Tylissos is reached today from Herakleion (7½ m. or 12 km.) by a winding road which continues on through picturesque valleys to the northern foothills of Mount Ida, which form a magnificent background for the Minoan ruins.

Their excavation by Hazzidakis (1909-1913) was occasioned by the accidental discovery of three huge bronze cauldrons (Fig. 142, G). Platon has recently made a restudy of the buildings, accompanied by further excavation, conservation, and restoration; he has generously allowed me to mention some of his findings, but for the revised plans we must await his publication.[14]

Two of the buildings, A and C, were no doubt houses, though A is so large that it is sometimes referred to as a Little Palace; much of their walls is built of excellently dressed and coursed masonry (Fig. 78). The other building, B, is a remarkably regular rectangular structure, but it has no clear features of Minoan domestic architecture, and may have been simply a storehouse for A.

11. HOUSE A, TYLISSOS

Largest of the houses at Tylissos, House A has a maximum length of about 115 ft. (35 m.) and a width varying from 54 to 60 ft. (16½ to 18 m.). It falls into two distinct halves, each fairly rectangular in outline, and each containing two sets of stairways; the northern half, on the ground floor, is the service quarter, while the southern contained the living quarters of the family (Fig. 19).

The most important complex of rooms includes the Hall, 6, which is paved irregularly with flagstones interrupted by two slightly raised rectangular platforms of unknown use. At the west end of the room is a slight variation of the plaster-floored light-well; the small extra portico on its north side was apparently intended to provide a covered passage from the Hall into the important room, 3. Other small rooms open off the Hall, including a possible toilet, 7, with a drain in the southwest corner, and a bathroom, 11, which, like the one in the South

---

[14] The new plans (by Piet de Jong) are now hung in the Herakleion Museum.

House at Knossos, was changed from a room with steps leading to a lower floor level to one with a floor level even with that of the Hall.

A group of small rooms, 12-14, with a corridor, A, is entered by a single door from the Hall. This is strongly reminiscent of the arrangement of the women's quarters in the residential area of the palaces, and the resemblance is strengthened by the private stairway to the upper rooms.

Room 3 with a central pillar was the Pillar Crypt; a pyramidal stand for a double-axe was found in it, and two smaller rooms, 4 and 5, opening off it seem to have been associated "treasuries." In 5 was discovered a bronze ingot like those from H. Triadha, and in 4 the three bronze cauldrons mentioned above.

In the northern half of the house a deep L-shaped portico, 15, faced on a small paved court into which the main entrance opened by way of a narrow corridor (not shown on our plan). The two large rooms, 16 and 17, north of this, contained many big storage jars. On their axes were two pillars each, and the finding of painted fragments of stucco in 17 suggests that there were two large and important rooms over them in the second storey, or more probably a single very large hall with two rows of three columns each. In its plan such a room would have resembled the banquet halls (as we have identified them) in the palaces (Ch. vi, 2); like the one in the palace at Mallia it would also have been accessible from two stairways. The stair adjacent to the west, located conveniently near the storerooms and a series of small rooms where food could have been prepared, would be used by household servants; the long stairway reached from the portico opposite the main entrance, and leading directly to the southwest corner of the room, would be used by guests.

12. HOUSE C, TYLISSOS

House C at Tylissos is considerably smaller than House A, but is better preserved; indeed many of its walls are intact almost to the second storey. Some remains at a high level, including two column bases and a cistern at the northeast corner, belong to a rebuilding of the house in the L.M. III period.

The house has the characteristic irregular outline with the various groups of rooms forming projecting wings (Fig. 20). Four quarters or groups of rooms may be distinguished: cult rooms, 2-3, in the southeast—one with a central pillar; a complex of storage rooms, 8-10, in the west; the living quarters, 12-15, in the north; and a central group, 4-6, of unknown use. To serve these rooms there was an extensive and remarkably preserved system of corridors, A to D, repeated no doubt on the second floor, which was reached by three sets of stairways.

The Main Hall of the Residential Quarter, 15, had a flagged floor and the usual pier-and-door partition (Fig. 77). A remarkably deep light-well opened on the east end of the Hall through the regular two-columned portico; on its south side a well preserved and now fully restored window, over eight feet (2½ m.) wide and divided into three openings, supplied light to Room 14. From the main part of the Hall a door opens into the more private quarters. The first room, 12, as Platon has discovered, in its original form contained a bathroom of the usual type with steps down to a lower level; later, however, like the one in House A, it was remodeled. Room 14 would presumably be the Women's Hall. A long corridor, D, secured by a door, led to a flight of stairs no doubt serving the bedrooms, and, at its far end, to a room, 13, with a toilet provided with a drain through the outer wall (Fig. 79).

A single large Hall presumably covered the area over Magazines 8-10, and four of the bases of a pier-and-door partition are preserved in position on the north-south wall between 8 and 9-10. The arrangement bears an obvious resemblance to the great public halls over the west magazines in the Minoan palaces.

13. HOUSES AT MALLIA

At Mallia, as well as at Knossos and Phaistos, the palace was surrounded by districts of houses, such as Quarter D to the west of the palace. Excavations have been made in various of these residential areas, but the only one which has been linked up directly with the palace itself is that currently being excavated to the east of the palace and known as Quarter Z (Fig. 24).

An irregular and not yet fully defined area along the east side of the palace forms a large cobble-paved "East Court," and through this, beginning at the southeast entry of the Central Court, runs a fairly straight, narrow street paved partly with cobblestones, partly with a line of stone flagging. On this street lie Houses Za and Zb, about 120 ft. (nearly 40 m.) east of the palace on the north side, and over 220 ft. (nearly 70 m.) on the south side, respectively.

Like the palace itself the houses at Mallia are of simpler quality than those at Knossos. Most have rubble foundations, floors flagged (at best) with irregular slabs of schist, and pillar bases of roughly rectangular blocks of stone. However they share many characteristics with the better houses at other sites, and two of them, Da and Za, provide very clear and typical examples of the upper-class Minoan house.[15]

14. HOUSE Dᴀ, MALLIA

Particularly well preserved is the ground plan of House Da (Fig. 22). Its indented outline reveals very distinctly the typical Minoan way of building houses, or palaces, in a series of "agglutinative" units corresponding to the arrangement of the rooms.

The entrance from the west opened into a probably unroofed vestibule, 1, with flagged floor and a doorway at the left giving access to a double storage room found filled with large jars. A double doorway at the end of the vestibule opened into a flagged corridor, 2, and so directly into the Main Hall, 5, entered through a four-bayed partition. Another four-bayed pier-and-door partition divided the Hall unequally into two parts, both

---

[15] Houses Za and Da are published in *Mallia, Maisons*, 1; Zb, House E, and a general discussion of the street and area to the east of the palace, in *Mallia, Maisons*, 11.

roughly flagged. The usual light-well at the end of the smaller part had a single central column and a drain through the wall at the northwest corner. A flagged corridor continues north from just outside the entrance of the Hall to a door controlling access to the private apartments. These consisted of a large flagged room, 6; a bathroom, 7, with the usual sunken floor; and a smaller room with a thin partition shielding the entrance to the toilet in the corner (Fig. 114), a toilet which has the distinction of being the best preserved one in Crete (Ch. v, 4). Another corridor, 4, leads directly into the private apartments through a double door.

The rooms in the south end of the house seem to have been used for work and storage. Near the entrance to the Hall a stairway with the unusual feature of "winders" at the bottom suggests that there was an upper storey of some importance.

To preserve the remains of this interesting house the excavators have rebuilt the walls in rubble and roofed it over at the level of the first storey. Our Fig. 21 attempts to restore the original appearance of the house with the aid of the "Town Mosaic" from Knossos (Fig. 103).

15. HOUSE Zᴀ, MALLIA

House Za has a remarkably regular rectangular outline for a Minoan building and measures about 80 by 57 ft. (24½ by 17½ m.). The part of the house used for living purposes was limited, at least on the ground floor, to about one-third of the total area, and was sharply separated from the rest, used for storage and work purposes, by a straight line of wall broken only by a single doorway (Fig. 25). This door, which seems to have been the only entrance to the living quarters, was reached by a long corridor, 2, from a roughly flagged vestibule housing a two-flight stairway, 15, to the upper floor.

The door at the end of 2 opened at right angles into a second corridor, 4, from which one passed directly into the Main Hall, 12. The walls of the Hall were stuccoed and the floors of both parts, on either side of the usual pier-and-door partition, were roughly flagged. At the west end of the room opened a plaster-floored, single-columned light-well; its walls should be shown on the restored plan (Fig. 25).[16]

Close to the entrance to the Hall a doorway opened into the private apartments, while just outside this door, and therefore conveniently located with respect to both the Hall and the Women's Quarters, was placed the usual bathroom, 11, with sunken floor. The principal room, 5, of the Women's Quarters was a kind of small edition of the Main Hall, with flagged floor and transverse pillar partition, and apparently a small light-well, 8, beyond; this is particularly surprising since the pillar partition and light-well do not otherwise seem to occur in the Women's Hall outside of the Palace of Minos itself. Reached from the far corner of the apartment was a narrow doorway to the toilet which projected entirely beyond the walls of the house in an extravagance of hygienic enthusiasm.

In addition to the entrance into the main part of the house an adjacent entrance into 21 retains in place a fine stone threshold with the door-pivot holes and mortises for the upright posts of the jambs (Fig. 110 and Ch. IX, 3). Room 24, apparently reached from this by a double doorway with three rough jamb bases in position, has certain features of interest (Fig. 26). In the center of the western part of the room is a round column base, and in line with this in the north wall is a flat block intended, it would seem, for a post; evidently a transverse beam to support the ceiling ran from the north to the south walls. Around the sides of the room against the foundations of the walls was set a low rubble wall; this was surely not part of the foundations, as treated in the restored plan, but a low bench of a type found not infrequently elsewhere. This bench is interrupted at the northeast corner of the room, but certainly not for a window, as proposed; a window in a corner with its sill at the floor level would be strange indeed, and there is no support for

---

[16] Part of the plaster floor of the light-well is actually preserved.

such a restoration in the appearance of the outer foundation wall at this point. The resemblance of the arrangement to that in the "Throne Room" at Knossos suggests to me that a wooden seat or "thronos" was placed in the gap between the benches. Whoever sat here was well placed to see all those sitting on the benches as well as to command the doorway. But the nature of the meetings or ceremonies that took place in this chamber is not explained by any objects found in it.

16. HOUSE Zʙ, MALLIA

House Zb is more irregular than the preceding houses and inferior in quality, but not without architectural features of interest.

As in Za there was a two-flight stairway opening off the vestibule, *a*, in the northeast corner of the house (Fig. 27). The entrance corridor turns into a central room whose roof was supported by a single column. Were it not for the column base and for the rarity of courts in Minoan house architecture the manner in which the other rooms revolve about and open off this central room would suggest that it was an open court;[16a] possibly, like the central hall of the Egyptian houses at Amarna (ca. 1375 B.C.), there was a clerestory above this room providing light and air to the surrounding rooms.

The space under the stairs, i, was used as a cupboard for the best pottery; vi, xv, and perhaps other rooms, served for storage; the presence of ashes in xii, unless they fell from an upper storey, may indicate that it was a kitchen.

The main living room or Hall, vii, served apparently by a private entry on the south, *b*, opened directly, without the usual portico-like section, through a pillar partition on a light-well. The excavators termed iii a weaving room since loomweights were found in it, but it is hard to see where there would have been space for a loom to be set up. The small, flagged room, ix,

[16a] Cf. Weinberg, *AJA*, 65 (1961), p. 318; he suggests that the irregular south half of the house was a later addition.

opening off the Hall, is called a bathroom; but the very large drain at floor level in the southwest corner suggests that it was really a toilet.

A few other points of disagreement with the restored plan may be mentioned. Along the east side of the south entrance, *b*, runs a low rubble bench, not shown on the plan; such benches are found at the entrance to House B at Palaikastro (Fig. 29), and in Room 53, the northeast entry at Phaistos (Fig. 4). In spite of the difference in levels it does seem that there was a doorway to xii from the southeast corner of xvii, and that xii connected in turn with xiv through a door at the west end of the wall dividing them. The proposed window in ii at a low level and directly on the street is most unlikely; though the sill is a little high for the threshold of a door this is not an unreasonable precaution against surface water running into the house from a flooded street.

17. HOUSE E, THE "LITTLE PALACE," MALLIA

It is not surprising that the excavators at Mallia have been tempted to refer to a large building, accidentally discovered about a hundred yards south of the palace in 1931, as a "Little Palace," for its area (so far as it can be defined) is nearly twice that of the Little Palace at Knossos, while the workmanship of certain features rivals that of the Mallia palace.

Nevertheless the plan is so unorthodox that the French archaeologists were still vainly attempting to make sense of its maze of irregular rooms a quarter of a century later. The official publication has now appeared and is a model of conscientious thoroughness, yet it asks almost more questions than it answers. Some of the confusion is due to the incorporation of elements of an earlier house (M.M. I), and to a late rehabilitation of parts of the building after a partial destruction. In Fig. 23 we present a "regularized" plan, based on a tracing from the excellent French "excavated condition" plan, in the hope of making it more intelligible.

67

The main entrance "sidles" in from the street on the north, much in the manner of the north entrance of the palace, to a paved vestibule, i.[16b] From this a corridor, ii, leads into a large flagged court, ii *bis*. Northwest of this a smaller court, v, has an L-shaped colonnade with four fine column bases in position. West of v only workrooms and storerooms seem to have existed, the clearest being a row of six rooms opening on a corridor, xlvii-xli. In the southwestern area of the house is a small impluvium-like court, xiv, with piers perhaps on all sides.

The south-central part of the house presumably contained the living quarters since ix is a bathroom of the usual type. In its west wall are two niches, not known elsewhere in a bathroom; a fine stone lamp (Fig. 140, G) and a fragment of an offering table were found in the room. The large room, viii, off which it opens, has none of the characteristic features of a "Minoan Hall," but the remains of plaster painted with plant designs found there has earned it the name of "Salle aux Fresques."

A number of other minor features of interest occur, but nothing that seems to throw further light on the nature of the building. No evidence was obtained for the existence of a stairway to a second storey.[16c]

18. THE VILLA OF THE LILIES, AMNISOS

Amnisos: one jar of honey to Eleuthia. (LINEAR B TABLET from Knossos)[17]

Amnisos is remembered in later tradition, and under its correct Minoan name, as a harborage for Knossos. Odysseus mentions it as the site of a cave where Eilithyia was worshiped,[18]

[16b] Seton Lloyd appears to have found a similar entrance in his palace at Beycesultan in Asia Minor, and he notes the Mallia parallel (it also appears in the palace and in House Db), *Anatolian Studies*, 6 (1956), p. 121. It is also common in the Amarna houses; cf. e.g. W. S. Smith, *Art and Architecture of Ancient Egypt*, fig. 70.

[16c] Weinberg suggests that there was a stairway in the vestibule, i, *AJA*, 65 (1961), p. 319; but I am inclined to suppose that this formed a passage to Court v, and that there may have been a stairway in ii, leading to a portico along the north side of Court ii *bis*.

[17] *DMG*, p. 310, no. 206.

[18] *Odyssey*, 19, 188.

a Cretan deity whose name has recently been read on a Linear B tablet from Knossos, and who survived into Greek times as a goddess of childbirth. The cave, containing stalagmites—one manifestation of the Cretan pillar cult—was explored as early as 1884, and its entrance is now marked by a fig tree high up on a hillside some distance back from the sea and within a few yards of a modern motor road.

A few yards from the sea a fine Minoan mansion was excavated and published by Marinatos in 1932.[19] Recently it has been further studied and restored by Platon, but since his findings and a revised plan have not yet appeared we can only describe it in a general way and illustrate it with a photograph taken in 1959 (Fig. 76).

The quality of the house is indicated by the massive outer walls built of huge dressed limestone orthostates marked with tridents and a star. Some of these blocks, in spite of their size, had been toppled out of position by a quake, or more probably by a tidal wave (Ch. 1), which destroyed the house around 1500 B.C. Graceful wall paintings of lilies have given the villa its modern name; and a large Hall in the northeast corner had a six-bayed pier-and-door partition with gypsum bases opening north on a flagged terrace with a fine view of the sea and the island of Dia. The rest of the Residential Quarter is badly destroyed, but Platon has succeeded in identifying a short flight of steps leading down to a bathroom. That there was a second storey is proved by the remains of a stairway.

19. HOUSE B, PALAIKASTRO

Excavations made by the British School at Palaikastro on the east coast from 1902 to 1906 revealed part of a small town with narrow, winding streets and a considerable number of small houses (Fig. 28). Few yield intelligible plans, and the site was completely ruined during the last war.[20]

[19] *Praktika*, 1932, pp. 76-94; cf. *BCH*, 57 (1933), pp. 292-295.
[20] *BSA*, 8 (1901-1902), pp. 306-316; 9 (1902-1903), pp. 277-296; 10 (1903-1904), pp. 192-226; 11 (1904-1905), pp. 272-290.

In the center of House B is a large rectangular room with an impluvium-like court having a column at each of the four corners; since there was no drain it may have been covered by a clerestory (Fig. 29). Two other houses at this site have similar courts, termed "megarons" by the excavators, and we have noticed a similar arrangement in House E at Mallia.

The smaller room, 2, off the court, with a stepped bathroom of the usual type, would apparently constitute the "Women's Quarters." The so-called bathroom, 15, in another part of the house, was perhaps a toilet. There are also remains of stairs leading to a second storey. One other feature of interest is the row of alternating pillar and column bases in front of the entrance (Fig. 28).

20. HOUSE AT SKLAVOKAMBOS

Some six miles (9-10 km.) west of Tylissos the remains of a large house were accidentally found by road builders in the 1930's, and much of the northern part was destroyed before archaeologists could be summoned to excavate the rest;[21] it was further damaged during the war. The site, impressive in its lonely isolation, lies near a small stream at the foot of a high rocky hill, with the nearest settlement, Gonies, visible on a hillside some distance to the west.

The southern half of the house was used for storage and service and had a separate entrance (Fig. 32). In the center is a small court, 15, with four pillars, resembling those at Palaikastro and Mallia E. Traces of a hearth were found in the portico and two rooms opening on the west side of the court seem to have been used in the preparation of food.

The main part of the house was entered by a double door near the southeast corner, 1. The largest room, 4, was badly destroyed; it opened through three bays on a narrow corridor, 5, at the west end of which was a group of three rooms. One of these, 12, was used for storage, and three jars were found in 11, which however seems to have served principally as a con-

[21] *Ephemeris*, 1939-1941, pp. 69-96.

necting link with a broad, pillared veranda facing the north and a fine view. Beneath the stairway, 6-7, was a toilet with a drain through the outside wall. Of the other rooms little is known.

21. PLATI, LASITHI PLAIN

In the plain of Lasithi near the cave sanctuary of Psychro in east-central Crete a one month campaign was conducted by the British School in May 1913.[22] A number of rather nondescript rooms were excavated around three sides of an open area; best preserved are those along the southwest side, at A on the plan (Fig. 30). Two periods of construction were distinguished: L.M. I and L.M. II. At the close of the excavation the remains were refilled (only a few blocks are visible today), and the report left it an open question whether part of a regularly planned Minoan town with a number of houses about an open area had been discovered, or whether the remains were those of a single unidentified building about a central court.

Our plan presents a redrawing of the published excavation plan with some simplification and omission of walls that do not belong to the main period of occupation. It will be seen that the various rooms appear to belong together in a unified complex rather than to be parts of separate houses, and, except for the orientation, which is more east-west than north-south, the plan bears a remarkable resemblance to the central court scheme of the major palaces. In particular it will be noted that though rather narrower than the courts of such palaces as Mallia—a little over 50 ft. (16 m.) instead of 80 ft. (over 24 m.)—it is, as preserved, about as long. Further, the pillared front at A, with the complex of rooms (13, 15, 17-20) behind it, is definitely reminiscent in form and position of the Tripartite Shrine at Knossos, Room 25 at Phaistos, Suite vi at Mallia, and a pillared portico at Gournia (Ch. vii, 2).

If not part of a palace, possibly we have here a court for the bull games surrounded by the suite of rooms needed to accommodate the bulls, performers, officials of the games, etc., and for the associated religious ceremonies.

[22] *BSA*, 20 (1913-1914), pp. 1-13.

22. OTHER SITES

Houses of the Minoan period have been excavated at many other sites, but because of poor preservation, architectural insignificance, or incomplete excavation or publication, they would not repay description here, though some may be referred to later for particular details. Among these we may mention Knossos itself, Mallia, Phaistos, Prasa and Katsamba near Herakleion, Kefala (southwest of Mt. Dikte), Pseira, Siteia, Zou (near Siteia), and Zakros in east Crete, and Apodhoulou and Monasteraki in south central Crete (Fig. 1).[23] The Italian School has also just excavated (1958) a large farmhouse near Gortyn, whose lower floor was almost entirely given up to store- and cult-rooms; no stairs were found, though it presumably had a second storey.[24]

In addition, remains of three large buildings, identified as "palaces," have been found southwest of Knossos: at Arkhanes, Vathypetro, and Kanli Kastelli. Evans suggested that the first was a summer palace for the lords of Knossos; the other two are candidates for the site of Lykastos, mentioned by Homer as one of the seven important cities of Crete.[25] Vathypetro was perhaps never completed. It has a marvelous view over the valley toward Kanli Kastelli, and is the most fully excavated; but Marinatos plans further excavation before publication.[26] Its most unusual feature is a grape or olive press (Fig. 94). Kydonia in west Crete, mentioned by Diodorus Siculus along with Knossos and Phaistos, has never been located; presumably it was near Khanea.[27]

[23] See Bibliography of Minor Sites.
[24] Levi, "La Villa rurale minoica di Gortina," *Bollettino d'Arte*, 44 (1959), pp. 237-268.
[25] *Iliad*, 2, 646-648.
[26] Marinatos, *C. and M.*, pp. 66, 68.
[27] Diod. Sic., 5. 78. 2.

THE CENTRAL COURT AND THE
BULL GAMES

THE IMPORTANCE of the central court is clear from a glance at the plan of any of the major palaces (Fig. 7). At Mallia, where an estimate can be made most accurately, it occupies, together with its porticoes, nearly a fifth of the total area (Fig. 6). Indeed the Cretan architects, at least at Phaistos and Mallia, seem to have laid out the court first and then to have employed two of its adjacent sides as base lines to develop outwards the various quarters of the palace (Ch. XIII, 1).

Perhaps there is no need to look far for an explanation of the existence of these large courts. Besides serving as the organizing nucleus of the plan, at once dividing and uniting the parts of the palace, they must also have formed, like the court of the Classical Greek house, the focus of much of the daily activities of normal palace life. The porticoes and galleries, which constituted an integral part of the court, provided a pleasant retreat from rain, wind, or the blaze of the summer sun. Palace domestics and artisans would have found the court a pleasant spot for some of their tasks, although at Phaistos and Mallia there were special service courts and areas, and the children of the royal household and their friends had ample space for their endless games.

Again as in the Hellenic house many of the rooms and groups of rooms faced on the central court and derived their light and air from it or from its porticoes. Nevertheless, since it was not shut in by contiguous structures as was the Greek town house, nor confined within high fortification walls like the Mesopotamian palace at Mari (Fig. 148), the Minoan palace was not entirely "introverted": the royal residential apartments looked outward through columned porticoes, and the great state halls in the Piano Nobile had large windows opening upon the west courts. Moreover a central court is not a characteristic, let alone invariable, feature of even the larger Minoan houses, suggesting that the inner court was not an indispensable and inevitable feature of Minoan domestic architecture. The more restricted "light-well" was perhaps more congenial to the Cretan climate.

It is probable, also, that entertainments such as boxing, a popular Cretan sport, and dancing, perhaps always a religious rite, took place in the central court, whose west side was lined by various shrines. Of course the "Theatral Areas" and the west courts must likewise have been the scene of various ceremonies, as in fact the "causeways" in the fresco of the "Sacred Grove and the Dance" indicate.[1]

However the central courts have certain peculiarities which seem to call for some explanation beyond what we have so far suggested.[2] For instance, it is a strange fact that the "central" court at Gournia lies actually outside the limits of the palace (Fig. 8), as if it were not so much a necessary and integral part of the palace structure itself as a large open area which provided for some form of activity associated with palatial or civic life. There may even have been, at times, a "central court" without a palace at all, a possibility we have mentioned at Plati (Ch. III, 21, and Fig. 30).

Peculiar likewise is the remarkable degree of similarity, in a number of respects amounting almost to identity, among the central courts of the three major palaces (Fig. 7). All were paved with flagstones; all had one or more porticoes, probably with upper galleries, on the long sides; all had their long axis

---

[1] *Knossos*, III, pl. 18; Evans takes the "causeways" to be low isodomic walls, and so Karo (*Greifen am Thron*, p. 50), but cf. Platon, *Kret. Chron.*, 13 (1959), p. 239.

[2] For a fuller discussion, with references, of the use of the central courts for the bull games see my article in *AJA*, 61 (1957), pp. 255-262.

running north and south;[3] and all measure about 80 ft. (24 m.) broad by 170 ft. (52 m.) long. This standardization, as it were, of the court might even suggest that it was built to definite specifications, like a football field or a tennis court.

In several ways the Minoan central courts resemble the long narrow public plazas or forums of early Italian towns with their surrounding porticoes and galleries. These were so designed, the Augustan architect Vitruvius tells us, not only to serve the traffic and commerce of everyday life, but also to double as a place for staging the favorite public entertainment of the time, gladiatorial exhibitions.[4]

If we take a cue from this and ask what was the favorite spectacle of the Minoan Cretans there can be no doubt of the answer. Over and over again in their wall paintings, their gems, and their minor arts, we see represented the famous bull games (Fig. 102). At least in origin these shows were no doubt of a religious nature, a form of sacred ceremonial, designed to please or to appease the gods; in actual practice they may have tended, like our Christmas celebration, to become more and more secularized. They were not bull *fights*, as they are sometimes carelessly called, for no weapons were involved, and the animals were apparently not injured in any way—unless it may be that they were sacrificed at the conclusion (Fig. 101). The performances were a test of skill and agility. Cretan youths, and girls too, no doubt after lengthy preliminary training, pitted their dexterity, strength, and courage against powerful bulls in a thrilling display of skilful manoeuvers which culminated in (the favorite moment for the artists to select for their representations) an almost incredible tour de force: the acrobat faced the charging animal head-on, deftly seized its horns and, as it angrily tossed back its head, used the impetus thus gained to perform a full somersault over the bull's back, and so alight on the floor of the arena behind. If the performer

[3] Conspicuously on the axis of the Central Courts at Phaistos and Knossos are the "holy mountains" Ida and Iuktas, respectively (Fig. 51, and *Knossos*, IV, fig. 7, and suppl. plate 56).
[4] 5, I, 1-2.

75

were killed—ritually immolated in effect to the Minoan goddess —perhaps he could look forward to the assured enjoyment of some Minoan Elysium.

Representations of the bull games sometimes hint at an architectural background, and Evans himself was of the opinion that the "Grandstand Fresco," as he called it, depicted a large crowd of Cretan men and women watching these sports in a setting of columns and a tricolumnar shrine (Fig. 133). He also fancied that this signified some kind of amphitheater with tiers of seats rising amid a grandiose architectural framework: a special arena somewhere outside the limits of the palace. But no traces of any such structure have ever been detected at the three major sites, and it is in fact plain that no specialized form of sports auditorium on such an elaborate architectural scale existed before the amphitheaters of Roman times.

Although the porticoes and galleries and (at Knossos) the Tripartite Shrine embedded in them irresistibly suggest themselves as the source of inspiration for the background architecture of the "Grandstand Fresco," it is sufficiently evident why Sir Arthur could not conceive of this rough-and-tumble sport taking place in the central court of the palace. For at Knossos he could see no sign of precautions taken to prevent a careering bull from penetrating into the surrounding porticoes or passages, with dire results both to the palace and to the spectators. But the boundaries of the Knossos court are very badly preserved, and the search must be extended beyond the Palace of Minos.

At Phaistos there are clear traces of doors to protect all the openings on the Central Court, although it is difficult to see their usefulness in the ordinary régime of palace life. The most extraordinary and significant instance is the façade of the large hall, 25, near the northwest corner of the court, which is composed of two great pillars on either side of an oval central column (Fig. 50). At some time after its original construction the intervals between the pairs of pillars were walled up, probably, we may imagine, for only four or five feet above the floor level; and doors were then set up to close the remaining space between the pillars and the column. The Italian publication comments on this astonishing architectural practice of closing a door against a column, but does not offer any explanation.[5]

An even more peculiar situation is found at Mallia, where the surroundings of the court are very well preserved (Fig. 6). On the west side of the court access to a flight of steps some 10½ ft. (3.20 m.) broad, leading to important rooms in the second storey, was controlled by a set of double doors. The French excavators remark on the strangeness of this feature, but do not attempt to explain it.[6] Along the north end of the same court runs a columned portico with another odd arrangement: a distinct threshold, and therefore a doorway, between the two columns at the west end (Fig. 57). This can only mean that passage between the other columns was not left free; what form the barrier between these columns took is not known, but one might conjecture a mud brick wall four or five feet high. On the east side of the court there is a well-preserved portico about 110 ft. (ca. 33½ m.) long, made up of alternating pillars and columns, a common Minoan arrangement. On the upper surface of the stone sill between each pillar and column are three circular cuttings, plainly sockets for the tenons of vertical posts some 9 in. (22 cm.) in diameter, capped no doubt by a horizontal railing. Such a balustrade in an upper gallery would be quite understandable as a means of protection against a fall, but here portico and court are practically on the same level. Nor can it be explained as a barrier to keep humans from entering the portico from the court (even if any reason were apparent for so doing), for the spacing of the posts is wide enough to allow even an adult to squeeze between them, and probably one could also have climbed over the railing. It seems difficult, then, to explain this barrier except as designed to prevent some large domestic animal from getting into the portico from the court.[7] But the palace court was certainly not the place for

[5] *Festòs*, II, pp. 71-72.   [6] *Mallia*, I, p. 32.
[7] There is a possible trace of a barrier in the similar portico on the east side of the Central Court at Phaistos, as I noticed in 1959: the top surface (1.20 m. above

stabling cattle, while the horse was still very rare in Minoan Crete.

Thus the rooms and porticoes surrounding the central court were in fact protected, which removes the objections felt by Evans and others to the otherwise obvious suggestion that the central court was also the bull ring. Since the animals were not goaded to fury by the tortures to which they are subjected in the Spanish arena the doors and railings indicated by the remains would no doubt have formed an adequate barrier. On a fragment of a mural painting from Knossos a Minoan lady is shown standing behind a fence similar to that suggested by the remains of the east portico at Mallia, while beside her enough remains to indicate a crowd of male spectators, as in the Grandstand Fresco (Figs. 133, 136, C).

A well-known gem which Evans described as "the finest combination of powerful execution with minute detail to be found, perhaps, in the whole range of the Minoan gem-engraver's Art" represents a bull with its forelegs up on a large rectangular object decorated by a series of latticed lines which follow the four sides and the diagonals of the rectangle; above the rectangle, at the upper left, a man in the usual Minoan toreador's costume is leaping head first on to the animal's head (Fig. 54).[8] The common but hardly possible explanation of this scene is that it shows a man capturing a bull which he has surprised drinking from a tank. Surely no bull would drink in such a fashion nor would a Minoan artist have so represented him!

On the diamond-cut-diamond principle we propose to solve this riddle by conjuring up a second. In the northwest corner of the Phaistos court is a construction which the official publication leaves as an "enigma" (Fig. 52). It consists of a carefully built platform of dressed masonry about 8 ft. 3 in. (2.50 m.) long by 2 ft. 8 in. (0.80 m.) wide by 3 ft. 8 in. (1.12 m.) high,

the stylobate) of the top block of the northernmost base shows, in the center of its south edge, the traces of a cutting 4½ cm. wide by 4 cm. deep.

[8] *Knossos*, III, p. 185, fig. 129. In the latest publication of the seal V.E.G. Kenna interprets the scene in the usual way without further comment (*Cretan Seals*, Oxford, 1960, p. 118, pl. 8, no. 202).

which narrows at its east end and drops down to a height of 2 ft. (0.60 m.). This gives it a step-like appearance, and in fact the upper edge of both the lower and the upper stone block at the east end is worn as if from frequent stepping up and down upon the platform. Yet as a flight of steps it makes no sense, for there are no openings at or near this level in the well preserved wall behind it. Can we suppose that one of the doubtless numerous manoeuvers which were devised to lend variety and interest to the bull games was one in which the acrobat, cornered, whether intentionally or not, in this blind angle of the court, quickly stepped up on this platform and, at the right moment, as the bull perhaps succeeded in getting his forefeet on the narrow end of the first step, bounded upon its back and thence to the ground behind the bull, safe from his apparent impasse (Fig. 50). In early Spanish bull baiting, it is interesting to note, vaulting over the bull from a chair or table was a recognized manoeuver.

That there is a significant correspondence between the scene on the gem just described and the platform in the Central Court at Phaistos is indicated by the fact that the distinctive pattern on the rectangular object on the gem (which represents, in our view, the stone leaping-platform) occurs nowhere else in Cretan art except painted at a large scale on the rear face of the two deep niches which, symmetrically set on either side of the great central doorway, are a very conspicuous feature of the impressive façade which formed the north end of the Central Court (Fig. 50), and on a similar niche just within the same doorway.[9] One of these niches is in fact but a few feet away from the stone platform in the northwest corner of the court (Fig. 53); small wonder that the gem-engraver associated the pattern and the platform in his mind! Indeed it is quite possible that the pattern had some symbolical connection, presumably religious, with the bull games.[10]

[9] Fragments of plaster apparently with a similar design were also found in the fill under Stairway 76, evidently from the ruins of an earlier palace, *Festòs*, II, p. 62.

[10] Cf. *Knossos*, I, pp. 375-376.

It is tempting to suppose that it is not merely coincidence that the main north-south axis of the Central Court of Phaistos, the scene of the bull games (Fig. 50), points directly toward the sacred cave of Kamares, much frequented from Early Minoan times, on the south slope of Mount Ida (Fig. 51). And surely the double-peaked crest of that mountain must have suggested to the Minoans, as it does to us, their sacred symbol the sacral horns, which are commonly supposed to have their origin in a conventionalization of the horns of a bull.[11]

It may also be due to some connection with the bull games that toward the north end of the west side of the court in each of the major palaces, and perhaps also at Gournia, Plati, and Vathypetro, there is a room where religious rites may have been performed. At Knossos this is the "Tripartite Columnar Shrine"; at Mallia, a large room with an altar (vi 1); and at Phaistos, Room 25 with its imposing façade of piers and central column (Fig. 50). Was the bull sacrificed here at the end of the performance?[12] Or was it the scene of certain preparatory rituals? One further conjecture: were some of the rooms facing on Corridor 26, which connects with the rear of Room 25 at Phaistos, temporary stalls for the bulls while awaiting the performances (Fig. 4)? They must have been kept somewhere nearby, and where else more suitably? This might also explain the curious ramp down into Room vi 12 at Mallia, one of the rooms behind the room with the altar (Fig. 6).[13]

Can we with the available evidence, and not a little fancy to eke it out, imagine what one of these performances may have been like—say at Phaistos?

The sun has just arisen, one early summer morning in the fifteenth century B.C., over the eastern hills. The sky is a bril-

[11] Nilsson, *MMR²*, pp. 185-186.

[12] Forsdyke interprets the scenes on the Chieftain Cup found at H. Triadha, as the presentation of the hides of sacrificed bulls to Minos, *Journal of the Warburg and Courtauld Institutes*, 15 (1952), pp. 13-19; Evans says that "the bull of sacrifice, in fact, is a bull of the arena" (*Knossos*, IV, p. 44). And see further discussion Ch. VII, 2 (end).

[13] *Mallia*, I, p. 24, fig. 3, pl. 15, 2.

liant blue unflecked with clouds, except to the north where the eternal bank slumbers on the ridge of Ida. But even at this hour groups of peasants in simple but brightly colored festive costumes are streaming forth from dozens of little villages across the fertile plain to Phaistos on its hilltop.

Cheerful chatter and country songs relieve the tedium of the trek along dusty paths converging on the long, low palace building. Here the staff of the royal household is already busily preparing for the oncoming multitudes and arranging for the games and ceremonies of the festival in honor of the Great Mother. A number of handsome bulls have been brought in from their pastures on the preceding day, and attendants are now feeding and watering them in their temporary stalls just off the Central Court, and giving them a final grooming with brush and comb to make them perfect offerings for the goddess. In the court, where the sun is just beginning to light up the western porticoes, gangs of men are spreading a thick coat of sand over the flagging to provide a softer footing for man and beast, and several youths and girls are already limbering up their muscles in preparation for the dangerous sport ahead.

By mid morning all is in readiness. The arena has been cleared save for the attendants who patrol it with long staves, and make certain that all the doors which open on it from the ground floor rooms of the palace are well secured. The long porticoes and the galleries above are overflowing with an animated and excited crowd whose voices fill the court with a babble of eager expectation. From the windows and balconies in the upper storeys gay throngs of aristocratic courtiers and their ladies look down: the men trim-waisted and proudly erect, with short wavy black hair, their handsome darkly tanned bodies set off by a scanty but gaily colored and patterned kilt; the ladies with their elaborately waved tresses, fashionably pale skin, reddened lips, gleaming necklaces, flounced skirts, and daringly cut boleros—a sight to have graced the court of the Grand Monarque himself.

The din of voices suddenly changes tone. A number of boxers

wearing a peculiar kind of tight-fitting trunks and a heavy leather helmet enter the courtyard and, pairing off, proceed to pummel one another with a vigor that brings cries of appreciation from the crowd, though their lack of strategy and of defensive tactics would shock the boxing-fan of today. After this sport has lasted for some time the boxers retire; there is a subdued hush of anticipation; and then into the arena, tumbling and cartwheeling in their exuberant vitality, come the star performers of the day, both men and girls clad only in the tight-fitting trunks worn also by the boxers.

Meanwhile the preliminary religious ceremonies are being conducted in the high-ceilinged room on the west of the court, and presently one of the great doors is opened and a powerful-looking bull with brown-spotted hide is led forth by the attendants. A cheer breaks from the spectators and several of the performers engage the beast in a series of preliminary encounters. Nimbly they dodge his lowered horns and flying hoofs, and the shouting of the onlookers rises and falls in swelling waves of applause as the daring and graceful execution of this or that spine-tingling manoeuver wins their noisy approbation.

As the sport warms up and the animal becomes more angry he pursues one of his elusive human opponents into the blind northwest angle of the court. Quickly the acrobat steps up on the stone platform in the very corner and, as the bull clumsily attempts to mount the narrow lower step, he lightly springs over the horns of the enraged creature and with a deft somersault leaps to the ground behind, amid the plaudits of the crowd (Fig. 50).

But the sport is now swiftly reaching a climax. In the center of the court, well within view of the expectant multitude, a black-haired, dark-skinned athlete is tensing his muscles for a supreme effort as the bull charges directly toward him, head down. Cool nerves this feat demands, and close timing. Watching his opportunity he suddenly seizes the horns in his hands, and as the creature's head is thrown upward in an angry toss he is hurled into the air. The cheers of the spectators rise to a crescendo—suddenly to subside in a hoarse moan, punctuated with not a few feminine shrieks, as the unlucky youth is impaled on the horns of the bull. But the crowd soon recovers its spirits and the participants appear undismayed by the fate of their comrade. A few minutes later aristocrats and peasants alike watch in breathless admiration as a slim and graceful maiden executes the same manoeuver with flawless perfection, nimbly somersaulting over the animal's back and, steadied by the outstretched hands of a waiting companion, landing unhurt amid an acclaim so tumultuous as to seem to rock the building to its foundations.

And so through the long summer day the sport goes on, varied perhaps by the sacrifice of the dedicated bull—after he had been ritually conquered by the climactic leap over his horns—by sacred dances in which the agile beauty of the Cretan youths and maidens is seen to splendid advantage, by picnicking in the heat of the early afternoon in the shade of the pines, on coarse bread, olives, and cheese, washed down with wine. And again wrestling, racing, and other sports continue until the sun begins to drop behind the hills.

Long after the crowds have left the palace hill the sounds of merry laughter and the raucous braying of donkeys, gradually mellowed by distance, float up to the open windows. In the growing dusk dim lights begin to flicker on the slopes of the distant hills as the villagers return to their empty homes. Presently the lights disappear one by one; the countryside is hushed in the stillness of a summer night.

And on the palace roof a lonely sentinel—like his fellow who, from the roof of Agamemnon's palace, kept watch that fateful night on which Troy fell—paces his beat and, now and then, pauses to gaze in wonder at "the starry conclave of the midnight sky."[14]

[14] Aeschylus, *Agamemon*, prologue (Morshead translation). For a fascinating re-creation of the bull games and the life of the performers see Mary Renault, *The King Must Die*, Pantheon Press, 1958.

CHAPTER V

THE RESIDENTIAL QUARTERS OF THE ROYAL FAMILY

1. GENERAL DESCRIPTION

Nowadays one is likely to think of a "palace" only as the dwelling place of the royal family. Webster, for example, defines it as "the official residence of a sovereign." But, as we have already seen, the Minoan palace was much more than that; the part used for the royal apartments occupied, in fact, but a small fraction of the total area of the palace. Yet they are of especial interest for several reasons. They give us an intimate glimpse into the life of the royal family—ever a subject of peculiarly engrossing concern to the "commoner"; they are often particularly well preserved compared with other parts of the palace; and they are amongst the most carefully built and decorated suites of palatial chambers.[1]

As the best preserved of all (even without the "reconstitutions") it is inevitable that we should visit first the royal apartments in the Palace of Minos, or as Evans called them, the "Domestic Quarter."[2] We prefer to avoid this term in order to prevent any misunderstanding that it was intended for the "domestics."

The Residential Quarter of the palace at Knossos was situated, as in the other palaces, well away from the principal entrances, in the *penetralia* of the building, east of the Central Court and just south of its mid point (Fig. 12). Here the

[1] For a fuller treatment of the palace residential quarters see *AJA*, 63 (1959), pp. 47-52.
[2] *Knossos*, I, pp. 325-359; III, pp. 282-390.

ground sloped off rapidly toward the east, and in a later phase of the construction of the palace a broad flat terrace for these rooms was created by cutting a great vertical scarp running along the eastern edge of the court and reaching a depth of nearly thirty feet (9 m.) below its flagged surface. This allowed sufficient space for two storeys below the court, and above it there must have existed at least two more, all probably forming part of the royal residence.

When this part of the Palace of Minos was destroyed the collapse of the upper storeys preceded that of the lower, filling them with debris almost to their ceilings; perhaps not until the slow decay of their woodwork did the lower piers and columns finally give way. The result was that when Evans dug into this part of the building it was a dramatic, almost eerie, experience. Approaching from the north, he found himself tunneling through a doorway to a landing from which stairs both ascended and descended. This was, of course, the "Grand Staircase," as he named it, the walls of which, starting at the level of the Central Court (though originally it went still higher), he supported and consolidated wherever necessary with remarkable skill (Fig. 38). In later years he went much further, rebuilding many of the piers and columns, heightening the remains of the walls, and constructing ceilings over the first storey rooms, employing, instead of the original wood and stone, modern structural steel and concrete. It is the fashion now to criticize him severely for this, and undoubtedly his reconstructions here involve some uncertainties and even errors; the new materials are somewhat disturbing, and at times it is difficult to be certain what is new and what is old. Yet if he had done nothing, much of what he uncovered would have been later destroyed by the weather and by the destructive earthquakes to which Crete is still subject.

At any rate it is an unforgettable experience for the modern visitor to descend from the Central Court to the "Hall of the Colonnades" at the foot of the Grand Staircase, where he finds four massive columns of the typical Minoan form, with bulging

convex capitals and shafts that taper downward instead of upward (Fig. 136, F). These columns (of course restored) flank
two sides of a small unroofed court about 11½ by 18½ ft. (3.50
by 5.65 m.), forming as Evans called it, a light-well or light
area. The stairway forms a third side, and a wall, with windows
on a smaller stairway, the fourth.

From the Hall of the Colonnades one passes through a doorway in its northeast corner into a long corridor illuminated by
two openings from another light-well on the right. A few feet
farther a door opens into the most impressive room preserved
(or reconstituted) in the palace. Evans dubbed it, with his ear
for the picturesque name, the Hall of the Double-Axes, from
the numerous double-axe symbols cut in the walls of the light-
well (Fig. 39). More simply, and to bring it into line with the
similar rooms in the other palaces, we may term it the Men's
Hall, for such it must have been, though this is not meant to
exclude the probability that women also used the room.[3]

Measuring about 26 by 40 ft. (ca. 8 by 12 m.) the hall was
floored with fine gypsum flagging laid in a regular pattern of
blocks; the walls were plastered above a high dado of gypsum
veneer, and perhaps hung, along the line of a painted spiral
band, with a series of large "figure-of-eight" shields consisting
of layers of bullhide stretched over a wooden frame. The inner
half of the room, lighted through a two-columned portico from
a light-well at its west end, was divided from the eastern half
by a row of five rectangular piers, restored on the stone bases

---

[3] Evans also called it the "Hall of State Receptions" (*Knossos*, I, p. 329), but
this was surely the main room of the private suite; there was ample provision
for public rooms elsewhere in the palace. He also referred to it in *Knossos*, III,
p. 481, as the Piano Nobile, but this is hardly a proper use of the term. The sign
now in the room calls it in Greek the Μέγαρον τοῦ Βασιλέως, and in English the
"King's Room." Marinatos (*C. and M.*, p. 126) also writes of the suites I (with
most others) identify as residential quarters, "these elegant rooms, which are
found in the best positions in all the palaces, must have been reception rooms
rather than private apartments. At Phaistos and Mallia they lie at the northwest
corner of the palace to face the cooling winds during the long and scorching
summer months." The position is "best," I agree, for the living quarters, but the
magnificent west façades and the position of the formal entranceways combine
with other evidence (Ch. VI, 1) to indicate that the reception halls were placed
along the west fronts of the palaces on the upper floors.

which were found in their original positions (Fig. 45). In each of the four openings between the five piers there once existed, as the pivot holes prove, a set of double doors which when open folded back flush into a panel in the face of each pier; when all the doors were closed it created a kind of temporary partition separating the two halves of the room. This pier-and-door partition, as we have called it, was a very popular feature of Cretan palace and house architecture, its purpose being perhaps partly to gain greater privacy for one part of the room, but probably it was chiefly a device to adapt the room to the extremes of Cretan weather (see Ch. v, 2). In the Hall of the Double-Axes there is another similar partition at the east end of the room and again along the east end of the south side, both of which open on an L-shaped veranda. Thus in pleasant weather all the doors could be left open for both air and view, while in bad weather as many doors could be closed as desirable, and the chill further tempered by portable charcoal braziers (Fig. 140, E, F). Above the doorways there was perhaps a series of "transoms" which may have been filled with waxed parchment to enable some light to filter through when the doors were closed (Figs. 45, 151).

The columned portico opened on what was probably a garden terrace, bounded on east and south by a low retaining wall and commanding a view over the valley beyond.[4]

From the southwest corner of the Men's Hall a narrow passage, turning at right angles and guarded by doors at both ends (Fig. 12), leads into a smaller but well decorated hall. This formed, as Evans recognized, the main room of a more private suite; it may therefore be called the Queen's Hall or Women's Hall (Fig. 43).[5] The floor of the room was flagged

[4] Evans would restore here a wall to the full height of the first storey (*Knossos*, III, p. 328), and it is in fact partly rebuilt; but there seems to be no evidence for more than a low parapet, or, as Dinsmoor (*Arch. Anc. Gr.*, p 9) says, "little more than a garden wall."

[5] Evans called it the "Queen's Megaron." But "megaron" should be reserved for the distinctive main room of the Mycenaean palace (Fig. 150), which bears no resemblance whatever to this room. This and the attached rooms were no doubt not exclusively used by the women (and so Lawrence, *Gk. Arch.*, p. 39); but

with gypsum, the walls beautifully painted in bright colors with scenes of marine life and figures of dancing girls, and the ceiling was decorated with an intricate spiral pattern. On two sides were light-wells with high stone sills forming convenient seats. From the northeast corner of the room the ladies could pass by means of a winding corridor, closable at several points by doors, into the area of the garden terrace and verandas to the east and south of the Men's Hall. One can hardly avoid seeing in this arrangement a nice respect for the privacy of the fair sex, as well as a due appreciation of their society.

Opening immediately off the Queen's Hall and lighted from it by a window is a small bathroom; the remains of a clay tub were found nearby (Fig. 81). South of this room another passage leads to still more private rooms, the general nature of which is indicated by the presence of a remarkably well designed toilet connecting with an extensive system of palace drains (Ch. v, 4).

A narrow stairway led directly from the Queen's Hall to rooms above, used perhaps as sleeping rooms, no doubt for both men and women. This upper floor was also accessible by another stairway that could be reached either from the inner rooms of the lower floor, or by a door opening off the southeast corner of the Hall of the Colonnades at the foot of the Grand Staircase.

The fact that the royal suites in the other palaces bear a remarkable resemblance to the one in the Palace of Minos makes it clear that the excellent planning of the residential apartments is not the result of chance, nor is it likely to be due to the happy inspiration of a single architect. Rather it seems the result of the combined and traditional experience of generations of island architects working wherever their services were from time to time required. If true, this has considerable bearing on our understanding of the relationship of the architecture of

---

since they must have been used particularly by the women we may, for the sake of convenience, continue to employ the terms "Queen's" or "Women's Hall," or "Apartments."

the palaces in general, and so it will be worthwhile to examine the private apartments of the other palaces with some attention.

Next, then, we turn to Phaistos. The principal royal suite—for there seem to have been two in this palace—is located well away from the public part of the palace and set on a terrace scarped out of the edge of the hill at the northern end of the building (Fig. 4).[6] The single approach to it was, as at Knossos, by way of a long stairway, descending however not from the Central Court but from the northeast corner of the Peristyle Court.

At the foot of the stairs a doorway opens to the left (north) into a large room, 77-79, which is remarkably like the Hall of the Double-Axes—clearly the Men's Hall (Fig. 47, at right). The entrance, as is normal in this type of room, is placed near the end of one long side. The floor is covered with a fine gypsum flagging laid in a regular pattern, the joints between the slabs being filled with red plaster (Fig. 127); the walls were wainscotted with the same material. Gypsum is indeed used with prodigality in the Phaistos palace for there were quarries providing a fine grade of gypsum, i.e. alabaster, in the neighborhood of H. Triadha and Gortyn. These are again being utilized in the work of restoration (Fig. 125).

The arrangement of the light-well with its two columns at one end of the room (the right on entering), and the four-bayed partition dividing the room into two parts, is virtually identical with that in the Men's Hall at Knossos. Along the whole north side of the room a similar pier-and-door partition opens on a colonnaded portico, and there was no doubt a terraced garden beyond.

The Queen's Hall, 81, is reached from the Men's Hall by way of a narrow corridor, 80, secured with doors at both ends, exactly as in the sister palace (Fig. 82). The floor and wall dado were done in alabaster veneering, and the plastered upper walls seem to have borne painted designs. As at Knossos the

---

[6] *Festòs*, II, pp. 254-304.

bathroom, 83, opens off the main room, but is here, as regularly elsewhere, at a lower level and reached by several steps; both steps and walls are lined with gypsum (Fig. 82). Another door led from the Queen's Hall to more private rooms, 82, incompletely preserved but retaining traces of a toilet arrangement. Still another door opened on to the veranda and terrace on which the Men's Hall also opened—again as at Knossos.

In addition this Residential Quarter included an extra room, 50, located south of the access stairway (Fig. 47). It was likewise lavishly decorated with alabaster floor and wainscotting, and part of the room had a gypsum bench around the walls. The position of the light-well is unusual, not at one end of the room but in the center, and apparently confined to the square space within the area enclosed by the four columns. A narrow stairway provided communication with the rooms in the storey above.

Anyone who has experienced the summer heat at Phaistos will understand why a northern exposure was selected for the main residential suite; but this exposure enjoyed the additional advantage of providing a magnificent panorama of the range of Ida (Fig. 51). At Knossos the pleasantest available view was also chosen.

A more modest but better protected suite was built to the east of the Central Court, 63-64 (Fig. 4).[7] Here we can recognize most of the elements familiar from the preceding examples: the Men's Hall, 63, with a small plaster-floored light-well with drain to the northeast but no columns, a pier-and-door partition across the middle and another opening on an L-shaped veranda, 64, with high polychrome bases set in a stylobate; also a Queen's Hall, 63b, entered by a simple doorway from the light-well and equipped with the usual bathroom, d, and with more private rooms, ce, beyond—the drain from e suggests the position of a toilet. The most interesting feature is the natural rock terrace, perhaps left for the picturesque effect, on which the

[7] *Festòs*, II, pp. 155-191.

veranda opens; along its southeast side several steps lead down to a lower terrace. With the help of the wall paintings from the palaces it is easy to picture here an attractive flower garden along the edge of the steep slope to the valley; the view must have been even more delightful in antiquity when the opposite hills were clothed with trees.

At Mallia the Residential Quarter is built in the northwest corner of the palace, well away from the principal entrances (Fig. 6).[8] In keeping with the palace as a whole it is less well decorated than the otherwise similar suites at Phaistos and Knossos, though there are remains of painted walls and floors. The Men's Hall, iii 7, is very like the Hall of the Double-Axes in plan, while the arrangement of the Queen's Hall, iii 1, is extraordinarily close to the corresponding room in the North Residential Quarter at Phaistos, 81: four doorways connect with the Men's Hall (via the usual corridor with doors at each end); with the bathroom, iii 4; with more private rooms, iii 2 (drains indicate the position of a toilet); and with the veranda on which the Men's Hall opens through a pier-and-door partition. There was also a private stairway at III *b* to the upper rooms. Beyond the long columned portico on the north there seems to have been an open area, probably a garden with a view over the bay a short distance away (Fig. 58).

The Villa at H. Triadha also had a fine residential suite set in an artificially leveled terrace at the northwest corner of the building;[9] they were reached from the upper level by a flight of steps lighted by a light-well at the bottom (Fig. 11). Here once again we find the L-shaped veranda opening on a terrace with a magnificent view toward Ida to the north (Fig. 65) and toward the valley and gulf to the west. Behind an unusually long pier-and-door partition is a Hall, 3, about 20 by 30 ft. (6 by 9 m.) in size, with a floor of regular gypsum flagging (Fig. 151). Combined with a space beyond a four-bayed parti-

[8] The Mallia Residential Quarter was first recognized by Platon, *Kret. Chron.*, I (1947), pp. 635-636; *Mallia, Maisons*, I, p. 105.
[9] *Guida*, pp. 30-32.

tion, 12, this evidently formed the Men's Hall. At the east end is the usual two-columned light-well, which however has two more columns through which to supply light in the opposite direction to Room 4 (Fig. 69). This room has a gypsum floor and paneled walls, as well as a stone bench around the walls; a smaller room off it has a low gypsum platform in one corner on which a bed may have been placed (Ch. XII, 1).

The vista of alternating light and shade created by the succession of rooms, light-wells, and porticoes from the east end of Room 4 to the west end of Room 3, a distance of nearly 75 ft. (23 m.) must have formed an architectural composition rivaled only by the suite of rooms in the Little Palace at Knossos. We have attempted to suggest the effect as seen from the west end of Room 3 in Fig. 151, bottom.

Through large openings in the walls the light-well also supplied light on the south to the stairway, and on the north, to 13, the Queen's Hall (Figs. 68, 70). What rooms there may have been beyond the pier-and-door partition on the north side of this Hall is unknown, nor is it clear what the area, 14, within a thin adobe brick partition east of 13, was used for, but fragments of the fine mural painting representing a cat stalking a bird were found here (Fig. 134). At the northeast corner stairs led down through a door, still complete with lintel (Fig. 154), to a small room with tiny columned court or light-well in the center and steps to rooms in the upper floor. No bathroom has been found in the preserved remains.

In the Little Palace at Knossos a suite of rooms along the east side (Figs. 13, 64) supposedly would constitute, on a sumptuous scale, the main living rooms of this aristocratic residence. The Men's Hall with its lavish provision of pier-and-door partitions, opens on a peristyle court. Immediately adjacent to this suite of rooms we again find a bathroom (it became a shrine in the last period of occupation) with several other adjoining rooms, but there is no clear "Queen's Hall."

Some other less pretentious dwellings present closer analogies to the residential quarter of the palaces. Perhaps the clearest instance is House Da at Mallia (Fig. 22). Room 3, with its floor paved with irregular flagstones, a four-bayed transverse partition, and a single-columned light-well, is the Men's Hall; adjacent to it and reached by either Corridor 4 or 5, is the Women's Hall, 6. It also has a flagged floor and off it opens the usual sunken bathroom, 7; a smaller space beyond 6, enclosed with a thin brick partition, has a toilet in one corner.

House Za at Mallia is similar in its layout (Fig. 25): 12, the Men's Hall; 5, the Women's Hall, with a transverse partition and a toilet at the far end; the bathroom, 11, is entered not directly from 5 but from a small passage, 4, between 5 and 12.

Other possible or probable examples may be seen in the Royal Villa E, F, G, H (Fig. 14); the House of the Chancel Screen, 4, 5, 6 (Fig. 16); House B at Palaikastro, 2, 3, 6 (Fig. 29); Nirou Khani 5 (the Women's Hall), 3, 6, 7, 8, 9, all reached by a corridor, 4, with doors at each end, from the Men's Hall, 2a, and with stairs, 10, to the second storey (Fig 31); Tylissos A with Men's Hall, 6, and bathroom, 11, off it, and three rooms and stairs reached from Corridor A (Fig. 19); and Tylissos C with Men's Hall, 15, and a suite of rooms, 12 (bath), 14, 13, and stairs (Fig. 20).

It is evident that the living quarters in the Minoan palaces follow the general pattern of contemporary Cretan houses of the well-to-do classes, though of course on a larger and more luxurious scale—or should we say that the houses ape the palaces in this respect? One is left with the impression that the design of the royal apartments was based on long experience and on a fine understanding of, and regard for, the needs of the two sexes in their domestic relationships. It is noteworthy that the lowest floor of the private apartments—and this was probably the most important one—was located, even in the palaces, at the ground level, not in the Piano Nobile as was the case with the principal public apartments. Surely this was done so that the royal family could enjoy the pleasure of the open porticoes and terraced gardens. The Minoan would not have cared to live in a modern skyscraper apartment!

2. THE MINOAN HALL

Most of the larger excavated houses of Minoan Crete possess one room which is outstanding for its size, decoration, and certain other fairly constant characteristics, which may perhaps be best designated by the term "Minoan Hall," the "Sala Minoica" of the Italian excavators. Unless we need to be particularly specific, however, "Hall" alone (with a capital H) will be sufficiently clear.

In some ways it would be convenient to have a more distinctive term, one that could be used internationally, and Evans and others have employed the word "megaron," or "Cretan megaron" (*mègaron à la crétoise*).[10] However, not only has megaron (big room) a Greek, and specifically Homeric, flavor, but it has already been appropriated (and probably correctly) for the large and dominating rectangular room with a central hearth surrounded by four columns and preceded by one or two shallow porches (Fig. 150), characteristic of Mycenaean palatial architecture, and occurring also in domestic architecture in a simpler form. On the other hand, it is perhaps well to be satisfied with a rather vague and general word, for the room we propose to discuss in this section, as we shall see, varies considerably in form, and no doubt also in function.

The mainland palace normally had but one dominating megaron, but the Cretan palace usually contained several Halls on the ground floor, and quite possibly still more in the upper storeys. The residential quarters naturally afford the best preserved specimens, and we have already met a good many in our study of that part of the palace. Let us, however, select one for examination in more detail.

A very normal example is the "Men's Hall" of the North Residential Quarter at Phaistos (Fig. 4).[11] The whole complex,

[10] It has sometimes been called a "Pillar Hall" (*Pfeilersaal*), but this risks confusion with other types of rooms containing pillars, such as the "Pillar Crypt," or such a room as ix 2, north of the Central Court at Mallia. *Salle à portes* (*Türensaal*) has also been proposed.

[11] *Festòs*, II, pp. 281-291.

as we may call it, is about 44 ft. long by 22 ft. wide (13 by
6½ m.), a simple relationship of 2:1 frequently approximated
in these rooms. Backed up against an exterior wall at one end of
the Hall is a light-well, about 22 by 9 ft. (6½ by 2¾ m.),
which transmitted light and air to the Hall through a portico
of two columns. The Hall itself is divided into two unequal
parts by a transverse pier-and-door partition with four bays; by
closing the doors in these openings the Hall could be quickly
converted into virtually two rooms. The larger and more important part was, as invariably, the one farther from the light-
well (see below); it measured in this case about 19 ft. (nearly
6 m.) long against about 11 ft. (3½ m.) for the other part of
the room. Both parts were paved with large slabs of gypsum,
but the paving of the larger part was more carefully executed,
consisting of two concentric rectangles enclosing a single central
slab of large size (Figs. 127, 136, N). The walls of the entire
room, as well as of the end of the light-well, had a dado of
gypsum veneer preserved to a maximum height of about 3 ft.
(1 m.) but perhaps originally ca. 6 ft. high; above this the
plastered wall was decorated with geometric and plant designs
in bright colors; the fragments were too few to permit a restoration of the whole scheme.

Except in the finest houses the walls of the Hall were usually
merely plastered and the floor laid with irregular flagstones.
Nor were the columned porticoes opening on garden terraces,
found in the Men's Halls of the palaces, a feature of ordinary
domestic architecture, although an example occurs in the Villa
of the Lilies at Amnisos (Fig. 76), and another in the Little
Palace at Knossos (Fig. 13).

The area of the main part of the Halls varies greatly. The
largest by far is in the Residential Quarter at H. Triadha (Fig.
151), which measures nearly 30 by 20 ft. (ca. 9 by 6 m.) or
nearly 600 sq. ft. (54 sq. m.). Next in size are the Halls in
the Little Palace at Knossos, the Phaistos North Residential
Quarter, and the Hall of the Double-Axes, all about 385 sq. ft.

(ca. 36 sq. m.). Smallest is the one in the South House at Knossos, about 10½ feet square or some 110 sq. ft. (10½ sq. m.).

As we have already noticed, there is almost invariably a light-well or similar source of light and air at one end of the Hall complex, and the room itself is also nearly always divided into two unequal parts by a transverse pier-and-door partition. It is an odd fact that, whereas one might expect the larger and more important part of the room to be located next the light-well, the reverse is true. And since there are some seventeen instances in which this peculiar dichotomy occurs, some explanation is required.

Why was the main part of the room *not* put next the light-well, where it would certainly benefit by the more direct reception of light and air? The answer must be that rain, wind, and cold could also enter without hindrance between the columns, with possible unpleasant or harmful effects to both occupants and furnishings. Indeed the purpose of the transverse pier-and-door partition was to exclude the unpleasant elements at times emanating from the light-well.

But when the doors of the partition were all closed what, we may ask, can have been the use of the smaller part of the room next the light-well, especially when, as so frequently, there was no entrance into it save from the main part of the room? Would it not have been more practical simply to have substituted the pier-and-door partition for the columns along the light-well, thus avoiding the waste of a considerable amount of space? That this solution was in fact rarely adopted—there is one instance in House Zb at Mallia (Fig. 27)—indicates that it would have been for some reason undesirable. Perhaps the effects of the weather, especially rain, on the valuable wooden doors, may have been thought a serious objection; but we may suspect that a more important reason was that it greatly increased the usefulness of the pier-and-door partition. For example, during a heavy but warm rainstorm, some or all of the

96

doors could remain wide open without danger that the water might splash into the main part of the room, and thus there would be little or no reduction in the amount of light and air entering the room. For the same reason the outer pier-and-door partitions in the palace residential quarters were always placed within a protecting colonnade.

Actually this involves the same principle that operated in the Mycenaean megaron where the main room was sheltered from the weather by a porch. This porch often had two columns, like the Cretan light-well, and in the palaces it was often doubled for extra protection. The main room was further protected by a door or, in the palace at Tiryns, by three double doors in a row between heavy piers (Fig. 150). The Tiryns scheme was surely inspired by the Minoan pier-and-door partition.

The Main Hall of the palace residential quarters regularly opened, as we have said, on a colonnade or colonnades which in turn faced on terraces and gardens. With such a bountiful provision of light and air why, we may ask, was it still felt necessary to provide a light-well at the *inner* end of the room beyond the transverse pier-and-door partition? Two frequently occurring situations may furnish an adequate explanation: on a cold and windy day when it would be necessary to close the pier-and-door partitions opening on to the colonnades, the transverse partition could still be left open since the light-well would be much less exposed to the wind; on the other hand, in hot weather the cross ventilation and updraught of the light-well acting like a flue would have greatly increased the comfort of the inhabitants. In fact the term "light-well" is properly too restricted in meaning, while "ventilation shaft" is open to the same objection; "light and air shaft" would be more expressive, though rather cumbersome for ordinary usage.

While most of the Minoan Halls can be classified, as regards form and function, along the lines we have followed so far, there are some interesting variations and exceptions, for example the tripartite complex of rooms, 50, south of the stairway lead-

97

ing down to the North Residential Quarter at Phaistos, and supposedly forming part of it (Figs. 4, 47).[12] In this the light-well, instead of being at one end, is interposed between the main and the smaller parts of the room (the "Sala" and the "Portico," as the Italian publication calls them) and supplies light to them both through two-columned openings on each face. There is thus no pier-and-door partition at all. A somewhat similar situation occurs in the Main Hall of the Residential Quarter at H. Triadha, though here there is also a pier-and-door partition (Figs. 11, 151).

At Nirou Khani the Main Hall is normal in most respects except that where we expect a light-well the two-columned portico opens directly on a stone-paved court (Figs. 31, 75). In fact the portico here is a "porch" in the English sense of the word, an "entrance"—the main entrance of the house. Superficially it bears a remarkable resemblance to the megaron at Tiryns, to which it has been compared. But it differs in several essential respects: unlike the Tiryns megaron it has doors from its inner corners leading to other parts of the house, while it lacks the Tirynthian hearth with four surrounding columns and the place for a throne.

Hall-like rooms were sometimes used for special purposes and were then furnished with special architectural features which alter their usual character. The Royal Villa at Knossos, with its balustraded dais and niche on the axis of the Hall for a formal seat (Fig. 74), has already been described (Ch. III, 4). Two similar arrangements occur in other houses—if they were really residences—in the vicinity of the Palace of Minos: the House of the Chancel Screen (Fig. 16), and the House of the High Priest.[13]

Finally, there is a unique agglomeration of no less than three Halls communicating with each other through pier-and-door partitions in the northeast corner of the Villa of H. Triadha (Fig. 10). All three have transverse pier-and-door partitions

[12] *Festòs*, II, pp. 258-268.
[13] *Knossos*, II, pp. 391-395; IV, pp. 202-215.

of two or three bays, two have light-wells and the third a window; some or all have gypsum-faced walls and floors. A broad stairway communicates with upper rooms and the general purpose is considered to be residential. For further details we must await the publication.

3. BATHROOMS OR LUSTRAL CHAMBERS?

One of the most disputed, yet least adequately discussed, questions in Minoan archaeology is the one which forms the title of this section. Everyone has an opinion on the matter, but who has taken the trouble to debate the pros and cons in detail? Certainly not Sir Arthur Evans anywhere in the length and breadth of *The Palace of Minos at Knossos*. He tells us what are bathrooms and what are lustral chambers, but exactly what, in his mind, distinguishes them he leaves to be inferred. Nilsson does devote two pages in his last edition of the *Minoan-Mycenaean Religion* (1950) to the question whether these rooms were used for cult purposes, but the treatment falls far short of his usual thoroughness.[14]

Of the many other scholars who have declared themselves in one camp or the other on the identity of these rooms R. W. Hutchinson has expressed himself (in 1950) at greater length than most. They cannot, he declared, be bathrooms because they have no drains or piping, and because they are lined with "gypsum which dissolves in running water. . . . The one certainty about 'lustral areas' is that they had some ceremonial significance. Their character and significant positions proves this. . . . In general they are rare and possibly confined to houses inhabited by princes of the royal line."[15]

The lack of a drain and the solubility of gypsum we shall discuss later. The meaning of "their character and significant positions" is not self-evident; but to this also we will return. As for rarity, at least eighteen of the familiar type with steps

---

[14] Nilsson, *MMR²*, pp. 92-94. "Bathrooms or Lustral Chambers?" was presented at the Meeting of the Archaeological Institute of America, Dec. 28-30, 1960, *AJA*, 65 (1961), p. 189.

[15] *Town Planning Review*, 21 (1950), p. 209.

down from an adjoining room are known, ten of these in private houses. "Princes of the royal line" must have been as common in Crete as "Kentucky colonels," and Minos as fertile as Ramses II.

Let us say a word now about the *probabilities* of the case in favor of the bathroom interpretation. First: In a southern climate bathing is a relief and a pleasure, whatever be the prevalent hygienic philosophy—so let us have no comparisons with modern Eskimos or with, say, King Henry VIII.

Second: Bathrooms are usually the easiest room to identify in the ruins of an ancient house, either by bathtubs (sometimes built in), or by special waterproofing of floor or walls, or both; position and size are also often clues.

Third: Bathrooms are common in ancient houses excavated elsewhere—Olynthos, of course, in the Classical Greek period, but they are found in the Bronze Age too. At Amarna in New Kingdom Egypt (ca. 1375 B.C.) the bathroom "was invariably a small room with a bath-slab of limestone fitted into one corner, and often two upright slabs to protect the walls from being splashed . . . the water ran off into a vase cemented into the floor . . . (or) across the floor and out through a hole in the wall."[16] In this simple shower bath a slave would pour water over his master. In the palace at Mari on the Euphrates, about 1700 B.C. (Fig. 148), there were numerous bathrooms with clay tubs and often a "Turkish" toilet conveniently alongside, and even the luxury of a small fireplace in the corner with a flue to carry off the smoke.[17] At Pylos in the Peloponnesus a fine bathroom has been discovered with clay tub in place,[18] and others have been recognized at Mycenae and Tiryns; surely if the Mycenaean Greeks had bathrooms it would be perverse to deny this amenity to their cultural mentors the Minoan Cretans who, tradition asserts, lived in the lap of luxury.[19]

We will describe briefly a typical, well preserved example of

[16] Peet and Woolley, *City of Akhenaten*, I, pp. 45-46.
[17] *Mari*, II, pp. 202-205, Room 7.
[18] *Archaeology*, 13 (1960), pp. 53-54.
[19] Diodorus Siculus, 5, 66, 6.

the disputed type of Minoan room, in the North Residential Quarter at Phaistos (Fig. 4).[20] A seven-stepped stairway in two short runs descends three feet from the Queen's Hall to the "bathroom"—as we shall call it for the present, without intending to prejudge the case (Fig. 82). The floor, lower walls, steps, and parapet along the steps and between the bathroom and the main room, were all faced with gypsum; the walls were lined with thin sheets of gypsum veneering of the fine quality known as alabaster (in the modern sense of the word). On the end of the parapet once stood a short marble column. The dimensions of the sunken floor of the basin are about 7 by 7½ ft. (2.20 by 2.32 m.).[21]

Other bathrooms are fairly constantly about this size, but the quality of the decoration varies widely. The upper plaster wall in the bathroom of the Residential Quarter at Knossos is painted with a spiral band, and one in the South House with birds and flowers; in simpler rooms the floor was sometimes of plaster or merely of clay. In a wall of the bathroom of House E at Mallia were two niches, in one of which a fine stone lamp found in the room was no doubt placed.

It is commonly believed that the Queen's Hall or Women's Hall is regularly a kind of private sitting room reached by a corridor with a door at either end from the larger "Men's Hall," which at Knossos has been called the "Hall of the Double-Axes." A similar relationship of bathroom, Women's Hall, and Men's Hall occurs in the East Residential Quarter at Phaistos and in the Residential Quarter at Mallia, as well as in some of the private houses. Surely the position, which Hutchinson says proves that these rooms had a ceremonial function, very obviously in these cases at least, suggests instead a domestic function.[22] The toilet, also, is often in a similar position, off the

---

[20] *Festòs*, II, pp. 299-303.

[21] The floor was surfaced with seven slabs not four, as stated in *Festòs*, II, p. 299.

[22] Hutchinson must have been thinking of a few exceptional instances which we discuss below; Platon, on the other hand, notes that they are found particularly in the principal living apartments, review of Karo, *Greifen am Thron, Kret. Chron.*, 13 (1959), p. 238.

Queen's Hall—in both cases at Phaistos, at Knossos, at Mallia, and in some of the houses; should we therefore reinterpret these toilets as some form of chthonic shrine?

Yet Evans, and many others, persist in identifying the type of room we have just described as lustral chambers, not as bathrooms: as being used purely for cult, not for domestic, purposes. Evans however did recognize three rooms at Knossos as bathrooms, and these seem to have been generally accepted. What then are the qualifying characteristics? Here, briefly, is a description of the three.

No. 1 was a small room about 6½ feet square (2 m.) in the southeast part of the Palace of Minos, with gypsum-faced walls and floor; the floor was not lower than outside the room, hence there were no steps or parapet.[23] Remains of a clay bathtub were found in the room (Fig. 140, C). It was not in a residential quarter, at least one of the usual type.

No. 2 in the South House at Knossos was a small room first built in M.M. IIIb with steps down to its floor and a parapet (Fig. 15); in L.M. Ia it was remodeled by bringing the floor up to the outside level, eliminating the steps but retaining the parapet.[24] The floor and lower walls were gypsum faced; no tub remains were found.

No. 3 is off the Queen's Hall at Knossos (Figs. 12, 81).[25] This room in position, size, character of floor and walls, parapet and column, is essentially indistinguishable from the room already described at Phaistos, and from the one at Mallia. The one point of difference is that the floor was not at a lower level and that there were consequently no steps. Remains of a clay tub were found just outside the door of the room.

Thus it is clear that for Evans the difference between "bathrooms" and "lustral chambers" did not consist in position, size, the use of gypsum for floors and walls, the existence of a parapet, the presence of a drain, or the finding of remains of a tub (for none was found in the South House). The sole point of

[23] *Knossos,* I, pp. 579-580.
[24] *Knossos,* II, pp. 378-380.
[25] *Knossos,* III, pp. 381-386.

distinction is in the level of the floor and the consequent presence or absence of steps.

Sir Arthur's viewpoint likewise involves the assumption that a room which started out as a lustral chamber (in the South House) later became an ordinary bathroom. In fact, as a result of recent investigations by Platon it must be assumed that this also happened twice in the houses at Tylissos; and a careful investigation, I suspect, might show that the same was true of the bathroom off the Queen's Hall in the Palace of Minos. Otherwise why the parapet? Was it not also a vestigial remnant as at Tylissos House A, and in the South House at Knossos? We should have to suppose, as Evans did, that in their later days the Minoans began putting cleanliness before godliness.[26] There is however no other indication of this hypothetical decline in religiosity.

The common "proofs" adduced today by scholars who favor the lustral chamber as against the bathroom theory are, nevertheless, not the level of the floor of the room but the lack of drains and the use of gypsum—particularly the latter. How then can the same scholars accept the three rooms identified as bathrooms by Sir Arthur Evans?[27] Yet they appear to do so.

In any case neither of the objections they urge is a valid one. Drains are not necessary, merely convenient.[28] More of the Olynthian bathrooms lacked them than possessed them. And to have installed drains and maintained them in working order in the low-floored type of Minoan room would have been extremely difficult. A little water splashed from a tub could easily be sponged up; how many modern bathroom floors possess a drain? As for the tubs themselves we, accustomed to pipes which supply and evacuate the water, must not expect such conveniences in the "good old days." The built-in tubs at Olynthos had no drains; they must have been emptied rather laboriously by dip-

[26] *Knossos*, II, pp. 379-380; and so Pendlebury, *Handbook*, p. 44.
[27] Platon also calls attention to this anomaly in his review of Karo (p. 238), "no drain exists even in the Queen's Bathroom at Knossos."
[28] Karo writes in 1959 (*Greifen am Thron*, p. 8), "the sunken space shows no drain; it therefore cannot have been a bath." *Non sequitur.*

ping and sponging. In Crete, however, the tubs had handles or ledges for easy carrying, and so could be taken out of the room for filling or emptying.

As for the solubility of gypsum, the objection is really ridiculous. When I mentioned the problem recently to a well-known geologist he laughed and remarked that in that case one should not keep water in glass containers. Gypsum is soluble—yes—but . . . there are several "buts." For one thing, varieties differ widely. Certain types of gypsum may, some have said, "melt like sugar." Omitting the rhetorical exaggeration we may admit that some gypsum bases lying out in the weather at Knossos for half a century have been "honeycombed" by the rain (Fig. 117). Other varieties, as Evans himself observed, have "an almost unlimited power of resisting the elements."[29] Gypsum blocks are much used in exterior walls, in the great orthostates on the west façade at Knossos, for example; and gypsum was actually used for the floor of the foot basin in the "Caravanserai" at Knossos, in which water stood or flowed constantly.[30] It is also a simple physical principle that the rate of solution is directly related to the area of exposure, so that we may feel sure that the finely smoothed vertical wall surfaces of the alabaster veneering of the bathroom would resist any normal splashing practically indefinitely. And if by any unlikely contingency the floor slabs needed replacing after several decades of use the Minoan housewife must have felt that the advantages of having a "tiled" bathroom were quite sufficient to justify an occasional renewal.

Actually this objection is a legacy from the early days of Minoan excavation when it was first suggested by Evans that these rooms were partially filled with standing water to serve as tanks for fish for the royal table, or—a later suggestion—for bathing; when they got too fetid they could be baled out.[31] But many evidently still fail to recognize that the problem has been completely altered by the realization that the bathing was done

[29] *Knossos*, III, p. 288. [30] *Knossos*, II, p. 119.
[31] *BSA*, 6 (1899-1900), pp. 38-39; 7 (1900-1901), p. 63.

in a tub.[32] It is perhaps strange that no remains of bathtubs seem so far to have been found in bathrooms of the low-floor type; but Minoan bathtubs, not being built in, were too portable and too valuable to leave in the ruins; they could be used not only to bathe the living but to bury the dead. Large numbers of such tubs have been found in L.M. III cemeteries.

It may be urged however that there is another plausible reason to suspect a religious rather than a utilitarian explanation of these rooms. The considerable additional labor needed to excavate them several feet deeper than the general level is, some may think, easier to explain if religiously motivated, and various explanations along these lines have been proposed: that it was done in order to get closer to the Powers of the Underworld that cause the dreaded earthquakes; or to provide congenial pits for the sacred snakes familiar in Minoan cult; or to imitate the popular natural cave sanctuaries.

On the other hand if we ask whether it is possible that the Cretans could have had any good practical reasons for making the floor of a *bathroom* lower than that of the surrounding rooms I think that the exercise of a little sympathetic imagination can discover several; in fact in this we may have still another illustration of the Minoan experience in urbane living. The problem which the Cretan solved with the simple means at his disposal was to build the bathroom in such a way that it could be lighted from the larger room from which it was entered[33] without running the risk of water seeping into, or being splashed into, the Queen's or Women's Hall to the discomfort of its occupants and the possible damage to its furnishings. At the same time the lower level of the bathroom would shield the bather from cold draughts, and, in combination with a parapet

---

[32] Even Pendlebury says of the north "lustral area" that "it can never have been filled with water—the gypsum paving and wall-slabs would not have stood it," *Handbook*, p. 44.

[33] He could have enclosed the room entirely and depended on artificial illumination, and lamps have indeed often been found in these rooms, but this would not have been a congenial solution to the Cretan, especially in view of the ineffectiveness of Minoan lamps (Ch. XII, 1); artificial daylight is a modern development.

and possibly adjustable hangings between the two rooms, provide a certain amount of privacy. Yet if we may judge from the bathing habits of the Homeric heroes such complete privacy as we prefer today may not have been considered necessary; indeed the Homeric hero was sometimes assisted in his ablutions by a favored daughter of his host.

Nevertheless, in spite of the evidence we have so far presented, which consistently permits or favors the interpretation of these rooms as bathrooms, there exists some evidence of a contrary nature that we have not yet touched on. For instance, we have not spoken of the famous "lustral chamber" off the so-called Throne Room at Knossos.[34] This room actually differs little in most physical characteristics from those we have discussed, except that on the parapet between the two rooms are several columns. But there *is* one significant difference: its location off a room which was surely used not for domestic, but almost certainly for cult, purposes. The recent thesis that a priestess, not a priest-king, sat on the throne, would not, if true, essentially alter the situation (see above, p. 31).[35]

A second room described as a lustral chamber by Evans is located at the north end of the palace, far from the Residential Quarter.[36] Its basin, larger and much deeper than usual, was reached by sixteen gypsum steps. There is the usual high gypsum dado with colored plaster above, while on the stair parapet stood three columns, with three more on the parapet dividing the two rooms. Vessels which Sir Arthur believed were of a ritual character were found within the basin, and he conjectured that the chamber was used for ceremonial washing before proceeding further within the palace to appear before the king, an idea, though often repeated, for which there is no clear evidence either here or elsewhere, though it remains within the realms of possibility. It is also possible, as I suggest elsewhere (Ch. v,

[34] *Knossos*, IV, pp. 907-908.
[35] Platon's recent study also upholds the cult character of the room, *Kret. Chron.*, 5 (1951), pp. 392-394.
[36] *Knossos*, III, pp. 8-12.

5), that the room formed part of an elaborate suite for the entertainment of distinguished visitors.

A third room with steps down to a gypsum-lined basin opens off what perhaps should be regarded as part of a suite of grand reception halls in the Little Palace at Knossos rather than as a residential quarter.[37] In most respects the room is of normal type except for a row of four convex-fluted columns on two sides of the sunken area. In the final period of the building's existence the space between the wooden columns was roughly walled up and, as the numerous ritual objects found in it clearly show, the room was used as a shrine. Did this continue an earlier practice?

But religious associations are not completely absent even in simpler examples of this type of room. For instance in the newly published and rather enigmatic House E at Mallia a broken libation table was found in the bathroom;[38] and in the bathroom of the East Residential Quarter at Phaistos there came to light a pair of stone sacral horns, a rhyton of fine quality, a terracotta bull's head rhyton, and nine small bronze double-axes.[39]

How are we to explain this apparent anomaly: that an essentially identical room form should have been used both for cult ceremonies and for domestic bathing?[40] The answer I think must lie simply in the similar physical process involved; the washing away or cleansing of sin is not a figure of speech in the ancient Near East but an actual effective process. Thus the household room could be at once "bathroom" and "lustral chamber." In taking a bath one cleansed both the body and the soul.

[37] *Knossos*, II, pp. 519-525.   [38] *Mallia, Maisons*, II, p. 136, no. 12.
[39] *Festòs*, II, pp. 171-178; but Miss Banti disbelieves in the ritual character of the room, p. 584 and notes; on the other hand Hood in reviewing *Festòs*, II, in *Gnomon*, 26 (1954), p. 376, declares that these objects "do surely indicate some sort of cult."
[40] "Many of the rooms characterized as lustral basins were in fact baths, since they are found especially in the principal living apartments; the form of the similar installations used for lustral purposes evolved directly from the bathrooms," Platon in a review of Karo, *Greifen am Thron*, *Kret. Chron.* 13 (1959), p. 238; and Hood in his review of *Festòs*, II (*loc. cit.*) says that the " 'Lustral basins' must have been used for anointings or washings whether ritual or not."

And so, as frequently happens when there has been a long and sharp division of opinion among competent scholars the basic trouble is with the formulation of the problem. The question should not have been whether these rooms were "bathrooms *or* lustral chambers," for they were both at once, though the relative emphasis doubtless varied in the individual instances.

4. THE TOILET

One of the peculiar hallmarks of western culture frequently used by the traveler as a handy touchstone with which to condemn as backward the "less fortunate" countries he visits is the modern sanitary convenience. He may succeed in avoiding the art galleries, theaters, and literature of the country in which he is traveling, but unless he keeps very close to base, i.e. the luxury hotel in which he resides, he can scarcely fail to come into contact with this homely object in its native form. It is only natural, then, that the kinds of toilets used by the nations of the past should likewise fascinate the average tourist, and there are many who will comment reverently on that small dark room in the Palace of Minos when they have quite forgotten the treasures of art in the Herakleion Museum.

And perhaps the ancient Minoan and the modern American would find this subject more mutually intelligible than many others. For the Cretan did seem to take a considerable interest in physical comfort, and it is perhaps a significant contrast that although something over a hundred houses have been excavated at the Classical Greek site of Olynthos there is remarkably little sign of provision for toilets,[41] whereas some half dozen can be identified among the score of comparable houses of Minoan Crete so far brought to light.

In several of the Minoan houses the toilet is quite clearly located in the private living quarters, and usually in as well removed a position as possible; in House Za at Mallia it projects entirely beyond the general line of the house walls. In most cases the evidence for the identification of the toilet is

---

[41] *Olynthus*, VIII, pp. 205-206.

little more than the existence of a large and carefully built drain at floor level passing through an exterior wall (Fig. 79). But occasionally there are traces of some sort of provision for a seat.

Toilets may be recognized in all three major palaces. At Mallia Room iii 2, next to the Queen's Hall, which has two drains through its outer west wall, is probably a toilet. And again 63e, off the Queen's Hall of the East Residential Quarter at Phaistos, has nothing to show but a careful drain in the solid rock on which the exterior wall is bedded. The toilet connected with the North Residential Quarter is more interesting. Located as far as possible from the main living room it is reached by a short corridor from a door in the southwest corner of the Queen's Hall.[42] About five feet wide by perhaps twelve long (1½ by 3½ m.), the room is paved with large square slabs of gypsum and divided from the corridor to the east by a thin adobe brick partition. In the northwest corner is a somewhat higher gypsum slab with a rectangular gap about 5 by 10 in. (ca. 13 by 25 cm.) in the middle of one end, opening into a fair-sized drain that continued northward to the edge of the hill. Presumably over the hole in the floor a wooden seat was built against the now missing north wall of the room.

The most elaborate Minoan toilet known is the water-closet in the Residential Quarter of the Palace of Minos (Fig. 12).[43] It consists literally of a "closet" about 7 ft. 3 in. long by 3 ft. 8 in. wide (2.20 by 1.11 m.), provided with a door and set against one wall of a larger room reached by a long corridor from the Queen's Hall. Like the Minoan bathrooms its floor and walls were faced with gypsum for easier cleaning as well as for appearance. Along the rear wall is a slot about 14 in. (35 cm.) wide over a drain which forms part of an extensive system of drains serving both toilets and light-wells in this part of the palace; a short branch of the drain has another opening outside the threshold of the closet to receive slops or water swept from the floor of the larger room. In the face of one of

[42] *Festòs*, II, pp. 296-299.
[43] *Knossos*, I, pp. 228-230.

the gypsum slabs on the south wall and at a distance of about 22 in. (55 cm.) from the east or rear wall is a vertical slot evidently designed to receive one end of the vertical facing of a wooden seat; the top surface of the seat would have been nearly two feet (60 cm.) above the floor. Below the opening is a curious projection from the rear wall which "may have been used for the attachment of a balance flap to shut off the escape of sewer gas."[44] Some confirmation of this conjecture of Evans is perhaps provided by the discovery in the sub-stairs toilet in a house at Sklavokambos of two clay objects which seem to have been used to plug the drain holes and thus prevent the backing up of odors.

One of the houses near the palace at Mallia, Da, contains a toilet seat in practically perfect condition, since it was made of stone, not of wood like the one in the Palace of Minos (Fig. 114).[45] The seat measures about 27 in. wide by 18 in. from front to back (ca. 68 by 46 cm.), and its surface is some 14-15 in. (35-38 cm.) above the floor. It is built directly against an outside wall through which passes a capacious drain. Like the example at Knossos it was evidently intended as a seat rather than as a stand, resembling therefore the Egyptian toilet more closely than the "Turkish" type found in the palaces at Mari and at Alalakh.[46]

At certain times of the year the drains in the Palace of Minos may have been adequately flushed out by the rain that fell into the light-wells; but in general we must imagine that water was poured into the toilets to flush them, and Evans observed that there was sufficient space at one end of the seat at Knossos for a large pitcher. He concludes with evident satisfaction, "As an anticipation of scientific methods of sanitation, the system of which we have here the record has been attained by few nations even at the present day."[47]

[44] *Knossos*, I, p. 228, note 2.
[45] *Mallia, Maisons*, I, p. 45, "un curieux massif fait de pierres et de terre: foyer ou latrines?"—how could a "hearth" have a drain through the wall?
[46] *Mari*, II, p. 203; *Alalakh*, pp. 123-124.
[47] *Knossos*, I, p. 230.

5. THE GUEST ROOMS

God forbid that you should go to your ship and turn your backs on my house as though it belonged to some threadbare pauper and there weren't plenty of blankets and rugs in the place for host and guests to sleep between in comfort! Indeed, I have good bedding for all; and I swear that the son of my friend Odysseus shall not lie down to sleep on his ship's deck so long as I am alive or sons survive me here to entertain all visitors that come to my door.—(Nestor urging Telemachos to stay for the night at his palace at Pylos, ODYSSEY, 3, 346-355, Rieu translation)

Aristocratic travelers in Bronze Age Greece were too few to encourage the development of hostelries adequate to accommodate them, but they could expect a hospitable welcome in the palaces of friendly monarchs. A suite of rooms near the main entrance and adjacent to the Central Court of the palace at Mycenae has recently been tentatively suggested as a guest suite.[48] The evidence is better, perhaps, for a group of rooms near the entrance of the newly excavated palace at Pylos, also on the Greek mainland.[49] The Pylos suite includes a good-sized room with painted cement floor and walls and a central hearth, two smaller rooms, probably sleeping room and toilet, and, at least conveniently near if not for its exclusive use, a bathroom. The location near the palace entrance was no doubt felt to be convenient for the guest, as well as safer for the host than bedding a stranger too near the quarters of the royal family.

In the north palace at Amarna (about 1375 B.C.) two structures which are virtually large houses, within the boundary walls of the palace, are usually supposed to have served as residences for some of the pharaoh's personal staff (Fig. 149, center right); but one might guess that they were used, at least at times, to accommodate important visitors to the court. At any rate the large homes in the vicinity of this palace, which

[48] Mylonas, *Anc. Myc.*, p. 49.   [49] *Archaeology*, 13 (1960), p. 53.

must have housed members of the imperial aristocracy, contained suites of rooms which the excavators have very reasonably supposed were for the use of guests. In House T. 36. 11, e.g., this suite includes a columned hall or living room adjacent to the central living room of the house; off this hall and completely separate from the rest of the house, runs a corridor serving a row of several small rooms which would certainly appear to have been bedrooms.[50]

The excavator of the great palace at Mari on the Euphrates (2000-1700 B.C.) has recently suggested that a suite of rooms, including a bathroom, court, and kitchen, near the main palace entrance, was used for the reception of distinguished guests (Fig. 148, at 160).[51] One might suggest further that a series of single rooms with attached bathrooms around Court 15 was also used for guests of lesser importance, though the publication prefers to believe that it was used by certain court officials (Fig. 148, below 106).[52]

Minoan Crete is not likely to have lagged behind Egypt or Mari in the amenities of civilized life, while one would expect her to have been well ahead of mainland Greece in this regard. I propose to recognize two such suites of guest chambers in the southwestern quarter of the Palace of Phaistos (Fig. 4). A long corridor, 12-13, opening off the main passage, 7, from the West Court to the Central Court, provides convenient and private access. A kind of anteroom, 15, serves both suites, each of which consists of two rooms and bath—sitting room, bedroom, bath? —namely 17, 18, and 19, to the north, and 16, 20, and 21, to the south.[53] Just south of these rooms are the remains of a pier-and-door partition running east to west; perhaps there was a broad veranda to the south of this for the enjoyment of the guests.

[50] W. S. Smith, *Art and Arch. in Anc. Eg.*, fig. 64; Frankfort and Pendlebury, *The City of Akhenaten*, II, pl. 12; E. B. Smith, *Eg. Arch.*, pl. 67.
[51] *Mari*, II, pp. 20-33.　　[52] *Mari*, II, pp. 192-205.
[53] *Festòs*, II, pp. 122-130. I find now that the idea has been previously expressed, though apparently long since abandoned; see C. H. and H. B. Hawes, *Crete, the Forerunner of Greece* (1911), p. 81.

At Knossos it is possible that the "lustral chamber" near the north entrance of the palace formed part of a fine suite of guest chambers.[54] Perhaps the fragment of an alabaster jar inscribed with the name of the Hyksos king Khyan found here was the relic of the visit of some high Egyptian official to the court of King Minos. Likewise in the southeast quarter at Knossos there are two suites of rooms, a good deal altered, it seems, in the L.M. III period, each with a bath, and each accessible from a southeast entrance. Evans himself remarked that the area had a decidedly domestic appearance and might have been the residence of a priestly functionary.[55]

Since the only recognizable bathroom in the Palace of Mallia is in the Residential Quarter no clue of this nature is available to help in identifying guest suites. In view of the modest character of the palace perhaps there were none. Nevertheless one might venture to suppose that two groups of rooms were so used, namely the suites entered by a door in the south exterior wall of the palace just west of the south entrance to the Central Court (Figs. 5 and 6, xviii 1-7).

Two of the finest private houses excavated at Knossos also have small suites of rooms including bathrooms, on the ground floor near the main entrance, which could with some plausibility be identified as guest suites, namely the Royal Villa, E H (Fig. 14), and the House of the Chancel Screen, 4-6 (Fig. 16), although we have preferred to suggest that they formed part of the "women's quarters" of these houses. There would seem to be no possibility of setting up a hard and fast distinction in all cases between these two types of suites, and it is conceivable that the East Residential Quarter at Phaistos was used, or at least could be used at times, as a reception suite for guests of distinction.

[54] *Knossos*, I, pp. 405-422; III, pp. 8-12.
[55] *Knossos*, I, p. 576.

CHAPTER VI

PUBLIC APARTMENTS

1. RECEPTION HALLS

To ANYONE familiar with the Bronze Age palaces of the Greek mainland the title of this chapter may seem rather pretentious. In the Mycenaean Greek palaces almost the only really large and well decorated room is the "megaron" or "big room," a room about 30 by 40 ft. (ca. 9 by 12 m.) preceded by a narrow anteroom and a two-columned portico facing on a small court (Fig. 150). Wall paintings and floor designs gave a rather splendid effect, but so much of the central area of the room was occupied by a hearth (13 ft. or 4 m. in diameter at Pylos), and by four columns, that the king's throne was crowded against the center of a side wall in a position more conducive to the royal comfort in cold weather than convenient for the reception of a foreign embassy.[1]

When Nausicaä tells Odysseus what he will see in the great room of her father's palace at Phaeacia she paints a very domestic scene indeed: "When thou art within the shadow of the halls and of the court, pass quickly through the great chamber (megaron), till thou comest to my mother, who sits at the hearth in the light of the fire, weaving yarn of sea-purple stain, a wonder to behold. Her chair is leaned against a pillar, and her maidens sit behind her. And there my father's throne leans close to hers, wherein he sits and drinks his wine, like an immortal."[2]

The megaron therefore ordinarily formed part of the domestic or private quarters of the palace, though it could be

[1] *Archaeology*, 13 (1960), pp. 46-54.   [2] *Odyssey*, 6, 303-309.

pressed into service as a place to receive and entertain visitors of distinction. No rooms specifically reserved for this latter purpose can be definitely identified in the mainland palaces so far excavated.

These palaces, however, were much smaller and more modest structures than those in Crete, and were hemmed in by great fortification walls. For analogies we should look rather to Egypt and the Near East, and there we find a very different picture.

Egyptian palaces of the eighteenth dynasty, such as that of Amenhotpe III at Thebes (Malkata), have large columned rooms identified as state reception halls,[3] while the South Palace at Amarna (ca. 1375 B.C.) has a colossal battery of hypostyle halls culminating in one around 225 ft. wide by over 400 ft. long (ca. 70 by 120 m.) and containing well over 500 columns.[4] In the Middle Bronze palace at Mari on the Euphrates the reception halls are smaller than the Egyptian, but the principal hall, 65, must have been in its way as impressive for it was over 30 ft. high, 85 ft. long, and 40 ft. wide (9 by 26 by 12 m.), without the use of a single supporting column (Fig. 148).[5]

It should not be surprising, therefore, if the Minoan Cretans built themselves rooms of considerable size and architectural pretensions as formal reception halls. Nevertheless, since very few rooms outstanding for size or quality of decoration are actually preserved in the ruins of their palaces, except for those already identified as forming part of the residential quarters, why, it may be asked, should we suspect that important public or state apartments did exist in the vanished upper storeys; and even if they did, how can we hope to learn anything about them?[6] Reasonable questions indeed—yet the case is not really

[3] W. S. Smith, *Art and Arch. of Anc. Eg.*, fig. 55.
[4] *Ibid.*, fig. 66.
[5] *Mari*, II, p. 143.
[6] The publication of the last Palace of Phaistos has very little to say about second storey rooms; their existence, to some extent, is admitted, but their importance is minimized (see especially *Festòs*, II, pp. 327-336). Both Banti (*Festòs*, II, p. 330) and Lawrence are very suspicious of the proposed restorations by Evans of the Piano Nobile at Knossos between the Central and West Courts, and the latter claims that "the plan above ground level is conjectural in almost every

as hopeless as it might seem; a certain amount of evidence does exist.

In the first place analogies may be found in many times and places, including the *palazzi* of Renaissance Italy, for the practice of putting the important public rooms in the storey above the ground floor. This storey was referred to in Italy as the *Piano Nobile*, or principal floor, a term Evans adopted for the corresponding feature of the Minoan palace. The main rooms may also have been located on the second floor of Cretan houses, at least in the more crowded urban districts, as is suggested by the houses of the "Town Mosaic," many of which have windows only in the second and third storeys (Fig. 103), and by the actual remains of houses along the narrow alleys at Gournia.[7] The better houses, however, at Mallia, Knossos, Tylissos, etc., certainly had important living rooms (lighted by light-wells, not by windows) on the ground floor, though possibly on the floor above as well.

Second: in all three major palaces there are broad flights of stone steps, far broader than would be necessary for ordinary daily use—in other words clearly designed for splendor of effect —leading up toward a second storey above the area of the palace west of the Central Court (Fig. 7). At Mallia several steps of two broad stairways are still in position west of the Central Court. At Knossos there is also a broad flight leading up from the Central Court (restored from slight remains), and another from the South Propylaeum, which was connected with the West Court by the Corridor of the Procession. At Phaistos the system of stairways begins at the West Court.

Third: fragments of plaster from elaborate figure compositions found in the storage rooms west of the Central Court at

detail" (*Gk. Arch.*, p. 36). Yet there is some evidence, and scholarly caution does not justify ignoring it completely.

[7] Weinberg, in a review of *Mallia, Maisons*, I in *AJA* 59 (1955), pp. 340-341, remarks that above the very irregular ground floor rooms of some rather large houses excavated at that site there must have existed larger and finer rooms. Putting the main living floor one storey above the ground is certainly a common practice in modern Greece; cf. Travlos, Πολεοδομικὴ Ἐξέλεξις τῶν Ἀθηνῶν. (Athens, 1960), p. 226.

Knossos must have fallen from important rooms above. Evans also found in this area stone door and pillar bases clearly derived from the same source; in fact they sometimes seem to have subsided merely a foot or two from their original positions and therefore provide valuable clues for the restoration of the plan of the missing rooms.[8]

Fourth: particularly at Knossos and Mallia the long narrow storage rooms along the west façade are grouped in more or less square "blocks" composed of from three to six magazines each, the outer walls of the blocks being usually distinctly thicker than those dividing the individual magazines (Fig. 83). This is not explained by the character or function of the magazines themselves; and it suggests that only the heavy boundary walls of the blocks supported walls in the storey above, and therefore that one large room in the Piano Nobile occupied the area of each "block" of the ground floor. This general principle was long ago proposed and has been widely accepted; in details there may be differences of opinion. That it provides the correct explanation for at least one block at Knossos, and for two at Mallia, is rendered a virtual certainty by the symmetrically placed rectangular enlargements of the dividing walls at two places in each block: clearly to provide a firm underpinning for pillars or columns to support the long transverse ceiling beams of the large rooms above (Figs. 84, 116).

Fifth: to anticipate the results of a later section (Ch. IX, 1), the broad shallow recesses, which are a characteristic feature of the west façades of the palaces, indicate the location of windows in the rooms of the Piano Nobile, and therefore sometimes provide further clues regarding their form.

Utilizing these various clues, a tentative restoration of the plans of the rooms of the Piano Nobile along the west front of the palaces at Knossos, Mallia, Gournia, and Phaistos is presented in Fig. 84.[9] The form of some of the rooms is not

[8] *Knossos*, I, pp. 442, 526; II, pp. 350-352, 716-718, 817-818, etc.
[9] For further details see *AJA*, 64 (1960), pp. 329-333, "Windows, Recesses, and the Piano Nobile in the Minoan Palaces."

clearly indicated by the available evidence and should be regarded as quite conjectural; this is particularly true at Phaistos.

The restoration of the three central rooms at Knossos given here agrees with Evans' restoration only for the middle room, whose two columns are vouched for by the two bases in the lower storey, as already mentioned (Figs. 85, 86, 116). As for the "Southwest Hall" over Magazines 3 to 5, Evans at first restored this as a single room in the Piano Nobile; the evidence he adduced in favor of his final version is certainly not decisive, while the position of the window as indicated by the recess supports the single-room restoration.[10]

The large room over Magazines 11 to 16 presents more of a problem. MacKenzie, Evans' right-hand man during the early years at Knossos, treated the area over 11-16 as a single room;[11] but Evans, in his final publication, broke this block up into several rooms entirely on the basis of a hypothetical Northwest Entrance which he conjured up out of a fragment of decorative stonework of a type sometimes used above doorways (Fig. 136, B, Ch. xi, 2).[12] If, on the other hand, we restore a single large room over 11-16, as MacKenzie did, the recess in its exterior west wall will be centrally located on the axis of the proposed Northwest Hall and indicates the position of a broad set of windows. In Evans' restoration this recess comes directly opposite a partition wall. A further important piece of evidence turned up during my visit to the site in 1959. Against the north face of the partition between Magazines 14 and 15 lies a large dressed limestone block certainly in its original position, and this is so obviously analogous to the enlargements in the walls between Magazines 7, 8 and 8, 9 that it strongly suggests that on the block stood a wooden pillar to buttress the wall at a point below a column in the room above (Fig. 115). No corresponding strengthening of the wall between 12 and 13 is visible, but this wall is considerably thicker than that between 14 and

---

[10] See note 17 in article mentioned in preceding note.
[11] *BSA*, 11 (1904-1905), p. 217.
[12] *Knossos*, II, p. 590.

15. This indicates that only two columns should be restored in the hall above (p. 156).

On the basis of this restoration we get three great halls over Magazines 3 to 16: the Southwest Hall, the Central Hall, and the Northwest Hall. The largest of these, the Northwest Hall, about 57 by 51 ft. (ca. 17½ by 15½ m.), would, appropriately for the bigger palace, be a little larger than the great Central Hall at Mallia, which was about 52 ft. square (ca. 16 m.) and whose existence is clearly attested by the two enlargements in the magazine walls already mentioned.

This process of "building castles in the air" involves us in complex but intriguing problems at Phaistos. The main problem is how to restore the upper floors over the great one hundred foot square including the Grand Propylon and the Magazines. The exterior walls of this block are so thick and so solidly and handsomely constructed, with massive facing blocks of finely dressed limestone, that they must have risen at least one and probably two storeys above the ground floor. Moreover the analogy of the position of the block to that of the rooms of the Piano Nobile at Knossos and Mallia strongly suggests that the state reception rooms were located in the upper storeys. Yet in the final publication of the palace recently published by the Italian excavators the view is put forward that the space above the Magazine Block was occupied not by public rooms but by a loft for the storage of grain.[13] Even on general grounds this would be highly suspicious, particularly in view of the regular Minoan practice of systematically assigning different parts of the building to specific functions (Ch. XIII, 3).

In a first study of the problem I attempted a solution which would not run counter to the peculiar conclusions reached by the Italian archaeologists. They could hardly be expected to advance a theory so derogatory to the dignity of their own palace

---

[13] *Festòs*, II, p. 330; however others have taken the obvious view that there were important rooms of a public nature here, notably Charbonneaux, *BCH*, 54 (1930), pp. 364-366, and so even the Italian *Guida* (1947), p. 52, written by Pernier and Banti.

without feeling that they had the strongest of reasons to do so;[14] and indeed the evidence of the excavations did clearly indicate that a large mass of grain had fallen from somewhere above the ground level. I was also influenced in the solution I proposed by the conviction that the ceiling above the magazines would have to be somewhat higher than the level of the floor of Room 70; but after a further prolonged visit to the site in 1959 I became convinced that the floor level of 70 could have extended over the whole area west of Room 25, as indeed the excavators maintain, without creating an abnormally low basement storage cellar. As for the presence of the grain, various explanations are possible; the simplest is that it represents an emergency measure, an emergency which in fact brought an end to the last palace. A pile of grain was also found by the excavators in the north portico of the Central Court at Mallia; but surely it was not normally stored there.[15] And grain was also found in an unlikely place in an Assyrian palace destroyed in the first millennium.[16]

The formal approach to the state apartments of the Phaistos palace was, without a doubt, the Grand Propylon. This consists first of a magnificent flight of steps in the best tradition of Minoan stair-building (Ch. x, 1); there is nothing to equal them elsewhere in Crete (Figs. 49, 137, 138). At the head of these steps is a deep landing and a broad portal over thirty feet (ca. 9 m.) wide, framed by projecting wall-heads at either end and supported by a very large oval column in the center. Beyond the porch, 68, was a cross-wall with a pair of large doorways opening into a vestibule, 69, illuminated by a light-well, 69A, fronted by three oval columns.

In spite of all this magnificent sequence of stairs, portals, and columns, none of the three exits from 69-69A displays either in its dimensions or in its position the architectural dignity for which the grandeur of the approach prepares us (Figs. 4, 48).

[14] *AJA*, 60 (1956), pp. 151-157.
[15] *Mallia*, I, p. 36.
[16] Conrad Preusser, *Die Paläste in Assur*, Berlin, 1955, pp. 19, 21.

It is not surprising, therefore, that some scholars, unable to accept the view that this complex was designed primarily as an approach, have tried to see in 69-69A a great hall where the king sat in state to receive important visitors.[17] For such a purpose, however, 69 and 69A are poorly arranged and proportioned, as well as quite un-Minoan in room form, and the floors and walls though well preserved show no sign of any place for a formal seat or thronos. The Italian excavators are surely correct in identifying 69A as a light-well.[18] Moreover, even if (and I think it a very large "if") on certain occasions the king did sit here in state, these rooms could not have taken the place of state apartments on the scale for which there is evidence at Knossos and Mallia.

Nor should anyone familiar with the vagaries of Minoan architecture (see Ch. XIII, 3) find it difficult to believe that any of the three doorways above mentioned could have formed the entrance to such apartments. Let us explore them in turn.

First, the door at the rear right corner of 69A. This opens directly on a landing from which a stairway descends to the important hall 25, and to the Central Court, while another ascends to Peristyle 74 and the large room with a pier-and-door partition, 93. Clearly, then, this doorway was an important one.

Second, the door at the south end of 69 and up three shallow steps into Room 70 with a stone bench along its west wall. This may have served as a guardroom for the control of the Grand Propylon, but must also have acted as an anteroom to the floor over Magazines 32-37 since there is no other route by which it could have been reached.[19] The plan of this area over the magazines should probably be restored as a great hall extend-

---

[17] So Platon (oral communication), and Dörpfeld, whose views were strongly opposed by MacKenzie, *Ath. Mitt.*, 30 (1905), pp. 257-297; *BSA*, 11 (1904-1905), pp. 181-223.

[18] It is drained, as light-well floors regularly are; Platon objects (orally) that the abundant light coming from the west would make such a light-well superfluous, but it would be useful in lighting rooms in the upper floors north of the Central Court—See *AJA*, 65 (1961), p. 167.

[19] The objections I mentioned in *AJA*, 60 (1956), pp. 152-153 are largely met by accepting the lower floor level over the magazines.

ing west from the rear of Room 25 to the west end of the building, with two rows of columns over the reinforced stone heads of the partition walls, and perhaps a pier-and-door partition on the line of heavy wall between Magazines 36, 30 and 37, 31.[20] Such a hall would surely have been suitable for important state functions.

But there is still another door, the widest of the three, that opens at the other end of 69 on a fine broad flight of steps, 71, ascending west to a broad landing, 72, from which a second flight would continue to the second storey. The probable height of the first storey, based on reasonable calculations for the height of the stairway and for the height of the columns would be in the neighborhood of sixteen to seventeen feet (ca. 5 m.). From the head of the second flight one could pass, no doubt, east to the gallery above Peristyle 74, but in all likelihood also to a portico above 68-69, which would have provided an excellent vantage point for viewing visitors or processions passing up the stairs of the Propylon (Fig. 48). A doorway in the south end of this portico would provide a convenient entrance into another hall directly above the one entered from Room 70, but extending also over Room 25, in other words all the way from the Central Court to the West Court, a distance of approximately one hundred feet. This great hall would presumably have constituted the principal room of the state apartments.

A general restoration of the Magazine-Propylon Block based on these results, and incorporating large windows for the two storeys of the Piano Nobile set in the pair of symmetrical recesses of the west façade, achieves a pleasingly harmonious and well proportioned effect which perhaps represents the high-water mark in Minoan architectural design (Fig. 48 and compare Fig. 50).

That the principal public rooms of the Cretan palaces were located above the ground floor seems well established. But the

[20] Cf. Charbonneaux, *BCH*, 54 (1930), pp. 352-366.

question *why* may very properly be raised. Some of our answers might well surprise the Cretan architect—if only because to him it was a well established tradition which he perhaps rarely, if ever, stopped to question.

From the negative point of view one might be tempted to reply that the "ground floor" was in effect the "basement," and was consequently given over largely to storage and service areas. To have stored heavy materials on the upper floors would have involved extra labor, and required stronger floors and walls. A considerable part of the ground floor was also given over to small shrines; especially in the case of the "pillar rooms," contact with Mother Earth was perhaps desirable. The main floor of the residential quarters was also apparently always put on the ground floor close to their terraced gardens.

But there must have been more positive reasons than mere lack of space on the ground floor to explain the preference for the second and third storeys for the main public rooms. There may have been such practical considerations involved as the desire to protect valuable furnishings from dampness, or to avoid possible damage from occasional floods to the wall and floor decorations, which could not be moved out of harm's way. Perhaps, too, flies and mosquitoes were less troublesome at the higher level.

Another important reason, I suggest, was that rooms on the upper floors could be equipped with numerous large windows providing abundant circulation of air and fine views over the surrounding countryside (Ch. ix, 2). At the same time privacy was secured by putting the windows sufficiently high above the ground to prevent the unauthorized multitude from viewing important official functions. Unglazed windows on the ground floor would offer a constant opportunity for prowlers.

Considerations of pomp and circumstance are also undoubtedly involved. Locating the state reception halls on the upper floors permitted the architect to design a splendid approach to the royal presence; the impressive effect, psychological as well as aesthetic, of a broad flight of steps ascending to the Piano Nobile, so skilfully employed in the Renaissance *palazzo*, no doubt did not escape the Minoan designers. The association in the human mind between royalty or divinity and a physically superior position is embedded in our very language: we are *elevated* to a peerage; we *raise up* our eyes unto the Lord.

The constant west orientation of the main suite of public halls likewise calls for some explanation. If it is not merely dependent upon the general orientation of the palace as a whole, or simply the result of following the pattern set by Knossos where the lie of the land favored such an orientation, it may be due to a desire to receive the benefit of the prevailing winds or to enjoy the maximum hours of daylight in the late afternoons and early evenings when most court functions would naturally be held. Artificial illumination in Minoan times must have been more attractive than effective.

Rooms used for public purposes were not necessarily restricted, however, to the series of rooms immediately facing on the west court. In fact Evans restored, no doubt correctly in principle though wrongly in detail, the plan of other large rooms, including the "Central Tri-Columnar Hall," between the north-south corridor serving the western rooms and the Central Court,[21] and it is probable that important rooms existed in this same position at Mallia. There may also have been large rooms in the upper storeys on other sides of the central court. At Knossos Evans considered that the plan of the basement rooms, and the masses of fine plaster relief fragments found fallen into them, on the east side of the Central Court, indicated the presence of "the most important of all the reception halls in the Palace area," which he termed the "Great East Hall."[22]

A special form of public room which it will be convenient to discuss separately is the banquet or dining hall, and to this we shall now turn.

[21] *Knossos*, II, plan C.   [22] *Knossos*, I, pp. 360-384.

2. THE BANQUET HALL

And so we sat the livelong day till the going down of the sun feasting on abundant flesh and sweet wine.—(ODYSSEY, 10, 467-468)

The tomb paintings of New Kingdom Egypt would assure us, if we needed assurance, that elegant dinner parties were already in vogue in the Bronze Age. We may feel certain that if the Minoans had fine large halls for the reception and entertainment of aristocratic or diplomatic guests or visitors they must also have had large dining halls in their palaces; we may likewise feel certain that such rooms would be on the lost upper floors. Shall we therefore leave the matter at this indefinite conclusion and resign ourselves to the futility of attempting to discover more?

Such is the prudent course of action, or rather of inaction, that has so far been taken. Might there not, however, be certain characteristic features of a dining hall which would leave recognizable clues in the surviving remains of the ground floor? For example, would it not be reasonable to look for: 1) indications of a large room in the second storey well removed from the main reception halls to avoid the odor of food and the clatter of preparation and of cleaning up; 2) the presence on the ground floor, beneath or near such a hall, of rooms suitable for the storage and preparation of food; and 3) adequate provision of stairways?

Somewhat scanty clues, perhaps, but surely worth a try![23] And where better to begin than in the Palace of Mallia whose ground plan is almost completely preserved (Fig. 6)? The entire area to the east of the Central Court of that palace is occupied by magazines, to the west of it by more magazines and small cult rooms with the state reception halls overhead. South and southwest of the court lies a maze of small nondescript rooms and no signs of a stairway or other indication of

[23] For a more detailed account see *AJA*, 65 (1961), pp. 165-172.

important rooms above. The northwest is occupied by the rooms of the Residential Quarter; and in the extreme north there is another row of storerooms.

Our search is thus quickly reduced to the area immediately north of the Central Court (Fig. 88), whose front on the court is formed by a fine columned portico.[24] Toward the west end of this portico a door opens into a long narrow room, ix 1, with a single square pillar base (Fig. 59). This room seems to have served merely as an anteroom to a larger one, ix 2, with six square bases in two rows. Some have called ix 2, on the grounds of Egyptian analogies, the Hypostyle Hall, but we shall refer to it simply as the Northeast Hall. There seems to be no real evidence that it was, as some have thought, an important cult room; in any case our interest in it is that its plan suggests the existence in the second storey of a large hall with two rows of four columns each. A broad stone stairway in two flights, ix *ab*, to the east of the hall, must have led to the upper gallery over the north portico; from this gallery a door, probably over that to ix 1, would have provided an approach to the Upper Northeast Hall.

It is an odd fact, however, that another two-flight stairway with no other destination than this same Upper Northeast Hall was built to the north of ix 1, 2 over xxii 1, 3 (Fig. 60). It seems difficult to think of an explanation of this duplication of stairways more likely than that the Upper Northeast Hall was a dining hall, accessible to the guests from the east stairway by way of the north portico, and to the service staff from the north stairway. The space between the head of the service stairway and the Upper Northeast Hall, that is over xxi 2 and xxii 2, would have been useful as a serving room. Directly at the foot of the service stairway was the "North Service Court," surrounded by magazines and small rooms well suited to the storing and preparing of food. No fireplaces were discovered either here or elsewhere in the palace, for the Cretans at this time seem to have used portable hearths almost exclusively. How-

[24] For what follows see *Mallia*, II, pp. 1-5, 19-24; III, pp. 15-17, 50-51.

ever, fragments of spit supports (Fig. 141, M) were found in xxi 2,[25] also grain mills and remains of grain in jars, and quantities of pottery were discovered in the "cupboards" in xxv 2 and xxvii 6 as well as in Rooms xxi 2, xxii 1, 2, xxv 3, and xxvii 2-5.

To the north of the Central Court at Phaistos certain bases and strong points in the walls of Rooms 58-61 and 91-92 indicate the existence of an "East Hall" in the second storey with two rows of four columns each (Fig. 87). In view of the remarkable resemblance between the various palaces in such features as the residential quarter, the virtual identity between the Phaistos East Hall and the Mallia Upper Northeast Hall, in location, plan, and dimensions, would suggest that they were used for the same purpose (Fig. 89). And this is supported, as we have seen in our study of the palace at Phaistos, by the existence of a fine stairway, by the finding of pottery and cupboards in the small rooms below, and by the identification of a large service area to the northeast in direct communication with these rooms (Ch. ii, 2).

Nor are we disappointed if we turn to the plan of the Palace of Minos for indications of a similar room, though the supporting evidence is less clear (Fig. 2). A considerably larger but similarly proportioned hall with two rows of five or six columns each, indicated by the square piers in the so-called Customs House at the North Entrance to the building (Fig. 40), forms an obvious analogy; furthermore it was entered by way of a portico or columned corridor leading directly from the north end of the Central Court, which was at a much higher level than the "Customs House."[26] The most we can say otherwise is that there were many small workrooms and storerooms on the ground level in this general area, and that it is perfectly possible that there was some direct means of access from them to the upper hall.[27]

[25] *REA*, 43 (1941), pp. 12-14.
[26] *Knossos*, III, p. 165 and fig. 106.
[27] Great masses of plain pottery were found in the nearby Northeast Magazines, *Knossos*, I, pp. 388, 390, 568-571.

As we have already seen there is evidence for a similar, though smaller, banquet hall in one of the Minoan houses, House A, at Tylissos (Ch. III, 11). The upper room in this instance would have had two rows of three columns each, and it would have been accessible from two stairways, one near the house entrance and the other near several workrooms and storerooms (Fig. 19). A further striking resemblance consists in the fact that this room would have opened off a gallery which faced south on a small courtyard, just as the Banquet Hall in the palace at Mallia opened on a gallery looking south over the Central Court.

Can it be only a coincidence that in the contemporary palaces of Amenhotpe III and of Tiy (?) at Egyptian Thebes two long rectangular halls with two rows of columns have been identified by the excavators as dining halls?[28] Monarchs did deliberately imitate each other's palaces, as we learn from ancient literary texts. Perhaps Cretan envoys to Egypt were entertained in such halls, and Minos paid Pharaoh the compliment of imitation.

[28] W. S. Smith, *Art and Arch. of Anc. Eg.*, fig. 55.

CHAPTER VII

OTHER ROOMS

1. STOREROOMS AND WORKROOMS

TANGIBLE evidence of the wealth of the Minoan princes is furnished by the rows of magazines in the palace "basements." No less than one-third of the ground floor area in the Palace of Mallia (exclusive of courts) was occupied by storerooms (Fig. 6).

Information available about Cretan storerooms is relatively abundant, thanks to their having been normally placed on the ground floor. This was done, among other reasons, to avoid unnecessary lifting, as well as to obviate the need to build stronger walls and floors in the upper storeys in order to sustain the greater weight. The discovery of a great pile of grain well above the floor level of Corridor 26 in the Magazine Block at Phaistos suggested to the excavators that the grain had been stored on the upper floor out of reach of dampness; but there is no other evidence to corroborate this, and it may have been done in this instance purely as an emergency measure (Ch. VI, I).

A favored position for the palace storerooms was along the west façade immediately beneath the great halls of the state apartments on the Piano Nobile. At Knossos, Mallia, and Gournia they consist of a series of long narrow rooms—over twenty at Knossos—served by a long north-south corridor. At Mallia there is also a row of seven such magazines east of the Central Court, which are of special interest and will be described in detail below. Other storerooms belong to a shorter, broader type, for example those in the Magazine Block at Phaistos (27-37), and those west of Court 90 (54-55), and at

Mallia a row (xxvii 1-6) at the north end of the palace, and three more (xii 1-3) east of the Central Court.

As for the private houses, storerooms of various sizes and shapes can be identified in most of them, but it is difficult to generalize about their position except to say that they were usually well separated from the residential part of the house. In House Da at Mallia (Fig. 22) two magazines filled with storage vessels were found immediately off the entrance passage; in shape and plan they resemble the East Magazines in the palace at the same site. House Za at Mallia is clearly divided on the ground floor into two parts, one residential, the other for service, each with its own entrance; the three magazines, 26-28, at the rear of the service half were found filled with a great mass of badly shattered pottery vessels (Fig. 25). In the service half of House A at Tylissos two large rooms, 16-17, with two central pillars each, contained numerous big jars or "pithoi" ranged along the walls (Fig. 19). In the southeast corner of 16 is a bin-like structure about 29 inches north to south, 37 inches east to west, and 48 inches high (74 by 94 by 122 cm.), smooth on the outside (toward the room), rough on the interior, and with a large opening, 18 by 21 inches (46 by 53 cm.), through the south wall at floor level. Could it have been a grain bin for current use with a slot for withdrawal?[1]

The commonest type of magazine, in the palaces as in the houses, is that used for the storing of pithoi. At Vathypetro these seem to have alternated with smaller jars set on wooden shelves. The West Magazines at Knossos, which vary from about 35 to 60 ft. in length (ca. 10½ to 18½ m.) and from 5 to 8 ft. in width (1½ to 2½ m.), could have held from thirty to forty jars apiece, ranged in single or double rows along the walls (Fig. 93). Estimating some 35 gallons (ca. 132 liters) as the capacity of an average jar, and the maximum number of jars at about 420, the total maximum capacity of the magazines might amount to over 16,000 American gallons (over 60,000

---

[1] *Tylissos*, pp. 21-23; the height is there given as 2 m.; perhaps it was better preserved at that time.

liters).[2] The contents were probably entirely olive oil, according to Evans, a commodity which was used by the ancients in tremendous amounts since it served as a food, as a soap substitute, and as fuel for their lamps. Pithoi were also used to store other substances, however, such as grain, beans, peas, and lentils.

A vivid picture of the efficient way in which the royal estates were managed is given by the arrangement of the compact rectangular block of magazines east of the Central Court at Mallia (Fig. 91).[3] A single doorway from the east portico controls a corridor which turns at a right angle to serve six identical magazines (one was later shortened by a cross-wall), each about 21 ft. long by 7 ft. wide (ca. 6.35 by 2.10 m.). Along both walls of every magazine is a low platform of cement about 2½ ft. (76 cm.) wide, which provided room for fourteen large and fourteen smaller jars, approximately 158 jars in all. Together with a score of jars in the long corridor and a single row in the entrance corridor, the total capacity of the block was about 190 jars, amounting possibly to some five or six thousand gallons (ca. 23,000 liters). Remains in the jars indicate that the larger ones contained wheat and lentils; the smaller, some liquid, probably oil. Particular pains were taken to avoid wastage of oil through spilling. Each platform was scored with fourteen transverse furrows carefully set at regular intervals with two different spacings for the two sizes of jars; these open into channels running along beside the platforms and emptying into a clay jar, embedded to the level of its rim in the cement floor, at the end of each magazine. Further equipment consists of a huge trough at the northeast corner of the long corridor, with two steps up to it; in the southeast corner is a great jar protected by a row of upright slabs. Beside the latter was a block of stone where, the excavators suggest, an overseer could have sat and kept his tally as the porters carried in their oil-filled amphoras to pour into

---

[2] My estimate reduces Evans' considerably; cf. *Olynthus*, VIII, p. 314, note 6; Ventris gives a higher estimate than Evans, *DMG*, p. 60, but Mr. Chadwick tells me he does not know how Ventris arrived at this figure.

[3] *Mallia*, III, pp. 1-5.

the jars. To judge by the inscribed tablets found in the palaces the records were kept in scrupulous detail.

Settling basins for oil seem to have been identified recently at Gortyn in a large farm villa, and oil separator jars have been found at several sites (Fig. 143, H).[4] An interesting feature, not yet noted in Crete, has been observed lately in a magazine at Mycenae, namely provision for heating one of the jars; this is said to be normal practice in present-day Tuscany to prevent the oil from congealing in cold weather.[5]

The size of these huge jars, which run up to seven feet (over 2 m.) or more in height, is a tribute to the skill of the Minoan potter (Fig. 92). But it was evidently something of a trial for the "shorties" of the day, for in Magazine 33 at Phaistos was found a terracotta stool about 16½ in. (42 cm.) high, with hand-holes for portability, to be used as a stand by one desiring to reach the contents of a tall pithos (Fig. 143, G). The potters, proud of the gigantic offspring of their craft, decorated them with loving care: rows of small handles, curving ropework in imitation of the actual ropes used in handling the jars, lines of impressed circles, "medallions," and even plant motives in re-lief were methodically planned and neatly executed in parallel zones of ornament. The Cretan pithos is a handsome piece of architecture.[6]

Another form of storage, common in the Palace of Minos but strangely enough not found elsewhere in Crete, is the sub-floor chest or "cist" (Fig. 93).[7] Even at Knossos they seem to have been predominantly a Middle Minoan III feature, after which many were abandoned. The Long Corridor of the West Maga-zines was closed off at this time by a block at one end and a door at the other and ninety-three cists were constructed beneath the floors of the magazines and of the corridor itself. Though dif-fering somewhat in size, all those in the magazines and seven in the corridor were of the same type and built with surprising

---

[4] *REA*, 43 (1941), p. 12; *Mallia*, III, p. 48, fig. 24.
[5] *BSA*, 48 (1953), p. 12; but Palmer now explains the heating as a step in the process of making unguents, *Mycenaeans and Minoans*, p. 108.
[6] *Knossos*, IV, pp. 633-648, for examples.   [7] *Knossos*, I, pp. 448-462.

care. A typical specimen from the corridor measures about 3 ft. long by 1 ft. 4 in. wide by 3 ft. 8 in. deep (ca. 92 by 40 by 112 cm.); the walls consisted of four gypsum slabs, the two end ones being mortised into the side pieces and all four mortised into a slab of limestone forming the bottom of the cist. All this was set rather loosely within walls of dressed stone and the intervening space packed firmly with red earth, the apparent intention being to help insulate the cists from dampness. They were likewise lined with sheets of lead, and of course covered by removable stone lids. Chests so carefully protected were evidently intended to shelter the treasure of kings, and, in spite of repeated plunderings through the ages, fragments of crystal, faïence, gold foil, and wooden boxes with bronze hinges were found in them by the excavators.

Four groups, each with five cists, in the Long Corridor are different in construction and more capacious. An average specimen measures about 3 ft. 3 in. long by 2 ft. 6 in. wide by 5 ft. 3 in. deep (99 by 77 by 160 cm.); the walls and bottom were of limestone and the whole was packed around with red earth. The cist was lined, however, with fine white plaster rather than with lead, suggesting that it was made to contain a liquid, which Evans supposes was oil. He further notes that a depression cut in the bottom of each cist would have served to catch sediment, so that the oil may first have been put in them and later skimmed off and stored in pithoi. The average capacity of these cists would be about 320 American gallons, amounting to perhaps 6400 gallons (over 24,000 liters) for the whole series.

Isolated rooms in various parts of the palaces and houses supplement though certainly do not complete the picture we have so far obtained of how the Minoans stored their property. For example, a room just behind the "Tripartite Shrine" on the west of the Central Court at Knossos was found to have two deep cists in the floor containing remains of a wealth of temple treasures; the larger measures 6 ft. 4 in. by 4 ft. 9 in. by over 5 ft. deep (195 by 145 by over 150 cm.).[8] Another cache, evi-

---

[8] *Knossos*, I, pp. 463ff.; the measurements are mine.

dently of a sacred nature, from two small rooms in House A at Tylissos, next to a Pillar Crypt, consisted of a bronze talent and three tremendous bronze cauldrons (Fig. 142, G). Nineteen other talents or metal ingots were discovered in a small room (7) in the Villa at H. Triadha; each weighed close to 64 lbs. (29 kg.), evidently the standard weight of a talent.[9] In one of the rooms (7) at Nirou Khani four very large bronze double-axes were discovered, while in another (18) quantities of stone altar tables were found neatly stacked (Fig. 31). It has been suggested that this building was a center for the distribution of Minoan cult apparatus. In one of its outer courtyards a series of storerooms had been built against one of the walls. Some contained large jars of the usual kind; more interesting is a space enclosed between heavy sidewalls and divided into five small bins (26-30) by thin partitions of adobe brick, which had been used for storing grain. Finally, in the northeast quarter of the Palace of Phaistos a long narrow room (88) was excavated several feet below the adjacent floor levels and reached by a short stairway; possibly it was a "cold-cellar" for keeping such foods as milk, cheese, or meat (see Ch. II, 2).

Pottery was of course often stored in ordinary magazines, as in House Za at Mallia. In the Palace of Mallia, however, large quantities were kept in two "cupboards," of which only rubble foundations remain, in Rooms xxv 2 and xxvii 6, in the northeast service quarter. At Phaistos pottery was kept in what must have been a cupboard beneath the stairs north of the Central Court;[10] and in the nearby rooms, 45 and 46, small stone-lined cupboards, built into the walls (Fig. 99) were evidently used for pottery.

A group of eight circular structures about fifteen feet (4½ m.) in diameter and arranged in two lines of four each was excavated at the southwest corner of the Palace of Mallia (Figs. 58, 62). What remains of each is built of rough stone, lined on the interior with plaster, and surely is to be completed

[9] *Guida*, p. 33, fig. 45; Matz, *KMT*, pl. 74.
[10] *Mallia, Maisons*, II, p. 10 and note 5 for other examples of understair cupboards.

in the form of a dome, supported on a central pillar of which the stump is preserved in most instances. The excavators have referred to them as cisterns, but the fact that they were built above ground renders this highly unlikely; their correct interpretation is surely indicated by their resemblance to contemporary Egyptian granaries.[11]

Also requiring careful storage were the clay tablets commonly used in Crete and Mycenaean Greece, as in the Near East, for keeping records (Fig. 147). "After writing, the tablets were dried (not baked) and then generally filed away in boxes of gypsum or wood, or in wicker baskets, and stacked on shelves in rooms set aside for the purpose."[12]

In the Palace of Nestor at Pylos there was a special "archive room," with an annex, opening off the main entrance, a "location very convenient for the supervision of incoming and outgoing goods and personnel";[13] and in the palace at Mari on the Euphrates some 20,000 tablets were found in a single small room (115 in Fig. 148) with two deep wall niches adjacent to the main court.[14] At Knossos, however, the tablets have been found for the most part at widely scattered points throughout the palace and its vicinity; often they seem to have fallen from upstairs rooms, and nowhere did the excavators find a room which had been definitely set aside for the exclusive storage of tablets.[15]

[11] In a letter of Aug. 19, 1960, M. Georges Daux writes, "Quant aux 8 pseudo-citernes, il s'agit bien entendu de silos à grain, comme vous le pensez." However M. Demargne (letter of Sept. 17, 1960) writes that he prefers to abide by Chapouthier's idea that they were cisterns, and that this is retained in the ms. for the forthcoming fascicle (*Mallia*, IV). Marinatos still refers to them as cisterns, *C. and M.*, p. 64. Lawrence argues with good reason that the "hypogeum" at the south end of the early palace at Knossos (*Knossos*, I, fig. 74) was a huge granary (*Gk. Arch.*, p. 298, note 3); Karo, however, calls it a cistern (*Greifen am Thron*, p. 32), while Matz thinks it may have been designed for the sacred snakes (*KMT*, p. 50). Hood also has recently referred to the Mallia structures as granaries, *Dawn of Civilization* (ed. Piggott, London, 1961), p. 223.

[12] *DMG*, p. 114.   [13] *DMG*, p. 117.   [14] *Mari*, II, pp. 80-81.

[15] *DMG*, pp. 114-117; the only deposit found *in situ* in the palace was under a small flight of stairs in a small room at the southwest corner of the Central Court. The accuracy of the find-records of tablets in the Palace of Minos has, however, recently been challenged; see Palmer, *Mycenaeans and Minoans*, especially Ch. VI. 4; Hood, *Antiquity*, 35 (1961), pp. 80-81.

Nevertheless the tablets at Knossos were occasionally found in groups of related content, and at least once they were discovered along with the type of object listed on them.[16] In the basement of a badly preserved building to the northwest of the palace termed the "Armory" or "Arsenal," there was found, fallen from an upper floor, a great quantity of bronze arrowheads, with remains of the wooden shafts, in two groups ten feet apart. They were embedded in the débris of two wooden chests with bronze loop handles which had been carefully sealed. A broken clay tablet from the same deposit lists two lots of arrows: 6010 and 2630, a total of 8640.

The newly, and still very imperfectly, deciphered Linear B tablets give some further indication of the range of objects stored in the palace magazines, although it is often far from clear that the tablets are in any sense actual inventories of the royal property. Classes of commodities mentioned include foodstuffs, textiles, furniture, pottery and metal vessels, and military equipment (see Ch. XII, 1). Tablets referring to the last item are particularly numerous and mention is made of arrows, spears, swords, horses, and chariots. Over four hundred chariots in various states of completeness are mentioned in the known Knossos tablets, often with considerable supplementary information, for example: "Three horse-(chariots without wheels) inlaid with ivory (fully) assembled, equipped with bridles with *cheek-straps* (decorated with) ivory (and) horn *bits*."[17] (The italicized words are regarded as uncertain).

Not much definite information about workrooms is available. A grape and an olive press was found in a room at Vathypetro (Fig. 94), but otherwise remarkably little specialized equipment (except religious) has been found, that can be distinctly associated with particular types of rooms. It seems clear that the northeast quarter of all three major palaces was used largely by the domestic staff, and evidence of the activity of potters, lapidaries, etc. has been observed at Knossos. Perhaps the best example is at Mallia, where there is a small court with

---

[16] *Knossos*, IV, pp. 836-837.   [17] *DMG*, p. 366, no. 265.

surrounding porticoes and nearby storage and workrooms, concerned primarily, if our identification of the Banquet Hall is correct (Ch. VI, 2), with the preparation and storage of food. Two hearths were found in a portico of the court of the house at Sklavokambos (Fig. 32), but fixed hearths seem rarely to have been used. Many years ago Hazzidakis remarked on their peculiar scarcity and on the difficulty of identifying kitchens in Minoan houses or palaces; his expectation that time would bring the solution[18] has not so far been realized.

Many objects which might be serviceable in identifying the use of particular types of rooms have not in fact proved helpful because their use is undeterminable or undetermined, because they have been found in rooms of unspecific function such as courts or storerooms, because their finding place is unknown or unreported, or because they have not been mentioned in published reports. Excavators who have a wealth of showy material to publish are prone to neglect the drab but often very informative objects of everyday life.[19]

2. CULT ROOMS

One does not need to read the entire three thousand pages of *The Palace of Minos at Knossos* to receive the impression that the building was a labyrinth of cult rooms from one end to the other; or, as the Master of Minoan Archaeology characteristically phrased it, "The cumulative results of the exploration of the great building at Knossos have served more and more to bring out the fact that it was interpenetrated with religious elements."[20] Yet Nilsson, that most careful and conscientious student of Minoan religion, discounts much of this; and Miss Banti, the writer of the major portion of the volume which so meticulously describes the last Palace of Phaistos, is of the opinion that this palace, otherwise so like its sister palace at

[18] *Tylissos*, p. 58. For the service area at Phaistos see Ch. II, 2, above, and *AJA*, 65 (1961), pp. 167f.

[19] Chapouthier studied some objects of this nature in *REA*, 43 (1941), pp. 5-15, "La vaisselle commune et la vie de tous les jours à l'époque minoenne." See Ch. XII, 1, below.

[20] *Knossos*, I, p. 4.

Knossos, contains no cult rooms at all.[21] Surely the truth must lie somewhere between these extreme views.

A careful re-evaluation of the whole problem, bringing together all the available evidence, not only from the form and position of the rooms but from the objects found in them, is being made by Platon, the Ephor of Cretan Antiquities.[22] These studies have only begun to appear, but he has already succeeded in establishing the religious nature of a large number of rooms of a type interesting to us because of its distinctive architectural character. A description of a few of the best preserved will bring out the typical features.

Most of the examples listed in Platon's first article belong to the type of room frequently mentioned on previous pages as the "Pillar Crypt," together with associated rooms. We shall begin with the complex of rooms in the northern half of the Southeast House (Fig. 17).[23] The central room, C 1, the Pillar Crypt, measures about 10 by 12 ft. (3.15 by 3.65 m.), and the single pillar in the middle is preserved to a height of just over 6 ft. (nearly 2 m.); on three of the blocks of the pillar double-axe symbols are lightly incised.[24] At its foot a stone base of a type known to have been used for setting up a double-axe (Fig. 100) was found in place, while a rough foundation running from this to the north wall supported a number of bases for vessels probably intended for food and drink offerings. In the west wall of the room was a deep niche, but there were no windows, and light was evidently supplied by a handsome pedestaled lamp carved from a purple stone. At the northeast corner opens D 1, a narrow room doubtless used for storage of cult apparatus, and at the southeast corner another room B 1, in which was discovered a curious plaster stand evidently for ritual usage. B 1 communicated by a narrow passage, controlled by doors at both ends, with a stairway which must have led, as is known from other examples, to a Columnar Shrine whose single

---

[21] *Festòs*, II, p. 582.

[22] *Kret. Chron.*, 8 (1954), pp. 428-483.   [23] *Knossos*, I, pp. 427-430.

[24] The publication mentions only one double-axe sign, but two on the north side and one on the east are visible.

column would be placed directly above the pillar of the Pillar Crypt. From this upper room had fallen a sacral knot made of ivory, and fragments of wall paintings including representations of lilies.

In the northwest corner of the South House (Figs. 15, 71), a Pillar Crypt, about 13 by 18 ft. (ca. 4 by 5½ m.), has a central pillar preserved to a height of about six feet (nearly 2 m.).[25] Close to one face of the pillar was a pyramidal base for a double-axe, and near the opposite face another base, with three holes perhaps intended for the sacral horns with a double-axe in the center. An adjacent stairway led to an Upper Columnar Shrine with a stone bench still in position against a wall. From the upper shrine had fallen a set of five silver vessels probably for ceremonial use. Off the Pillar Crypt opens a storeroom.

The Pillar Crypt in the Royal Villa has already been described since it is so closely associated with the Main Hall and its balustraded area (Ch. III, 4, and Figs. 14, 97).[26] The crypt resembles those in the two preceding examples in its single central pillar and stairway to a Columnar Shrine. But it differs in the provision of a rectangular channel surrounding the pillar and deepening into two basins on opposite sides of it; presumably this was designed to catch liquid offerings (cf. Fig. 100) poured before the pillar—"Jacob . . . took the stone . . . and set it up for a pillar, and poured oil upon the top of it" (Genesis 28: 18). The floor was made of gypsum slabs and the walls of coursed blocks of gypsum; no cult objects were found.

A large Pillar Crypt, about 13 by 27 ft. (4 by 8.20 m.), west of the Central Court in the Palace of Mallia, contains two pillars on the long axis (Figs. 6, 95).[27] One pillar is marked with two double-axes and a star (Fig. 98), the other with a trident and a star, and a wall block also with a star. The floor was paved with flagstones in a regular scheme. Three of the West Magazines, which are walled off from the rest, are easily accessible from this room.

[25] *Knossos*, II, pp. 386-387. [26] Ch. III, 4; *Knossos*, II, pp. 406-408.
[27] *Mallia*, I, pp. 27-28.

Finally let us examine the rectangular complex of rooms occupying the center of the west side of the Central Court in the Palace of Minos (Fig. 2).[28] Two small connecting Pillar Crypts, each about 11 by 16 ft. (nearly 3½ by 5 m.), set end to end, contain a single pillar each, preserved, it seems, to its full height of 5 ft. 9 in. (1.75 m.). Each is made up of four blocks of limestone and all four faces of each block, except the west face of the east pillar and the top surface of the west pillar, were inscribed, according to Evans (some are difficult to see now), with double-axe signs, twenty-nine in all. Adjacent to the eastern pillar are two shallow, stone-lined basins evidently intended for the same purpose as those in the Royal Villa. Associated with these Pillar Crypts are several storage rooms, in the floor of one of which were two shallow stone-lined cists found empty; beneath these two earlier cists, much larger and deeper than those above (Ch. vii, 1), were discovered, and in and above them a mass of fragmentary objects of a ritual character, including snake-goddess figurines, a marble cross, quantities of painted shells, faïence plaques with a cow suckling its calf and a goat its kids, etc. (Ch. ii, 1).[29]

Easily accessible from the West Pillar Crypt was the Corridor of the Magazines, and it is possibly significant that the head of the partitions of the two nearest magazines (4 and 5) were marked with double-axe symbols which, as we have seen, were so generously distributed over the two pillars. To the east of the East Crypt was a larger anteroom, variously referred to as the "Room of the Stone Seat," because of a stone bench along its north wall, or as the "Room of the Column Bases," from the two round stone bases found in it, fallen from the Columnar Shrine above, which could be reached by a small stairway to the south. Just north of the steps that led up from the anteroom to the Central Court, on the line of foundations marking the west border of the court, Evans noticed faint traces of a series of four columns which he ingeniously, and perhaps correctly, in-

[28] *Knossos*, I, pp. 425, 441-442.　　[29] *Knossos*, I, pp. 463-523.

terpreted as marking the position of a "Tripartite Columnar Shrine," whose appearance in elevation is possibly represented, with variations, by the columnar shrine seen in the Grandstand Fresco (Figs. 44, 133). The actual remains, reversing the arrangement in the mural, allow for two columns in the wings and only one in the center, where Evans supposes the shrine or cella of the goddess was located. In a narrow area behind the right wing of the Tripartite Shrine was discovered a mass of sealings representing the goddess standing on a mountain guarded by two lions, with a worshipper in front and a shrine with columns and sacral horns behind.[30]

Thus, including the "Throne Room" complex at the north, which was perhaps used exclusively for ritual purposes (Chs. 11, 1 and v, 3), most if not all of the west side of the Central Court at Knossos (except for the stairs to the Piano Nobile), was occupied by a series of shrines. At Mallia the situation seems to have been similar: a complex of cult rooms at the north (vi), already described (Ch. 11, 3); the Pillar Crypt, vii 4, in the center; and an area with a round table of offerings south of the great stairway near the south end of the court (Figs. 6, 61, 95). At Phaistos Rooms 23 and 24 in the center west of the Central Court seem to have been cult rooms, and possibly the ruined rooms to the south of these were also (Figs. 4, 96). By analogy of position, then, Room 25 might likewise be expected to have a religious destination and, though no cult objects or features of a definitely religious nature seem to be associated with the room, its façade, composed of a very large central column flanked by massive piers, is not at all inappropriate (Fig. 50). Certainly with its handsome alabaster walls and floor, its niches and interior columns, it was no ordinary room, no mere anteroom to the magazines as the Italian publication describes it. I have already suggested, without, I admit, any specific proof, that it had certain functions in connection with the ritual of the bull games, and that some of the magazines behind it were used to stable the bulls at the time of the games (Ch. iv).[31]

[30] *Knossos*, II, pp. 796-810.   [31] *AJA*, 61 (1957), p. 261.

The position of Room 25 and the form of its façade bear a general resemblance, already remarked on (Ch. IV), to an open-fronted and pillared room at Mallia (vi 1), at Gournia (near the north end of the west side of the "Public Court"), at Plati (at "A"), perhaps at Vathypetro, and at Knossos (the "Tripartite Shrine" or possibly the "Throne Room" complex); compare Figs. 2, 6, 8, 9, and 30. In view of the many architectural analogies between the various palaces, this resemblance is not likely to be altogether coincidental. Is it not possible that all these rooms were in some way connected with the bull games, if these, as I believe, were put on in the central court? Let us add one further possibly significant circumstance: immediately north of the pillared portico at Gournia, mentioned above, lies a huge flat stone slab nearly 9 by 7 ft. in length and width and about 8-10 in. thick (ca. 2.75 by 2.15 by 0.23 m.), pierced obliquely by a large hole from top to bottom.[32] Can this have been an altar stone on which the bull was sacrificed after the ritual games (cf. Fig. 101)?

[32] This block is not described in the publication.

CHAPTER VIII

BUILDING MATERIALS AND FORMS

1. MATERIALS

THE BUILDING materials available to the Cretans of the second millennium B.C. were those in general use throughout the Bronze and Iron Ages until in the Roman imperial period the development of structural concrete and of window glass revolutionized the art of architecture. The use by the Minoans of stone, wood, lime mortar, clay, and reeds will be discussed in that order.

STONE. Gypsum, hydrous sulphate of calcium ($CaSO_4.2H_2O$), is very easy to work since it is so soft that, especially when fresh from the quarry, it can be scratched with the finger nail. When very pure it is snow-white, but it is generally clouded or veined by iron or other impurities, which may however increase its beauty. Coarser varieties of the mineral are used today for "plaster of Paris" by driving off 75% of the water content; it was commonly used by the Egyptians for ordinary plaster, but not by the Cretans, who preferred lime plaster. Thin cleavage plates can be employed, like mica, as a substitute for window glass; but no instances of its use for this purpose in the Bronze Age seem to have been observed.

Gypsum was extensively used at Knossos, where "inexhaustible" quarries occur on the neighboring hill of "Gypsadhes," for wall blocks, pillars, step treads, floor flagging, column and pier bases, etc. Except for outside wall blocks, where the exposed surface was vertical and was often shielded by a thin coat of stucco, gypsum was restricted largely to uses where it was protected from the weather because of its slight solubility in water.

The visitor to Knossos will see some gypsum bases honey-combed by the weather after half a century's exposure (Fig. 117); but some varieties are very resistant to water, as we have already noted in speaking of palace bathrooms (Ch. v, 3).

A fine-grained, marble-like variety of gypsum, capable of producing a very smooth, lustrous surface, is known today as alabaster, and was greatly prized by the Minoans for facing floors and walls in halls, bathrooms, and other important rooms. With bronze saws five feet or more long, they were able to saw this soft stone into sheets over six feet (2 m.) square and often little more than an inch (2½ cm.) in thickness (Fig. 125). Although the Egyptians from Early Dynastic times had used "ancient alabaster," a form of calcite closely related to marble, in slabs for lining passages and rooms, the Cretans were the first, so far as I can discover, to use stone essentially as a thin veneer to conceal a wall of inferior material. This very practical and economical method of achieving a fine effect with a minimum consumption of high quality stone was apparently not commonly used again until Imperial Rome learned to build its tremendous structures by combining the strength and economy of brick and concrete with the beauty of a thin revetment of marble or other fine stone.

Alabaster veneer was used with particular prodigality at Phaistos and H. Triadha. Near the latter an ancient quarry for alabaster of fine quality has been discovered and this (Fig. 125), as well as one near Gortyn, is being used by the Italian archaeologists in the work of repairing and restoring the two palaces. So lavish was its use—even occasionally for magazines —that the rulers of Phaistos and H. Triadha almost literally "dwelt in marble halls."

Limestone was the most widely used stone in Minoan build-ings. It usually took the place of gypsum whenever there would be direct exposure to the weather. Outside stairways and pave-ments, for instance, were always made of limestone; the central courts at Knossos and Phaistos were paved with rectangular slabs of this stone. Carefully dressed blocks were extensively employed for pillars and pillar bases, column bases, door and window facings, walls, etc.

Numerous grades and varieties of limestone were in use. A very hard type of a gray-blue color, known as ironstone (*sidheropetra*), was common at Knossos in the earlier period for pavements (*mosaiko*), and in the later period it was frequently employed for the central panel of a floor with a border of gypsum. It was also much used in the form of large rough blocks at the base of the outside walls of the houses at Mallia. On the other hand a soft, poor quality of white limestone, known as *kouskouras*, was also commonly employed at Knossos and elsewhere. Marble, which is a fine crystalline form of limestone, is comparatively rare in Crete.

Sandstone, in a soft, brown, very friable variety (*ammoudha*) was used extensively in the Palace of Mallia for exterior, and for some interior, walls. Obviously its use was dictated by the fact it was easily worked and locally available; traces of ancient quarries have been found close to the modern beach. The use of a building stone so inferior in quality is in keeping with the modest character of this palace.

Other stones such as schist (slate), marble, and breccia, had a more limited architectural usage, the first for flagstone paving, the other two for column bases.

WOOD. Since well preserved remains are rare we must depend largely upon inference, conjecture, and analogy for a study of the use of wood in Minoan architecture. More will be said in the next section on construction.

Considerable carbonized remains of wooden columns have been discovered at Knossos and Mallia, one shaft in the Palace of Minos being preserved to a length of over eight feet ($2\frac{1}{2}$ m.).[1] This and the remains of other heavy timbers used in the construction of the Grand Staircase were found to be of cypress wood, and, although today Crete is badly deforested and the cypress has almost disappeared from the island, in ancient times it was evidently abundant, for Pliny says that Crete was the

[1] *Knossos*, III, p. 321.

native home of the cypress,[2] and it "supplied materials for the temples and cult-statues of Mainland Greece."[3]

Wood was in common use for columns (which were never made of stone), ceiling and roof beams, flooring in the upper storeys, stairs (especially the upper flights), door and window frames and the doors themselves, and in the form of long timbers to strengthen adobe brick and stone walls. Empty beam-sockets in the upper part of masonry walls, such as the Pillar Crypts of the Royal Villa and the Temple Tomb at Knossos, also furnish evidence regarding the size of the timbers used and the form of the construction (see next section for details).

LIME MORTAR, PLASTER, STUCCO, CEMENT. Minoan builders did not use a gypsum mortar, as the Egyptians did, but a lime mortar, composed of slaked lime, sand, and an aggregate of pebbles, potsherds, or the like. There is now apparently conclusive evidence that they also knew how to make a true cement by adding an element resembling the Roman "pozzolana," namely the Greek "Santorin earth" from the island of Thera (modern Santorini).[4] In this book the terms "plaster" or "stucco" (a finer form of plaster) are used for wall facings, and "cement" for floor surfaces; but in view of the impossibility now of determining in each case whether it was composed of plain lime mortar or of true cement, these terms are not intended to be understood as necessarily accurate.

A fine smooth stucco excellent for wall paintings was ob-

---

[2] *Nat. Hist.*, 16, 141; Evans claims that "the material of the columns, as tested by expert examination of charred specimens, seems in all cases to have been cypress, which also supplied the massive beams and framework" (*Knossos*, I, p. 344); yet Marinatos asserts that the carbonized remains of ancient columns in the Palace of Minos are fir (*C. and M.*, p. 12).

[3] Evans (*loc.cit.*); he cites Hehn, *Kulturpflanzen*, pp. 244ff.

[4] The Gournia publication states that a cement was used at that site which contained "Santorin-earth" (*Gournia*, p. 21); no analysis or other proof, however, is given. Doro Levi also refers to the use of a true cement at Phaistos, *Nuova Antologia*, 467 (1956), p. 230, and cf. *PdP*, 71 (1960), p. 113; by letter he reports that several analyses of mortars from Phaistos and elsewhere have been made, and that a member of the Italian School has nearly completed "a comprehensive study on the Minoan architecture and building techniques," to be published in the *Annuario*. See also *Festòs*, II, pp. 347, 422.

tainable from limestone quarries, producing a very pure chalk lime, within a couple of miles of the Palace of Minos. Rough walls of adobe or rubble were often faced with stucco or thick plaster which, thanks to the cohesive force of the plaster, had a considerable structural as well as decorative value. Even the massive dressed masonry of the palace façades was surfaced with a thin layer of stucco, not however to conceal the joints for they were deliberately emphasized by incised lines (Fig. 121); the purpose of the stucco coat was perhaps rather for color since it was sometimes, at least, painted red. Red stucco was also employed to fill the joints between the gypsum flagstones of floors like that in the Main Hall of the North Residential Quarter at Phaistos in order to emphasize the pattern (Fig. 127). Cement or plaster floors were regularly used for light-wells, sometimes for open courts like the large West Court in the period of the last palace at Phaistos, or for rooms where liquids might be spilt, as in the East Magazines at Mallia (Ch. VII, 1). Stone or clay receptacles such as the sub-floor cists in the West Magazines at Knossos could be made tight with a thin coating of stucco, while thicker plaster was used to line the early "keeps" (cisterns?) northwest of the Central Court at Knossos, and the granaries at Mallia (Fig. 62).

None of the uses of stucco or plaster mentioned so far can be regarded as at all unusual. But at Phaistos one quite remarkable use of true cement (*calcestruzzo*) has been brought very forcefully to the excavators' attention: a very coarse concrete, often two to three or more feet thick, was used to cover over and seal in part of the ruins of earlier stages of the palace and thus provide a firm and relatively even surface on which to rebuild.[5] This process, it has recently been discovered, was repeated no fewer than three times, presumably after catastrophic earthquake shocks had destroyed the earlier palaces. While this has made the archaeologist's task a difficult and expensive one, the labor expended in cutting through and removing these masses of

---

[5] *Festòs*, II, pp. 10, 422.

concrete has been amply rewarded by the remarkable preservation of the lower portion of the ground floor rooms and their contents, belonging to palaces built as early as the beginning of the second millennium.

CLAY. Clay was used principally for the making of sun-dried or adobe bricks, of which the walls of ordinary buildings and much of the upper walls even of palaces were composed; at Phaistos, however, the excavators claim, the walls were generally of stone or rubble, while adobe is not known to have been used except for thin partitions.[6] The bricks were rarely, if ever, baked in an oven, although the conflagrations in which many buildings perished have often produced this effect.[7] Both straw and seaweed have been reported used with the clay as a binder, and the bricks generally measure about 18 to 24 in. long by 14 to 16 in. wide by 4 to 5 in. thick (46-61 by 35-40 by 10-13 cm.).

Clay was employed as a cohesive element between courses of adobe brick and in walls of rubble stone; it was also used between courses of dressed masonry.[8] Clay mixed with straw was used to face rough walls, sometimes itself serving as a backing for stucco. A special kind of impermeable, bluish-black clay was laid in a thick coat over the roof to prevent leakage, as indeed it still is, under the name of *lepidha*, in present-day Crete.

Water pipes were made of terracotta, as in the Near East (Fig. 139, A); but terracotta tiles do not seem to have been known, since the roofs were universally flat.

[6] *Festòs*, II, p. 421.   [7] *Festòs*, I, p. 228.

[8] The use of clay between courses of masonry was regarded by Evans as a mark of earlier date, but Levi's recent excavations and further studies at Phaistos have cast doubt on this and many other chronological criteria of an architectural nature used by Sir Arthur. Levi writes in *PdP*, 71 (1960), p. 107, "Certain technical criteria which used to be regarded as characteristic of the second palace today should be abandoned: such as the pavements and the alabaster dadoes of the walls, the wall surfaces, the pavements in regular oblongs of rectangular slabs in comparison with the polygonal 'kalderim' pavements, these latter for the most part of limestone, the painted stuccoes of walls and pavements, the shapes and heights of the column bases of hard stone; nor is it possible, on the basis of the difference in technique between courses of limestone blocks separated by a layer of clay and structure in blocks with a framing of wooden beams, observable throughout the constructions at Knossos and Phaistos, to establish the point of separation between the first and the second palace."

REEDS. Reeds were used abundantly in the river valleys of Egypt and Mesopotamia for purposes of building; even today large structures are built entirely of reeds near the mouth of the Tigris-Euphrates.[9] Considerable use was probably also made of reeds in Crete though definite evidence is slight. No doubt the commonest architectural purpose served by reeds in palaces or large houses was that reported from Gournia, namely as a backing for plaster ceilings.[10]

2. CONSTRUCTION

In the present section we are primarily concerned not with the form and material of such features as doors, windows, stairs, or columns, but with the actual structure of the houses and palaces: with pillars and columns as supporting members, with ceilings and roofs, and with walls and foundations.

Traditional Minoan construction paid little heed to the strength of foundations. Even the imposing walls of the west façade of the palaces at Knossos and Mallia were merely bedded on a few layers of small irregular stones or simply on tamped earth, and, given the characteristic lightness of the upper walls, this was adequate under normal conditions. But Crete was subject to violent earthquakes, and they exacted a heavy toll. The Palace of Phaistos was leveled time after time and though, as we have seen in the preceding section, the ruins were sealed in with a heavy layer of concrete to create a stable base over part of the area, yet it was not until the final rebuilding that adequate measures were taken. The builders now began to construct foundations of heavy blocks of limestone considerably broader than the walls they were to support, and to extend these downward, on the west and south sides of the palace where an artificial terrace had been built on the fill, to a depth of some six to eleven feet (2 to 3½ m.); even the foundations of the interior walls were sunk, where necessary, to a comparable depth.[11] At Tylissos, also, some of the exterior house walls built

[9] *Ill. Lon. News*, 226 (Jan. 19, 1955), p. 317.
[10] *Gournia*, p. 28.   [11] *Festòs*, II, pp. 425-428.

in the later period were supported on a rubble foundation carried down to bedrock.[12] That the construction of sound foundations, when felt to be needed, was well understood even at an early date, however, is illustrated by the heavy underpinning, running down ten feet (3 m.) or more to hardpan, which was provided for the individual columns of the stepped portico, erected according to Evans in M.M. Ia, mounting the steep slope below the Palace of Minos at its southwest corner.[13]

The construction of the walls varies almost infinitely, being dependent on such factors as the availability of materials, the resources and technical knowledge of the builders, the type of building, the height and weight of the superstructure, the degree of exposure to the weather, the danger from earthquakes, the position of the wall—whether interior or exterior, façade or rear, on a slope or on level ground, and so on—and often enough, it would seem, on the caprice of the builder. To give a reasonably brief and intelligible account of Minoan wall construction is correspondingly difficult.

As we have seen in the preceding section walls were constructed of a variety of materials, two or more often being combined in the same wall. Wood was probably never used alone, but was very commonly introduced into walls of adobe brick, rubble, or dressed masonry. The purpose of this "half-timber" construction was to provide a sort of semi-rigid framing which would unite and compact the other materials yet permit the wall to retain sufficient elasticity to absorb and resist the shock of earthquakes, so common in this region. It is a method of construction which has been widely used throughout the Aegean area from at least the third millennium B.C. to the present day (Fig. 124).

In the houses at Tylissos, for example, the regular practice was to run a short horizontal beam transversely through the thickness of the wall near the floor level, and on each end of this to support a vertical post flush with the wall surface on

[12] *Tylissos,* p. 48.
[13] *Knossos,* II, pp. 144-145.

each side; presumably one or more such transverse beams at higher levels would help to brace the posts firmly together.[14] In the rubble wall on the south side of Room 3 at H. Triadha a series of three sockets spaced about 4½ ft. (1.35 m.) apart on centers and about 7 in. (18 cm.) square, in the north face of the wall, correspond to three similar sockets opposite these on the south face (Fig. 67). Pairs of vertical posts rested directly on flat pieces of gypsum at the bottom of each socket, and must have been joined at intervals through the adobe wall above by transverse wooden bars.[15] Good examples of horizontal beams set flush into the wall faces, along with vertical posts and transverse tiebeams, can be seen in the ashlar masonry walls in the Hall of the Double-Axes and in the adjacent east-west corridor at Knossos.[16]

The upper parts of the walls, both exterior and interior, in all types of buildings, must have been normally built of adobe brick.[17] In ordinary houses the stonework was limited to a mere base or foundation of rough stone (rubble) leveled with clay on the top surface to receive the mud bricks; the outer face of the exterior walls of the houses east of the palace at Mallia is built of large boulders, a sort of rustic imitation of the palace orthostates. Occasionally interior walls, intended as light partitions and not to be continued beyond the first storey at most, were constructed of bricks laid on edge without any stone foundation at all. Examples of such walls, some only 4 to 5 in. thick, can be found in a storeroom for ritual double-axes (7) and in a series of grain bins (26-30) at Nirou Khani, in a bathroom (63d) and a toilet (82) at Phaistos, and in a number of small rooms at the southeast corner of the palace at Mallia.

Rubble masonry, ranging from small rough fieldstones compacted with clay to larger blocks with flattish surfaces due to natural cleavage, was also much used, either alone or in con-

---

[14] *Tylissos*, pp. 49-50.
[15] *Festòs*, II, p. 434.   [16] *Knossos*, I, pp. 347ff., figs. 250ff.
[17] The excavators believe that the walls of the Phaistos palace were entirely rubble, not mud brick, *Festòs*, II, p. 421.

junction with other materials. Sometimes it might serve, as already mentioned, as a foundation for adobe brick, or it might be continued up at least through the first storey; this is particularly common throughout the Palace of Phaistos and at H. Triadha (Fig. 67).

Masonry of dressed stone was used for strength, resistance, and appearance. Along the base of the principal (west) façade of the palaces, and occasionally elsewhere, as on the north façade of the Central Court at Phaistos (Fig. 122), a course of massive orthostates of dressed stone was regular. It was usually two feet or more high, and the individual blocks, sometimes exceeding six feet in length by three to four feet thick, might weigh several tons; they rested on a low projecting plinth or "euthynteria" (leveling course).

Yet these orthostate blocks, and the same is true of wall blocks of dressed stone in general, were finished smooth only on the front, top, and bottom surfaces, and not more than the front half of the ends. The rear was left quite rough since it was normal practice to complete the thickness of the wall with rubble masonry. A variation is seen in the orthostate course of the west façade of the Palace of Minos, where the walls are six feet thick (nearly 2 m.), and are completed with a series of upright blocks of the same height as the orthostates on the outer face (Fig. 118); the two faces were united by a series of transverse cross-bars of wood set in dovetailed mortises cut in their top surfaces, and the irregular space between the blocks was filled with rubble.

In a few of the finest houses part of the exterior walls was constructed of dressed stone laid in fairly regular coursing, for example in the Little Palace, Royal Villa, South House, and Southeast House at Knossos, and also at Tylissos (Fig. 78). The rear wall of the South House is built of quite massive blocks preserved, in the lee of the cutting for the artificial terrace on which it stands, to a height of eight courses (Fig. 72). The rear wall of the Southeast House is composed of an odd mixture of stones (Fig. 80): the lowest course is limestone, the next three gypsum, and the upper two preserved are limestone again. Normal wall courses of this type are usually from 1 to 1½ ft. high (30 to 45 cm.).

Interior walls were also sometimes built of dressed stone masonry, particularly where the wall was exposed to the weather, as in the unroofed passage which led up to the Central Court from the North Entrance at Knossos, in the small court (48) at Phaistos, and in the light-well of House A at Tylissos. A good illustration occurs in the Residential Quarter at H. Triadha where the north and south walls at the ends of the light-well east of Room 12 are of dressed masonry, but as soon as these walls pass beyond the limits of the light-well they abruptly relapse into ordinary rubble construction (Fig. 70).

Sometimes it would seem that the interior walls were faced with dressed stone just for the sake of appearance, as in the Pillar Crypt of the Royal Villa (Fig. 97), and perhaps this is also the reason for its use in the rooms of the Residential Quarter of the Palace of Minos. Since the stonework in the latter case would have been concealed behind alabaster paneling or plaster, however, perhaps the true explanation for its employment here was to give greater strength to walls which had to support at least two and probably three upper storeys.

A thin bedding of clay was sometimes used between the wall courses; but mortar was not used, as in modern masonry, to hold the blocks together.

A thorough examination of the remains could probably provide us with a fuller picture of the technical processes involved in preparing and laying Minoan masonry. Stone quarries have been observed in several places and the usual method of getting out the blocks seems to have been to bore rows of round holes, some 6 in. deep and 6 to 9 in. in diameter, into which posts were driven and soaked with water; the resulting expansion of the wood split away the blocks along prepared lines of fracture.[18]

[18] *Knossos*, II, p. 233; Chapouthier, *Les écritures minoennes au palais de Mallia*, pp. 87-88, Figs. 32-33.

Large numbers of bronze chisels, saws, and double-axes have been found, especially at H. Triadha. Pernier has noted the abundant traces of the strokes of the double-axe on the faces of the west orthostates of the "Primo Palazzo" at Phaistos; he would even see the origin of the term "labyrinth," applied to the Palace of Minos, in the fact that the palaces were, so to speak, the creation of the double-axe (*labrys*), which first made possible the production of dressed stone masonry and so the appearance of monumental architecture in Crete.[19] Bronze saws, some of them more than five feet (1½ m.) in length, must have been employed in cutting the great sheets of gypsum used particularly for paneling the interior walls.[20] Chisel-strokes an inch or so wide (ca. 2 cm.) are apparent everywhere on the stones at Phaistos, both on surfaces that would be concealed by other blocks and, much more lightly, on important visible surfaces such as the orthostates at the north end of the Central Court (Figs. 120, 122). Small round holes have sometimes been observed on the sides of blocks; these have been explained as lifting-holes, but certainly the common method of moving large blocks of stone during the Bronze Age was to slide them into place by means of temporary ramps.[21]

While speaking of stone masonry we may mention one rather mystifying feature, the so-called mason's marks.[22] In the early period of the palaces these are often very large and deeply cut —a "thunderbolt" at Phaistos reaches a length of 28 in. (72 cm.);[23] later they become smaller and shallower, though rarely as tiny as a "star" in the west recess north of the Central Court at Phaistos, which measures barely 1⅜ in. (3.5 cm.) in width (Fig. 119).[24] The signs, which appear on walls, pillars, etc., of both palaces and private houses (Fig. 78), include the double-axe (particularly common at Knossos), the trident (frequent at Phaistos), stars, crosses, branches, thunderbolts, and many less

---

[19] *Festòs*, I, p. 441, Fig. 77. [20] *Knossos*, II, p. 632. [21] *Mallia*, III, p. 20.
[22] *Festòs*, I, pp. 399-415; II, pp. 423-424; *Knossos, Index Volume*, pp. 98-99; Chapouthier, *op.cit.*, pp. 75-95.
[23] *Festòs*, I, p. 400, no. 2b.
[24] *Festòs*, II, p. 60, fig. 24.

easily describable forms. They sometimes concentrate in a particular part of a palace, for example tridents near the "sea gate" (North Entrance) at Knossos,[25] and since some appear to have been cut at the quarry it is frequently claimed that they were truly mason's marks, cut by the quarryman for the guidance of those who were to use them. But the twenty-nine double-axes cut on the eight blocks of the two pillars in the Pillar Crypts west of the Central Court at Knossos must have had a religious or magical significance. The problem is however far too complex to discuss here in detail, especially since it appears to offer little hope of providing information useful to the student of Minoan architecture.

The thickness of Minoan walls depends on a number of factors most of which cannot be closely calculated. In general, exterior walls are thicker than interior. At Sklavokambos, for example, the outer walls are usually about 3 to 4 ft. thick (rather over a meter), while the partition walls are only about 1½ to 2½ ft. (45 to 75 cm.); but extreme examples may vary from 8 ft. (2½ m.) in parts of the west façade at Knossos, to 4 in. (10 cm.) for minor adobe partitions. Walls intended to be continued in the upper storeys are generally thicker than those limited to the ground floor; we have already noticed the difference in thickness between the walls of the two-storey block north of the Central Court at Mallia and the three-storey block in the same position at Phaistos (Fig. 89).

The frequent practice of facing all types of walls with a layer of stucco or plaster, sometimes painted, has been mentioned in the preceding section; the cohesive force of thick plaster would add considerable strength to a wall of loose rubble.

Pillars and columns were extensively employed as supporting members in Minoan architecture. Columns, except very short ones, were made of wood, not of stone; this may be due largely to the fact that it is far easier to make a round column out of a tree trunk than to shape it out of stone. Fragments of the

---

[25] *Knossos*, I, p. 394.

carbonized cypress-wood column shafts have frequently been found, one at Knossos having a length, as preserved, of more than 8 ft. (2½ m.). The capitals were doubtless made of separate blocks of wood. The lower diameter of three of the largest Minoan columns known at Phaistos seems to have measured between 3½ and 4 ft., giving a bearing of around 11 sq. ft. (ca. 1 sq. m.). Occasionally the base was mortised to receive a tenon on the lower end of the column, and in the court of House E at Mallia the central area of the bases was left rough, apparently also with the purpose of preventing the wood column from slipping on the stone base.

Columns rather than pillars were used in locations where appearance and not merely support was considered important. Columns are therefore regular in light-wells and porticoes of the residential quarters, in the porticoes of the central courts (often combined with pillars), in peristyle courts, on stairway parapets, and in formal entranceways. At Phaistos the great oval column of the Grand Propylon (67) supports the center of a free span of 32 ft. (9.75 m.); a round column divides the wide opening of 75 on the Peristyle Court, 74; and a pair of columns is placed on the axis of the large hall, 25, west of the Central Court, with an area of over 750 sq. ft. (72 sq. m.). This last example, the use of columns within a room, is almost unique in Minoan architecture on the ground floor;[26] but on the upper floors pairs of columns made possible the great halls, with areas of nearly 3000 sq. ft. (270 sq. m.) in some instances, along the west façades (Ch. vi, 1), and two rows, of four or five columns each, supported the ceilings of the banquet halls (Ch. vi, 2), which at Phaistos and Mallia had an area of about 1200 sq. ft. (115 sq. m.), and at Knossos of nearly 2600 sq. ft. (240 sq. m.). Columns will be further discussed in the section on architectural decoration (Ch. xi, 1).

Pillars, that is vertical supports of rectangular cross-section, were not infrequently made of stone. In Minoan architecture

[26] There seems to have been a single column in the center of the central room of House Zb at Mallia (see Ch. iii, 16).

156

the pillar was usually, if not always, a plain straight-sided shaft without decoration of any sort, and purely utilitarian in function. Neither decorative nor strictly utilitarian, however, are those pillars used in the "Pillar Crypts," for these rooms were rarely so large as to require any sort of interior support.[27] The pillars must therefore have been added purely for religious reasons (Fig. 95), and their religious character is confirmed by the sacred symbols frequently cut on their blocks (Fig. 98); twenty-nine double-axes arc incised on the two pillars in the pair of Pillar Crypts in the Palace of Minos (Ch. II, 1).

Examples of purely functional pillars of stone are the seven in IX 1, 2, north of the Central Court at Mallia, which in addition to supporting their own cciling no doubt took the weight of corresponding columns in the room above (Figs. 59, 88); the single one in the Corridor of the Magazines (26) at Phaistos; and the "built-in" piers in the west magazines at Knossos and Mallia, used solely to carry columns in the halls of the Piano Nobile (Fig. 116). Similarly four piers in Magazines 16 and 17 in House A at Tylissos were not needed because of the size of these rooms, but presumably to support columns in a large hall overhead (Ch. III, 11, and Fig. 19). Stone piers were also used in long porticoes, alternating with columns, especially in the central courts; and as angle piers in two-sided porticoes in the residential quarters.

Stone pillars frequently had a mortise on their upper surface for securing in position the horizontal beams that rested on them —often a useful indication that the pillar is complete in its present condition.

The numerous instances where a rectangular stone base is preserved, but no trace of any pillar remains, indicate that they were not always of stone. However they were not made entirely of wood, as we might expect, except perhaps very small ones,

[27] These cult pillars were functional to the extent that they did commonly support, it is generally believed, a column in the room overhead (cf. Fig. 71), but the presence of the column was also dictated by religious rather than by functional considerations (Ch. VII, 2).

but rather of vertical wooden posts with the spaces between filled in with clay or rubble. Commonly these posts were erected on the corners of a thick block of wood secured to the stone base by tenons and mortises. On the large stone base in the center of the doorway between 68 and 69 in the Grand Propylon at Phaistos masses of the clay packing were found in place, and the imprint of a nest of vertical posts each with a cross-section about 4 in. (10 cm.) square.[28]

A similar technique was often used to reinforce wall angles. A rectangular, or triangular, block of stone was built into the corner with mortises for securing a horizontal block of wood; on this probably rested three posts, one at the corner, and one at a short interval on either side, the spaces being packed with rubble.[29] The method of strengthening the ends of walls at door openings will be discussed in connection with doors (Ch. IX, 3).

A word should be added in regard to the structural purpose of the pier-and-door partitions characteristic of the Minoan Halls (Ch. v, 2). In several instances where the width of the Hall was unusually great the presence of the partition made it possible to run shorter ceiling beams parallel with the length of the room, and support them midway on this partition. For example, the Hall of the Double-Axes is about 26 ft. (8 m.) wide (Fig. 12), but this long span could be reduced to 18 or 19 ft. (5½ m.) by running the beams from the ends of the room to the transverse partition. However the width of the Hall is frequently no more, and sometimes even less, than the length of the main part of the Hall; this would indicate that the primary purpose of the pier-and-door partition was not to reduce the free span of the ceiling beams, but rather, as we have seen (Ch. v, 2), to control the "weather" within the room.

[28] *Festòs*, II, pp. 313, 317, 335, 436, and fig. 197.
[29] *Festòs*, II, pp. 434-435; *Tylissos*, p. 51. The southwest corner of ix 1 (north of the Central Court) at Mallia was reinforced by a pillar set on a stone base, not in the wall but in the corner of the room.

Remains of wood, usually cypress, used for horizontal beams supporting the floors and ceilings have been found in the area of the Grand Staircase at Knossos and elsewhere, and the empty beam-sockets in masonry walls are to be seen in some excavated buildings.

One of the most interesting examples of this is the Pillar Crypt of the Royal Villa (Fig. 97). The sockets in the top course of the walls show that the main ceiling beam consisted of a huge tree trunk which had been sawn in two and still retained its original taper from a width of about 28 in. (71 cm.) at one end to about 22 in. (56 cm.) at the other. Its free span between the wall faces amounted to about 13 ft. 9 in. (4.20 m.), but it received support at its center from a heavy gypsum pillar which was apparently needed for cult reasons. Three sockets in each of the other two walls show that three smaller beams, also retaining much of their original shape in cross-section, spanned the 13 ft. (4 m.) distance which represents the width of the room, and were socketed into the top face of the great transverse beam at their centers.[30]

The ceiling of a basement room in the "Temple Tomb" at Knossos (Fig. 113, C), with two large gypsum pillars on the east-west axis, was supported on ponderous cypress beams about 1 ft. 8 in. square (40 cm.) in section resting on the pillars and in sockets in the north and south walls; the length of the beams was between 18 and 19 ft. (ca. 5.60 m.). Eight smaller transverse beams, about 20 ft. long (6.10 m.), rested on these two beams and in sockets in the top wall course.[31]

The heavy character of these floor girders suggests the splendid resources in timber upon which the Minoan architect could draw, but he was surely accustomed to spanning far greater spaces with horizontal beams. In five of the Halls with pier-and-door partitions the minimum span is over 16 ft. (5 m.), and in one instance, Room 3 at H. Triadha (Figs. 11, 151), it

[30] *Knossos*, II, p. 408.
[31] *Knossos*, IV, pp. 968-970.

reaches a length of almost 20 ft. (6 m.). Wide spans are also common in the great public rooms of the Piano Nobile. The longest for which there is practically certain evidence are the spans from the east and west walls to the central pair of columns in the Central Hall at Mallia (Fig. 84), which was in the vicinity of 23 ft. (7 m.); in the Northwest Hall of the Palace of Minos, according to the restoration proposed above (Fig. 85), the span would be slightly greater still, about 25 ft. (ca. 7½ m.).[32] Yet this falls 13 ft. (4 m.) short of the span which the excavator of the somewhat earlier palace at Mari on the Euphrates believes the Throne Room (65) must have had (Fig. 148).[33]

The corbel principle, used in masonry spans at least early in the third millennium in both Egypt and the Near East, was certainly familiar in the Late Minoan period to the Cretan architects who employed it in the stonework of large underground tombs (Fig. 136, M), and apparently also in the great viaduct south of the Palace of Minos. Corbeled doorways, vaults, and superb domes are common in Mycenaean Greek architecture at a slightly later date (Fig. 135).[34] Yet for the use of corbeling in Minoan palaces or houses, where dressed stone masonry was rarely if ever carried as high as the door lintels, there is at present no evidence. As for the true arch, long employed on a modest scale for underground structures in Egypt and the Near East, there is no certain evidence whatever either in Minoan or in Mycenaean Greek architecture.[35]

Except for a slight slope for drainage the roofs of both Minoan palaces and houses seem to have been uniformly flat. All the available evidence points to this conclusion: the lack of roof tiles in the ruins, the shape of the ground plan with its multitude of projecting elements (Ch. XIII, 3), representations such as the

---

[32] Yet *Mallia, Maisons,* II, p. 12, note 2, refers to the "faible longueur des bois de l'île."

[33] *Mari,* II, p. 143.   [34] *Archaeology,* 13 (1960), pp. 46-54.

[35] In *Festòs,* II, pp. 447-450, two small rough arches are described; the first (fig. 278) is possibly Hellenistic rather than Minoan; the second (fig. 279) seems to be Minoan, but is hardly more than rough corbeling.

Town Mosaic (Fig. 103) and mural paintings, and actual remains of roofs, if recognized correctly, found in the fill.

The method of constructing the roof and making it watertight was probably much the same then as now. The modern procedure has been described by a native Cretan archaeologist as follows: "Throughout Crete in order to roof the houses, after having set the beams of the framework in place, a bed of thatch is strewn—brushwood or the foliage of the oleander. . . . On top of this a coat of earth two or three inches thick is laid . . . , and above this again a coat of impermeable clay called *lepidha*, which is tamped down again and again."[36]

[36] Xanthoudides, quoted in *Tylissos*, p. 54.

CHAPTER IX

WINDOWS AND DOORS

1. THE MEANING OF THE RECESSES

A STUDY of the shallow recesses which are such a distinctive feature of the outer walls of the Minoan palaces presents some interesting problems and leads to certain important conclusions, one of a very unexpected nature.

A striking feature of these recesses is that they are so absolutely limited to palaces that we might fancy them a kind of hallmark of the residence of kings, a prerogative of royal authority. They occur only in the palaces at Knossos, Phaistos, Mallia, and Gournia in Crete, but we may add that a typical recess has lately been discovered in the fine stone façade of the Palace of Nestor at Pylos on the Greek mainland.[1] A further peculiarity is that the recesses occur, with one exception, only on the west, or principal, façade of the Cretan palaces. The exception is the very carefully designed façade at the north end of the Central Court of the Palace of Phaistos, where a symmetrical pair of recesses occurs on either side of the axial doorway (Figs. 50, 51, 122).

In their present state the recesses start at the ground level and continue upward only as high as the stone masonry is preserved; but there is no reason to doubt that they originally extended to the top or near the top of the building in the structure of the adobe brick or rubble wall. The length of the recesses varies from less than eight to about twenty feet ($2\frac{1}{4}$ to 6 m.); in depth they measure fairly constantly about five to seven inches

[1] *AJA*, 59 (1955), pl. 28, fig. 15.

(12 to 18 cm.). In the plinth course the recess frequently extends a few inches wider at each end.

Agreement is quite general on one point: that the purpose of the recesses must be purely aesthetic—to relieve the monotony of the large wall surfaces. In ultimate origin they probably go back to the paneled façades, common in Egyptian and Mesopotamian architecture from early times, which seem to have developed in imitation of construction in other materials such as reeds where, to form the walls of simple buildings, sheets of reed matting were stretched between upright posts made of reeds tied in compact bundles.

It has often been suggested or assumed, for reasons obviously both aesthetic and structural, that if there were windows in the palace façades they would be located in the recesses. But Pendlebury, long Evans' principal assistant at Knossos and author of the standard handbook on Cretan archaeology (1939), came to doubt that windows could really have been located in the recesses. This opinion was the result of his failure to take adequate account of the evidence from Phaistos and Mallia, for he claimed, on the basis of what he saw at Knossos, that the recesses never bore any relation to a room behind, as they should of course have done if they contained windows. In fact he carried this argument to its logical conclusion by declaring that, in view of the recesses in the façade, it seems necessary to suppose that the main reception halls in the Piano Nobile did not have windows at all: "outside windows seem to have been avoided wherever possible." Light, he claimed, must have been furnished by clerestories and light-wells.[2] The Phaistos excavator, Miss Banti, evidently agrees with these conclusions for she states that "the idea has now been abandoned that (the recesses) indicate windows in the upper storey."[3]

But surely this conclusion is needlessly perverse. As in the problem of the location of the bull games and the existence of the Piano Nobile at Phaistos, the obvious and reasonable solu-

[2] *A. of C.*, p. 186.   [3] *Festòs*, II, p. 431.

tion has been rejected because of what superficially seemed to be insurmountable objections.[4]

But the objections are far from being insurmountable. For at Phaistos and Mallia the recesses *are* carefully related to the rooms behind them (Figs. 83, 84). Even at Knossos the southernmost recess is fairly closely centered on the room behind, although it is considerably displaced from the center of its façade unit (owing to the additional wall thickness at the south end). The recess to the north of this has a unique and unexplainable jogged form, but there are various possible solutions permitting the use of windows here, so it cannot be used as an argument one way or the other. The northernmost recess would actually be very closely centered on the single great hall which I feel should be restored here (Ch. vi, 1, Fig. 85).

In favor of the theory that windows were placed in the recesses there is a piece of negative evidence which gains considerable force from the fact that there are a score of available examples: in no case does a recess occur at a point where there is good reason to believe that there would have been a partition wall directly behind it in the upper storey. In one of the very few instances where walls abut against the rear of a recess on the ground floor, namely in the Magazine Block at Phaistos, these walls were almost certainly replaced by rows of columns on the floors above (Figs. 83, 84).

A detailed investigation of the recesses has also led to interesting conclusions regarding the unit of length used by the Cretan builders, but it will be better to return to this in a later section (Ch. xiii, 1).

2. LIGHTING AND VENTILATION

It is difficult today, in our northern climate, fully to appreciate the lighting problems of the ancient Mediterranean architect. Without window glass it was hardly possible for him to admit

[4] For further details and illustrations see "Windows, Recesses, and the Piano Nobile," *AJA*, 64 (1960), pp. 329-333.

light without also admitting air, but fortunately the generally mild climate prevented this from being a severe hardship.

The idea of windows without glass is to us almost paradoxical. Yet the Classical Greeks, for example, had numerous windows in their houses and controlled the amount of light and air with wooden shutters.[5] Whether the Minoans used shutters is not clear, but windows were certainly common, at least in the upper storeys, to judge by the "Town Mosaic" (Fig. 103), which represents the façades of a number of two- and three-storey town houses. Many of the windows on these façades seem to be divided into "panes," as many as six to a window, and some are colored red. It has been suggested that some material like an oiled parchment was used, which would at least be translucent though not transparent. Fragments of wall paintings from Crete and from Mycenaean Greece also show windows, and women looking out of them.[6]

Interior windows were probably fairly common. A number of examples of openings to transmit light from light-wells are known; there are, for example, five in the Residential Quarter of the Palace of Minos (Fig. 12, W). At Tylissos, in House C, a window over eight feet (2½ m.) wide, divided into three openings, lights a large room from the light-well of the Hall (Fig. 77), and in House A a window over five feet (ca. 1½ m.) wide also opens from a light-well (Fig. 19). The light-well in the Residential Quarter at H. Triadha has windows about five feet (1.49 m.) long and with sills over five feet (1.65 m.) above the floor, to light the stairs to the south and the Queen's Hall to the north (Figs. 11, 70, 151). Light is borrowed from the porticoes of Peristyle Court 74 at Phaistos to light the stairway, 71, through two large openings.

Evans believed that there was evidence for a series of openings ("transoms") above the doors of the pier-and-door partition in the Hall of the Double-Axes (Fig. 45),[7] and this prob-

[5] *Olynthus*, VIII, pp. 264-266.
[6] *Knossos*, I, p. 444, fig. 320; II, p. 602, fig. 375.
[7] *Knossos*, III, pp. 341-342; the transoms would admit some light when all the doors were closed.

ably was in general true of the pier-and-door partitions (Fig. 151). It must also be emphasized that the function of these rows of doors was to provide and control the admission of light and air rather than to furnish so needlessly many entrances or exits; they were in fact essentially shuttered windows, and by their use "infinite gradations might indeed be secured in regulating both temperature and ventilation."[8]

Exterior windows on the ground floor, for reasons of safety and privacy, were no doubt in general avoided. Yet some examples are definitely known and there may have been many more; the walls are rarely high enough to be sure. The rear walls of the South House at Knossos, of which eight courses remain in position, reveal the location of three windows: one into the Main Hall, one into a lavatory, and one opening on a stairway (Figs. 15, 72). Two windows are still to be seen in the northeastern quarter of the Villa of H. Triadha, and the French excavators believe there was one in the east wall of the palace at Mallia in room-group x. Outside windows have also been reported in the Little Palace, the House of the Frescoes, and the House of the Chancel Screen at Knossos, and in Houses Za and Zb at Mallia, but the last two are in my opinion doubtful.

Storerooms on the ground floor may have been ventilated and dimly illuminated by narrow slit-windows resembling those on some ivories recently found at Knossos.[9]

The position of windows in the second storeys of the west fronts of the palaces is indicated, we believe, by the recesses discussed above (Ch. IX, 1); and it is possible that the great halls in the upper storeys also received light from clerestory windows as suggested in our restoration of the Palace of Mallia (Fig. 58). And one of the principal considerations, as we have said (Ch. VI, 1), for putting the important reception rooms of the palace above the ground floor, may have been the desire to light them adequately by means of windows.

[8] *Knossos*, III, p. 340.
[9] *Ill. Lon. News*, 229 (Feb. 22, 1958), p. 301, fig. 11; also Edward Bacon, *Digging for History*, London, 1960, pl. 19. Vents of this type are suggested in our restorations, Figs. 48, 58.

◄ However the usefulness of windows without glass is limited, and Minoan architects learned to depend for much of their lighting on open courts and airshafts of various forms and sizes. The large dimensions of the palace central courts may have been dictated by their use as an arena for the bull games; but there can be no doubt that many of the inner rooms received most of their light and air directly from the court or indirectly through the long porticoes that opened upon it.

The Knossos palace possessed but one court. Mallia had a second very much smaller one with short porticoes on two sides, on which a number of storerooms and workrooms opened. Phaistos had two smaller courts within the walls of the palace: one, 48, served partly for communication, but mostly, it would seem, as a source of light for two of the large rooms in the upper storeys of the block north of the Central Court, and for some of the upper rooms of the North Residential Quarter; the other, 74, had porticoes on all four sides, with a very large hall, 93, which perhaps formed part of the living apartments of the royal family, opening on the north portico (Fig. 4).

The court was not, however, an indispensable element of domestic architecture as it was in Classical Greece, for example, for it is rarely found except in the largest houses, such as the Little Palace at Knossos, House A at Tylissos, and House E at Mallia. To some extent even the ground floor rooms of Cretan houses may have depended on windows for light and air; but for the Main Hall these were normally supplied, or supplemented, by a vertical airshaft, generally known as a light-well.[10] The light-well, in its usual form, extended across one end of the Hall on which it opened for its entire length of some 15 to 20 ft. (4½ to 6 m.), support for the lintel being provided by one or usually by two columns. The area between the columns and the back wall, some 6 to 10 ft. (2 to 3 m.) broad, was often floored with cement and regularly furnished with a drain. The shaft extended up through however many

[10] The distinction between a court and a light-well is a matter of size, and so must to a certain extent be arbitrary.

storeys the house, or palace, may have had, and is usually regarded as having been completely open at the top. But it is also possible that the opening was roofed over at the top and space left for wide openings at the sides, amounting to a kind of clerestory arrangement (Fig. 21); perhaps this explains the curious "penthouse" projecting above many of the roofs of the house façades in the Town Mosaic (Fig. 103 at right).[11] In the Egyptian upper class dwelling of this period the roof of the main hall in the center of the house (which is one-storeyed) is loftier than that of the surrounding rooms, and openings in the clerestory thus formed provide light and ventilation; the resemblance in principle, though not in detail, may indicate some relationship between the Cretan and the Egyptian house,[12] seen also, perhaps, in the common lack of a court.

It is sometimes supposed that light-wells were developed to solve the problem of lighting the inner rooms in large buildings like the palaces, yet, although they were in fact useful for this purpose, it is true that commonly in Minoan houses not only the room which is lighted by the light-well, but also the light-well itself, is adjacent to an outside wall. Why was light and air not provided simply by windows in this wall? The answer must lie partly in the inadequacy of the unglazed window. The light-well, while ensuring privacy and security, provided light without the full blaze of the sun, and air without the full blast of the wind. It was admirably suited to the Cretan climate.

Instead of the usual form described above, the light-well sometimes appears as a tiny court with columns or pillars on two, or on all four, sides. The type with a column at each of the four corners of the opening (like a "tetrastyle atrium") is to be seen in Room 50 of the North Residential Quarter at Phaistos, and in House B and two other houses at Palaikastro; the

---

[11] Lawrence, *Gk. Arch.*, pp. 27-28. Marinatos suggests, on Egyptian analogies, they may represent "summer bedrooms" (*C. and M.*, p. 48). Experiments with a model show that except when the sun is overhead and shining directly down into it the amount of light entering by way of an unroofed light-well is not very much greater than when the light-well is roofed; see *Hesperia*, 27 (1958), p. 320.

[12] Smith, E. B., *Eg. Arch.*, p. 207.

other type is represented by House A at Tylissos, the South-east House at Knossos, and the Queen's Apartments at H. Triadha—each of these with three columns about an angle—and by the Hall of the Colonnades, that is the light-well beside the Grand Staircase at Knossos, which has four columns. House E at Mallia possibly had eight pillars about a small court (xiv).

In the palaces light-wells occur almost exclusively in the residential quarters; does this mean that the scheme originated in domestic rather than in palatial architecture? No less than five light-wells are to be found in this quarter at Knossos, since its two lowest storeys had been constructed in a great cutting which extended to a level of nearly thirty feet (9 m.) below that of the Central Court, thus severely restricting its available light (Fig. 12). The bottom of the light-well beside the Grand Staircase measured about 11 by 18 ft. (3½ by 5½ m.) and lighted not only these stairs but a smaller set to the south. A second light-well served the Hall of the Double-Axes and, through a window, the Lower East-West Corridor. The Queen's Hall was equipped with light-wells on both east and south sides, the former also lighting a narrow flight of stairs through another window. The fifth light-well in this quarter, immediately south of the Grand Staircase, had two windows but no columns, and lighted and ventilated the secluded rooms amongst which was the "water-closet" already described (Ch. v, 4).

We have left the largest light-well in Minoan architecture for final mention. It forms the rear of the Grand Propylon at Phaistos (69A), and measures about 45 ft. long by 19 wide (ca. 13½ by nearly 6 m.), or some 855 sq. ft. (over 80 sq. m.) in area. The next largest light-well, at the south end of the South Propylaeum at Knossos, as restored by Evans, would amount to about 310 sq. ft. (nearly 30 sq. m.), while that at the west end of the Hall of the Double-Axes, which with three others ranks next in size, amounts to only about 225 sq. ft. (over 20 sq. m.).

Although 69A forms a passage from the Grand Propylon, by way of a small door in its right rear corner, to a double flight of steps leading to the Central Court in one direction and to Peristyle 74 in the other, yet it is clearly also a light-well, for its floor is surfaced with cement and there is a drain near the southwest corner (Ch. XI, 4). In keeping with its superior size it is fronted by three large oval columns.

Nevertheless, in spite of its evident importance, one may wonder why there was any need of a light-well in this position at all. The stairway, 66, and the landing, 67, were surely open to the sky as well as for forty-five feet along the front. This would certainly have furnished ample light to the two shallow vestibules 68 and 69, and to the area 69A itself, for almost the whole width of the opening between 67 and 68 was left free of any obstruction, and the two doorways in the wall between 68 and 69 are each eight feet ($2\frac{1}{2}$ m.) wide and were never closed by doors. The real reason for the existence of this light-well, it would seem, was to supply light to some room or rooms in the storey above, and this in fact agrees excellently with our restoration of the important group of rooms north of the Central Court (Figs. 87, 90).[13]

We have spoken in this section only of natural illumination; something will be said later of the large stone lamps with which the palaces were well supplied (Ch. XII, 1). But even state functions must have been conducted largely during the daylight hours. The Minoan Cretan surely slept far more of the dark hours than does twentieth century man, with his ability to turn night into day by means of the electric light.

3. DOORS AND LOCKS

The excavator of the palace at Mari on the Euphrates was fortunate in discovering the carbonized remains of a large wooden door, which in burning had retained its original size and form to a remarkable degree.[14] No such windfall has oc-

[13] *AJA*, 65 (1961), p. 167.
[14] *Mari*, II, pp. 268-270, figs. 322-323.

curred in Crete. However, one of the doors on the house façades of the Town Mosaic, though at a very small scale, does seem to represent a door composed of a number of overlapping vertical planks quite like the batten door at Mari (Fig. 136, D).

A wide variety of uses, sizes, and forms of doorways is indicated by the remains of the Cretan houses and palaces. As a means of protection when the Central Court was in use as a bull ring, doors were used at Mallia even to close off a broad flight of stairs to the second storey, and at Phaistos, for the same reason, a large pair of doors closed against a column (Ch. iv); both these instances are decidedly unusual. The most distinctive use of doors in Cretan architecture is their employment in "batteries" in the ubiquitous pier-and-door partitions (Figs. 45, 151), where they function essentially as shuttered windows for as doors their number is quite superfluous (Ch. ix, 2). In the Main Hall (77, 79) of the North Residential Quarter at Phaistos and in the one at H. Triadha (3, 12) there were no fewer than ten sets of such double doors (Fig. 151), while the corresponding Halls at Knossos and Mallia contained eleven.

In regard to the position of doorways it has often been noted as a distinctive feature of Minoan planning that in large rooms the door is placed not on the axis but generally near the end of a long side. This may be true of the informal residential quarters of the palaces, but there is no compelling reason to suppose that it holds good for the formal public halls in the Piano Nobile as well. The windows seem to have been axially placed in these rooms (Ch. ix, 1); the doors, we may suspect, were also. The axial doorway at the north end of the Central Court at Phaistos is an instructive example (Fig. 50).

Small metal hinges were in use in the ancient world from early times for boxes and chests, but the regular system for doors was a vertical wooden pivot, one end of which revolved in a hollow in the threshold, the other in a hole in the lintel. This was the common, if not invariable, method used in Crete; but it must be admitted that in some instances there is no trace of the pivot holes we should expect to find in the stone threshold.[15] The Minoan pivot holes commonly measure 2 to 4 in. (5 to 10 cm.) in diameter, and are rarely more than 1 in. (3 cm.) deep, sometimes less than ¼ in. (1 cm.). One at Mallia seems to show two stages of use (Fig. 107). Big doors like those at the foot of the ten foot (3.20 m.) broad stairway west of the Mallia Central Court had pivot holes nearly 6 in. (15 cm.) in diameter, though still very shallow.

The bottom end of the pivot, which bore the whole weight of the door, was sometimes shod with a "shoe" of bronze, as in Classical Greek times. Bronze Age specimens have been found at Alalakh in Syria (Fig. 104, C),[16] and at Mycenae in mainland Greece.[17] Only two seem to have been preserved in Crete, both for large heavy doors: the Mallia doors just mentioned, and those from the Central Court to Room 25 at Phaistos (Fig. 104, A, B).

Minoan doorways vary in width from 2 ft. (60 cm.) or even less to 6 ft. or more, but ordinarily measure from 3 to 4 ft. (90 to 120 cm.). It is not often that the height of a doorway is preserved or can be estimated. Two doorways in the basement of the South House measure about 5 ft. 3 in. (160 cm.); one in the Residential Quarter at H. Triadha (Fig. 154), 6 ft. (1.85 m.); and others in the palace and Royal Villa at Knossos, about 6½ ft. (2 m.).[18] Formal doorways like that on the axis of the Phaistos Central Court (Fig. 50) may have been considerably higher; the width of the Phaistos doorway, over 6 ft., suggests that its height may have been as great as the height of the first storey would allow, i.e. around 10 ft. (over 3 m.).

[15] *Mallia, Maisons*, II, p. 9, note 2, when no pivot holes are found "it must be supposed then, as J. Hazzidakis does with regard to Tylissos, that the doors turned on hinges fixed in the doorjamb"; the reference is to *Tylissos*, p. 55. But Miss Banti writes (*Festòs*, II, p. 590, note 289), "I do not believe possible the hypothesis of Hazzidakis, of bronze hinges which would have disappeared without leaving any trace."

[16] *Alalakh*, p. 118, fig. 48.   [17] Mylonas, *Anc. Myc.*, p. 53.

[18] The door of the "Tomb of the Tripod-Hearth" measures 1.90 m. high and tapers from 0.72 at the bottom to 0.51 m. at the top, and the two doors of the niches in the forehall of the "Isopata Royal Tomb" measure 2.03 and 2.05 m. high (*Archaeologia*, 9 [1905], p. 425, fig. 32, and pls. 96, 97).

Double doors were very common. There were two advantages: by reducing the width and therefore the weight of the door the wear on the pivots and their sockets was diminished; and in the pier-and-door partitions there was room to close the leaf neatly back into the face of the jamb (Figs. 106, 151).

Let us examine some typical examples of doorways commencing with one at the southeast corner of Room 22 near the southwest corner of the Central Court at Phaistos (Fig. 105).[19] The threshold, which was of gypsum instead of the limestone more usual for thresholds at this site, was laid at approximately the same level as the flagged floor of the room; this was common practice, though sometimes the threshold was a little higher. The L-shaped jamb bases, of limestone instead of the gypsum more frequently used for jamb bases at Phaistos, rested on the ends of the threshold and rise 3 to 4 in. (8 to 10 cm.) above it. The gaps for the pivot sockets, measuring roughly 3 in. square (one is 8 by 7 cm., the other 9 by 6 cm.), are so placed behind projecting "tongues" that the pivots would have been concealed and protected by the wooden doorposts or jambs.

In Corridor 62 at the northeast corner of the Central Court at Phaistos a single pivot hole shows that there was only one leaf, over 4 ft. (1.30 m.) long (Fig. 111). The projecting tongue on the south jamb base, which rests on the threshold and is 7 in. (18 cm.) high,[20] marks the lower end of a rebate against which the door closed.

The north door of the Queen's Hall (81) in the North Residential Quarter at Phaistos had a double door each leaf of which was about 20 in. (50 cm.) long (Fig. 109). A bolt hole in the threshold shows that the left-hand leaf (on entering the room) was the "sleeping" leaf ordinarily kept closed.[21] Such bolt holes have also been reported from Knossos.

Evidence preserved at Phaistos shows that the usual method

[19] *Festòs*, II, p. 143. In this and the following examples the details and drawings are from my notes made at the sites.

[20] Contrary to the statement in *Festòs*, II, p. 438, "Gli stipiti laterali non posano mai sulla soglia."

[21] *Festòs*, II, p. 283.

of constructing the doorjambs was to cover the stone base with a flat block or "cushion" of wood about 4 in. (10 cm.) thick, and to erect on this a number of vertical posts some 6 to 8 in. (15 to 20 cm.) thick.[22] The same method of construction was employed at Mallia where, however, separate doorjamb bases were rare in the palace, and the woodwork consequently rested directly on the threshold. A well preserved example is illustrated in Fig. 108. The threshold consists of a heavy block of "ironstone" with two pivot holes and clear traces of the circular scoring caused by the dragging of one of the leaves of the double door; indeed the pivot hole on this side shows signs of readjustment (Fig. 107), perhaps intended to correct this defect. In the wall-heads on either side are gaps for the vertical posts, one at each corner, and one in the center. Probably the two corner posts were provided with projecting rebates, corresponding to the tongues on the stone jamb bases, to protect the pivots, as shown in the restored plan (Fig. 108).

A final example of a well preserved threshold in a private house, Za at Mallia, may be illustrated (Fig. 110).[23] On the main body of the threshold two small pivot holes show clear traces of wear on the edges. At the ends the block of ironstone was cut down about a quarter of an inch (1 cm.) along a straight line, and the rectangular area, about 12 by 20 in. (30 by 50 cm.), used for the setting of the doorposts. Two matched sets of holes appear on this area. The two smaller holes being very shallow were probably abandoned as too small and too near the edge; the larger pair, 2 in. (5 cm.) in diameter and 1¼ in. (3 cm.) deep, have sharp unworn edges and were evidently not pivot holes but mortises to receive round tenons on the underside of the doorjamb blocks and keep them from shifting. Such care for the stability of the jambs is uncommon, but can be paralleled for example in a pair of bases at H. Triadha (Fig. 123). The distance of the pivot holes from the doorposts suggests some such framing as shown in the plan (Fig. 110).

[22] *Festòs*, II, pp. 440-441.   [23] *Mallia, Maisons*, I, pp. 65-66, figs. 6, 7.

Rarely the whole doorframe was made of stone (Fig. 154). Examples such as the two doorways in the basement rooms of the South House and the inner doorway of the Temple Tomb at Knossos, make it perfectly clear that the projecting tongue of the characteristic stone jamb bases is but the lower end of the vertical rebate against which the door closed or which sheltered the pivot.

Two of the doors just mentioned provide somewhat enigmatic information on methods of door closure.[24] Both are very similar in detail. In both the left-hand side (on entering) was the hinge side, though no pivot hole is to be seen. On the right-hand jamb both are rebated, and just far enough beyond the edge of the rebate to allow for the thickness of the wooden door (1 to 2 in.; 2½ to 5 cm.) is a deep rectangular cutting (Fig. 113, B); there can be no doubt that this formed a socket for a horizontal bolt in the form of a wooden bar. Another inch or two beyond the cutting a hole about ⅜ in. (1 cm.) in diameter pierces the stone obliquely and penetrates the side of the cutting. This was certainly designed to receive a metal pin to be inserted into a corresponding hole in the side of the bar when it had been thrust into its socket (Fig. 112, A, B). Several bronze pins of appropriate dimensions have been found, including one in the Temple Tomb and one in the South House.

But what was the purpose of the pin? Sir Arthur Evans' answer was that it was inserted "into the wooden bar so as to prevent its withdrawal."[25] Quite so. But withdrawal by whom? Certainly not, as Evans assumed, by someone *inside* the door, since all he need do in order to be able to withdraw the bolt was to remove the pin again. On the other hand, if it was possible for someone to move the bolt from the *outside* of the door by means of such a simple device as a knob fixed in the bar and protruding through a long narrow horizontal slot in the door (Fig. 112, C, D),[25a] then the insertion of the pin

[24] *Knossos*, II, pp. 382-384; IV, pp. 993-995.
[25] *Knossos*, II, p. 382; cf. III, p. 13.
[25a] The model shown in Fig. 112 was made to prove the feasibility of such a

would have a purpose. In fact it would lock the door and prevent its being opened from the outside, and this could be useful even in a storeroom, when someone was working inside.

This same door was likewise provided with a hole for the pin running obliquely through the stone jamb from the *outside* of the door into the same bolt-socket (Fig. 112, C, D). Thus it would have been possible to come out the door, shut it, push the bolt home, and by inserting the pin prevent anyone *inside* from releasing the bolt.

The arrangement served, as Evans remarked, as a "primitive lock," a lock in which the "key" must be left inserted. The "key" could therefore be effective only against an attempt to open the door by someone on the opposite side. It would serve a useful purpose in the residential quarter, for example, where a person could lock it from the inside, the private side, to prevent intrusion. To secure a storeroom door from the outside the time-honored system of "sealing" the door must still have been relied on; sealing did not prevent a door from being opened, but it did prevent it from being opened without detection.

Whatever its efficiency as a lock the locking pin was evidently merely an added refinement, an "optional feature"; essentially the device was a *latch*. It was operated, if our deductions are correct, by pushing the bolt into position by means of a knob from either side of the door, and released in similar fashion; the modern latch is usually controlled by a revolving knob. The need for the Minoans to invent some practical form of latch is clear when we consider the ubiquitous pier-and-door partitions. The ingenious system of weather control, made possible by their use (Ch. ix, 2), depended on being able to close some or all of the doors as desired; moreover the closure must be such as to prevent the doors being opened by air currents yet be readily controllable from either side for passage. A bolt

---

latch. I have since learned that this type of latch was in actual use in pioneer days in Canada, and I have seen it employed for both outside and inside doors (for rustic effect) in a summer hotel in Ontario.

operated in the way we have described was a simple answer to the requirements, and was as suitable for double as for single doors.[26]

Let us return to Sir Arthur and the puzzles he created for himself by his failure to see that the existence of the locking pin pointed inevitably to the conclusion that the bar could be operated from both sides of the door. His belief that the "locks" (essentially "latches") could only be worked from the side of the door on which the bolt was placed made it in fact impossible for him to understand the bolt on the *inside* of the door leading to the sepulchral chamber of the Temple Tomb (Fig. 113, C) for, as his workmen sagely observed, "the dead could not lock themselves in!"[27] As a way out of the dilemma he momentarily suggested the possibility of a trapdoor and ladder exit to the room above, but discarded this explanation in favor of a side exit by way of a flight of stairs. Unfortunately Evans appears to have forgotten that the stairs in question ascended not from the room behind the door with the bolt, but from the room in front of it. Sir Arthur had evidently become confused, quite understandably, because the stairway was indeed behind a doorway, but it was an outer doorway, not the one leading to the sepulchral chamber. That he undoubtedly was confused about these two doorways is shown by his further statement that both had the same sort of locking device, for in reality the outer one was not rebated and possibly contained no doors at all; in any case the cuttings on the jambs of the two doorways are of quite a different nature.

Viewed however essentially as a *latch*, which could be operated from the outside as well as from the inside, the "Mystery of the Tomb Door" seems solved. As for the locking pin on the inside of the door we grant that it is unlikely that the corpse availed itself of the device to prevent intrusion upon its eternal slumber, but it may have been useful for the tomb officials to

[26] Only one door in a series would *need* to have a bolt that could be opened from either side; the rest could be closed by simple horizontal bars or by vertical bolts.

[27] *Knossos*, IV, p. 993.

be able to guard against casual intruders when preparing and furnishing the burial chambers before the interment. Or it may be that the simple process of boring the small hole for the pin was done by some workman accustomed to do so as a matter of normal building practice and not specifically instructed to omit this detail in a burial chamber. Modern workmen have been known to commit comparable lapses. At any rate no provision for a locking pin was made on the outside of the door; in other words it was considered unnecessary to lock the dead man in. As a measure of precaution against robbers the latch control on the outside of the door could have been removed after the final closing of the tomb chamber, and a crossbar wedged in the jamb-cuttings visible on the rebates on either side of the door-way would have completely concealed the horizontal slot in the face of the door. Quite possibly a guard was mounted in the entrance portico.

Finally let us return to the South House, for not all the puzzles have been solved by the hypothesis of a latch controlled from either side of the door.[28] We have suggested that the ability to lock the door into Room A (Figs. 112, 113, A) from the inside would have been useful when someone was working within. Yet it must be admitted that it seems natural to suppose that, since the room probably was used to store valuable property, it would also have been useful to be able to have the door locked when no one was in it. But, as we have seen, this had to be done from the inside, and therefore the person locking the door had no available exit from A except into Room B. This small room, however, had no door other than that into A, and a further complication is introduced by the fact that, as can be seen from cuttings in the jambs, there was a bar set slantwise on the inside face of the door from A to B. Sir Arthur's explanation was that the person who locked the door at the foot of the stairs into A then passed into B, barred its door from the inside, and left by way of a ladder and trap-door in the ceiling. Thus both rooms were secured from intrusion, and the importance of this

[28] *Knossos*, II, p. 384.

is underlined by the discovery in B of a valuable collection of bronze saws, axes, and knives, "sacerdotal treasure," Evans called it.

Sir Arthur's solution may seem somewhat arbitrary, and there is of course no positive evidence in favor of the trap-door; but what are the alternatives? I see two possible explanations of the bar on the inside of the door into B. The first is that the room was used for some purpose, probably of a cult nature, which made it desirable to be able to prevent anyone entering B from A;[29] yet the small size and plain character of B renders this suggestion implausible. The second alternative is that the slanting bar on the inside of the door was controlled from the outside (from A) on the same principle as outlined above but with a slot in the door in the shape of a "7"; this solution, however, also appears unsatisfactory since, to mention but one objection, a simple bolt on the side of the door next Room A would have served the same purpose.

We return then to the trap-door proposed by Sir Arthur as the least objectionable explanation of the enigma. The existence of trap-doors in Minoan architecture need scarcely be doubted since other excavators have been led to suppose their presence in order to explain how cellar rooms without openings in their well preserved walls were made accessible.[30]

[29] *Kret. Chron.*, 8 (1954), p. 441, no. 12.
[30] *Gournia*, p. 21.

CHAPTER X

STAIRS AND STOREYS

1. STAIRWAYS

Aesthetically as well as practically the designers of the Minoan palaces and finer houses displayed a remarkable appreciation of the possibilities of stair architecture, although we need not go so far as to claim, with Rodenwaldt, that "the motif of stairs and staircases could be made the center of a system of Cretan architectural aesthetics."[1]

Outside stairways, though often intended to be impressively monumental, were very simple in construction. The steps, usually made of a resistant stone such as limestone, were simply bedded firmly on a natural or artificial sloping mass of rock or rubble. Shallow risers and deep treads, each with a downward slope, were normal in Cretan stair building, and these features were often particularly prominent in outside stairways, sometimes to such an extent that they resemble stepped ramps (Fig. 138). Such stairs as the set to the east of the H. Triadha Villa may have been designed for the passage of animals as well as of humans.

The exterior flights of steps which make up the "Theatral Areas" northwest of the Palace of Minos (Fig. 41) and at the north end of the West Court at Phaistos are bleachers for watching a performance of some sort rather than true stairways; in fact the one at Phaistos terminates at the top in a blank wall (Fig. 49).[2] The height of the steps in the latter is about 9 in. (23 cm.), possibly high enough for sitting; but those at Knossos,

[1] *Gnomon*, 11 (1935), p. 331.
[2] *Festòs*, 1, pp. 185-190.

less than 5 in. (12 cm.), must have been designed only for standing (Fig. 41).[3]

A typical outside stairway, 6, connects the West Court with the Upper Court at Phaistos (Fig. 138). The steps are about 12 ft. (3½ m.) wide with treads varying from 21 to 24 in. (53 to 61 cm.) and risers 4 to 5½ in. (10 to 14 cm.) high.[4]

Most monumental of all Minoan stairways—and an outside staircase in the sense that it was open to the sky, though it lay within the palace façade—is the one (66) which formed the approach to the Phaistos Grand Propylon and the State Apartments (Figs. 48, 49, 137, 138).[5] The twelve limestone steps which compose it have sloping treads only 5 in. (13 cm.) high and some 28 in. (71 cm.) deep, and a width of no less than 45 ft. (13.70 m.). Clearly this magnificent stairway, unrivaled in the Bronze Age, was calculated to impress the visitor with the splendor of the monarch of Phaistos. Even Knossos had nothing comparable.

But this stairway exhibits an architectural subtlety which emphasizes the remarkable aesthetic sensitivity of the Cretans, namely the distinct "crowning" or upward curvature of each step toward the center (Fig. 137). This would appear to have been intended, as in the case of the well known convexity of the steps of the Parthenon and other Greek buildings, which it anticipates by over a thousand years, to produce a certain feeling of elasticity and life, as well as to offset any tendency for the long horizontal lines to appear to sag in the middle due to an optical illusion. There appear to be no other instances of such "refinements" (as they are known) in the monuments of Minoan architecture available to us.

Interior stairways may be built, like exterior ones, simply of blocks of stone laid on a solid base, for short runs like the familiar bathroom steps (Fig. 82), and occasionally even from one storey to another when these lie on different terraces, like

[3] *Knossos*, II, pp. 578-587.
[4] *Festòs*, I, pp. 190-191 (stairway "XXXI"); II, pp. 27-35 (stairway "6").
[5] *Festòs*, II, pp. 306-311.

Stairway 39 leading from the Central Court to Peristyle Court 74 at Phaistos.

Normally it was not practical to build a solid base to support the whole length of a stairway from one storey to another, though often the lower part was so constructed. Nor was it usually practical to build such stairways all in one run. The two-flight stairway was normal, occasionally with the two flights built at right angles to each other against adjacent sides of a room, as in Za and Zb at Mallia;[6] but far more commonly the two flights are built parallel to one another and connected by a landing. The two types may be spoken of as the L and the U types respectively. In the U type the second flight seems normally to have been approximately the same length as the first. But there is one exception of some interest: the builders of Stairway 42/43, north of the Central Court at Phaistos, took care, even to the extent of inserting two extra steps at the turn, to attain the second floor level with a very brief second flight, terminating just short of the window whose position is indicated by the recess in the west half of the north façade of the court (Figs. 50, 87).[7] The reason for doing so was surely in order that the window might be available as another vantage point from which to watch events in the Central Court, such as the bull games.

In both the L and the U type of stairway the inside of each flight was built against a regular partition wall, while the outside was supported by a special wall. Sometimes this wall may have been only high enough to carry the outer edge of the stair, though this is not provable from the remains in any known instance; usually or always it may have extended as a solid wall to the ceiling, as in the L-shaped stairway running up from Room 50 at Phaistos, especially when it carried a stairway directly overhead in the upper storey. A solid wall, however, would have created a very dark stairway, and it may be that it

---

[6] For the use of stairs in a vestibule, as in Zb, *Mallia, Maisons*, II, p. 10, note 3, compares *Gournia*, p. 21, and Palaikastro, *BSA*, 9 (1902-1903), p. 292, Block D, and p. 295, Block E, 36.

[7] *Festòs*, II, pp. 244-245.

was usually pierced with openings; in the Grand Staircase of the Residential Quarter at Knossos the builders boldly substituted freestanding columns for such a wall (Fig. 38).

For some distance above the solid base the steps were sometimes continued in stone; but probably they were usually of wood. How these upper steps were supported is rarely clear, but those in 42/43 at Phaistos rested on sloping beams, the sockets for which were visible in the walls, and this has also been reported at Amnisos. Whether these beams resembled our modern "stringers" is not clear.

The space under the stairs, where not occupied by a solid base, was often utilized—for a toilet at Sklavokambos (Fig. 32), and under 42/43 at Phaistos as a closet where a mass of domestic pottery was found (Fig. 4).

The nature and position of stairways often provide useful clues regarding the character and extent, and even the plan, of the upper storeys of Minoan palaces and houses. For example, as we have seen, the two sets of stairs north of the Central Court at Mallia furnish some evidence for the position of the Banquet Hall (Ch. vi, 2).

We close with a description of a few of the better preserved and more interesting palace stairways.

A typical bathroom stair is that in the North Residential Quarter at Phaistos (Fig. 82).[8] Each of its seven steps is composed of a single block of gypsum a little over 3 ft. long by 16 to 21 in. wide by about 5 to 6 in. high (100 by 40-53 by 13-15 cm.); and the landing between the upper five and the lower two steps is also a single block of gypsum. A gypsum parapet beside the steps supported a column at the end.

The stairway in the northeast quarter of the Palace of Mallia (xxii 3, 1) is a typical example of the U type (Fig. 60).[9] Eight stone steps, each about 6 ft. 6 in. long, with treads averaging 17 in. deep and nearly 6 in. high (200 by 44 by 14 cm.), remain in position on a solid base composed of rubble at the

[8] *Festòs*, II, pp. 299-301.
[9] *Mallia*, II, p. 21.

bottom and clay or mud brick above. The first run, and presumably the second also, contained approximately fifteen steps, giving a total height for the stairway of around 14½ ft. (4.40 m.).

An interesting variation in stairway arrangement occurs in the Royal Villa at Knossos.[10] From the ground floor a narrow flight of stairs ascends to a landing from which two flights of similar width proceed upward, one on either side of the stair-wall over the first flight (Fig. 73). One of these upper stairways opened into the second storey rooms; the other continued via a flight over the stairwell, directly to the third storey (Ch. III, 4).

Lastly the Grand Staircase leading down to the Residential Quarter in the southeast area of the Palace of Minos (Figs. 12, 38).[11] As a feat of engineering it is a remarkable achievement for the age; Evans referred to it as "the most daring exhibition of Minoan architectural enterprise."[12] Its excellent preservation, plus bold restoration, adds much to its interest. It was discovered in the process of excavating through a doorway from the north which opened upon the landing at the level of the second storey. In dramatic fashion, and at considerable risk, in view of the delicately balanced masses of tottering masonry above, Evans proceeded to tunnel downward following two long flights which were supported on a solid ramp. Later he straightened up and resupported the upper parts of the walls, replacing the wooden beams and columns with stone, steel, and concrete disguised so as to simulate the original appearance. Even the third flight and part of the fourth (connecting the second and third storeys), which consisted of gypsum steps resting on cypress beams whose charred remains were often distinctly visible, were found nearly in their original positions and were maintained there until they too could be resupported. Evidence was also discovered of two

[10] *Knossos*, II, pp. 398-399.
[11] *Knossos*, I, pp. 325-326, 337-342; III, pp. 301, 481-482, Plan D; but certain promised revised drawings seem never to have been published, III, p. 482, note 2.
[12] *Knossos*, I, p. 337.

higher flights leading to a storey above the level of the Central Court, and it probably originally continued at least one more storey.

The stairway was built on the U plan, and the supporting wall along the outside edge was carried up only a little above the level of the steps to form a continuous stepped parapet; on the top surface of the parapet a series of circular holes were sunk to receive columns used to support the edge of the flight of stairs immediately above. Thus the stairs were abundantly lighted by the adjacent light-well.

Today the descent from the Central Court down the four long flights with the short intermediate flights at the turns—fifty-five steps in all—to the Hall of the Colonnades at the bottom of the light-well is an impressive experience. It is easy to sympathize with the fantasy of Sir Arthur who was tempted, one warm moonlight night when he was sleeping nearby during a bout of fever, to look down the well of the staircase: "the whole place," he writes in that monumental prose epic *The Palace of Minos at Knossos*, "seemed to awake awhile to life and movement. Such was the force of the illusion that the Priest-King with his plumed lily crown, great ladies, tightly girdled, flounced and corseted, long-stoled priests, and, after them, a retinue of elegant but sinewy youths—as if the Cup-bearer and his fellows had stepped down from the walls—passed and re passed on the flights below."[13]

2. HEIGHT AND NUMBER OF STOREYS

From a ruinous ground plan and a few unprepossessing fragments of stone an archaeologist dealing with the Classical Greek period can frequently deduce with almost complete assurance what the building he has excavated looked like when newly built. This is because of the symmetry and regularity which prevailed in public buildings in that period, and because of the standardized system of proportions regulating the dimensions of columns and superstructure.

[13] *Knossos*, III, p. 301.

The restoration of Minoan buildings is, unfortunately, quite a different matter. Yet how very vague must our conception of the Cretan palaces and houses be unless we can form some idea of their appearance in elevation! Luckily we are not entirely without clues. Occasionally, for example when built against a sloping hillside, actual traces of the upper storeys may be preserved. Thus we may be sure that the Royal Villa and the South House (Fig. 71) at Knossos had at least three storeys, while the Residential Quarter of the Palace of Minos had two storeys below the Central Court and one, probably two, above.

A valuable and unexpected source of information is provided by the discovery in the Palace of Minos of a number of fragmentary little pieces of faïence showing what are evidently the street fronts of urban houses (Fig. 103). These characteristically have a door at the street level and two rows of windows in what must be the second and third storeys.

The thickness of the walls in the palaces and houses may provide some indication of their height, but so many factors enter into this that its value is limited. One instance is the block of rooms north of the central courts at Phaistos and Mallia (Figs. 87-89). The difference in the wall thickness between these two does suggest that there were more storeys in one than in the other, which helps to corroborate what we had guessed for other reasons.

The most useful clues for the restoration of the upper floors of the palaces are those provided by remains of stairways. For example at Mallia stairways indicate that there was at least a second storey in the part of the palace west and north of the Central Court, but probably none over the small irregular rooms at the southeast corner of the palace. Other instances of this kind have been mentioned frequently in our descriptions of the various palaces and houses.

The height of the ground floor storey is occasionally indicated by remains of the floor above preserved at or near its original level, as in the Residential Quarter of the Palace of Minos—

a little over 13 ft. (4 m.); the Royal Villa—about 10 ft. (3 m.); and the South House—nearly 9 ft. (2.60 m.). At Phaistos the floor level of the rooms of the second storey of the North Residential Quarter is probably given by the adjacent Peristyle Court 74; the height of Room 50 should then be a little over 11 ft. (3.39 m.), and that of 77-79 about 12½ ft. (3.82 m.). For similar reasons the height of the ground floor rooms immediately north of the Central Court in the same palace (Fig. 90) was apparently about 11 ft. (3.35 m.).[14]

Sometimes the stairway to the second floor is preserved complete, or at least sufficiently to be able to calculate its original height. The floor-to-floor height of the main storey of the Little Palace at Knossos is thus given as 13 ft. (3.95 m.). At Mallia north of the Central Court are two stairways serving the Upper Northeast Hall, each of two flights and each with several of the first steps preserved (Fig. 88). The height of the first flight in both can be calculated at over 7 ft. (2.20 m.), and since the plan suggests that the second flight was of similar length, the total height of the first storey may have amounted to over 14 ft. (ca. 4.40 m.).

At Tylissos the northeast stairway in House C had a first flight of nearly 5 ft. (1½ m.); the second was probably similar, amounting in all to about 9 ft. 9 in. (3 m.). A stairway in the southwest corner having ten risers of 6 in. (15 cm.) each in the first flight yields similar results. In a room in the southeast corner of the same house is a stone pillar approximately 6 ft. (1.80 m.) high with mortises on the top face, suggesting that on it rested the wood timbering of the ceiling. How much should be allowed for the thickness of the timbering and of the flooring? The answer may be approximately supplied by the Pillar Crypt of the Royal Villa where the pillar is 6 ft. 6 in. (2 m.) and the known first floor height is about 10 ft., a difference of 3 ft. 6 in. Applying this to House C we get 6 ft. plus

---

[14] The figures for Phaistos are derived from the levels marked on plate 2, *Festòs, Tavole*. Most of the other heights given in this section have been either measured or checked by the writer.

3 ft. 6 in. = 9 ft. 6 in. or very nearly the 9 ft. 9 in. indicated by the stairways. Tylissos A, whose Pillar Crypt pillar was about the same height as that in House C, should have had a first storey height similar to that of the other house. In Houses Za and Zb at Mallia the maximum (and probable) run of the stairs was some 21 to 23 ft. (6½ to 7 m.), which, with treads and risers suitable to such houses (being of wood the steps are not preserved), would yield a floor-to-floor height of around 9 ft. (2.70 m.).

We may conclude, then, that the height of the first storey of the usual better-class Minoan house and that of the service rooms on the ground floor of the palaces might amount to about 9 to 10 ft. (2.75 to 3 m.); and that the better rooms in the palaces and outstanding mansions were often between 12 and 14 ft. (nearly 3½ to 4½ m.).

Where it was desired to obtain an impressive architectural effect, however, as in the Propylon and Room 25 of the Palace of Phaistos, much greater heights were reached, in these cases perhaps 16 to 23 ft. (5 to 7 m.). No direct estimate of the height of the State Reception Halls in the Piano Nobile is possible, but the fact that the Central Hall in the Palace of Mallia would have an area nearly three times that of the Hall of the Double-Axes indicates a great difference in scale between these public rooms designed to accommodate large crowds and even the finest private rooms of the residential quarters; that their ceilings were also much loftier is therefore not an unreasonable conclusion.[15]

As for the total height of the palaces, what conclusions can be reached? At Knossos the Residential Quarter probably consisted of four storeys, but this was built on the slope of a hill and two of these storeys were below the level of the Central Court. The maximum elevation above the general ground level was probably to be found on the west fronts of the palaces at Knossos and Phaistos, where there is fairly reliable evidence

[15] *AJA*, 60 (1956), pp. 156-157.

that there were two storeys in the Piano Nobile plus the magazine or basement storey; the Mallia palace was probably nowhere more than two-storeyed. The total height of the façade at Knossos and Phaistos is not likely to have exceeded 40 to 45 ft. (12 to 13 m.). Considering the large area they covered and the flat roofs, the general effect of the Cretan palaces must have been low and spreading. The proportions represented in our restored views of the palaces at Phaistos and Mallia, Figs. 55 and 58, are in accurate perspective and are based on the conclusions outlined in this section.

CHAPTER XI

DECORATIVE FEATURES

1. COLUMNS AND PORTICOES

THE MINOAN CRETANS anticipated the Classical Greeks in many of the forms and uses of the column, although in palace architecture it never became the principal decorative feature of the exterior that it was in the Greek temple and many other public buildings. The structural uses of the column have been discussed in a previous section (Ch. VIII, 2); its place as an element of architectural decoration will be considered here.

One area in which the Minoans showed themselves sensitive to the possibilities of the column is in the formal entranceway, where, treated monumentally, it could add greatly to the impressiveness of the approach, as the Mycenaeans and the later Greeks were also well aware. The outstanding example in Cretan architecture is the single massive column at the head of the Grand Stairway which formed the principal entry to the Palace of Phaistos (Fig. 48). The portal in the center of which this column stood was thirty-two feet (9.75 m.) wide, and the column itself measured perhaps fifteen feet (4½ m.) high.

A somewhat similar arrangement is found at Knossos where, on the stairway leading up to the Piano Nobile from the Central Court, we find two columns placed in the center of the stairs one behind the other (Fig. 44). A single great column also stood in the center of the front of the West Porch, the main approach to the Palace of Minos, which is about thirty-seven feet (11.25 m.) in width (Figs. 2, 128). Still another monumental treatment is the façade of Room 25 on the Central Court at

Phaistos, with a large central column between four massive piers (Fig. 50). On a smaller scale is the entrance to the rather enigmatic building at Nirou Khani, where we have a two-columned porch which contrives to resemble at the same time a typical Minoan light-well and the entrance to a Mycenaean megaron (Figs. 31, 75, 150).

The porticoes and peristyles of classic architecture likewise occur in Minoan, though with less prominence. We have already spoken of the porticoes, usually L-shaped, of the residential quarters (Ch. v, 1). They faced outward to command the finest view afforded by the particular site; H. Triadha is the outstanding example (Fig. 11). A long apparently continuous portico with a good view ran along the east side of the magnificent suite of rooms in the Little Palace at Knossos (Figs. 13, 64). The longest colonnade preserved is the one with eleven columns across the north end of the Central Court at Mallia (Figs. 6, 57). An even longer portico, nearly 110 ft. (ca. 34 m.) in length, extends along the entire east side of the court of the same palace, but here the columns alternate with square piers. The east side of the court at Phaistos is treated in similar fashion. This alternation of pillars and columns is a favorite and distinctively Minoan scheme, occurring at Phaistos, H. Triadha, Mallia, Gournia, and Palaikastro, but not at Knossos. The most remarkable instance is in a building at H. Triadha, which was built at a slightly later period (L.M. III) than that to which we have in general limited this survey.[1] This building bears a peculiar resemblance to a Greek "stoa": a long series of small rooms (shops?) at the rear all open on a portico nearly 150 ft. long (about 46 m.), fronted by an alternating series of eight pillars and nine columns.

Above the porticoes on the central courts of the palaces were, in all likelihood, colonnaded galleries, and probably the same was often true of the porticoes associated with the residential quarters.

---

[1] *Guida*, pp. 37-38; Lawrence, *Gk. Arch.*, p. 51 and fig. 32.

Two instances are known of the complete interior peristyle, that is with porticoes on all four sides of a court.[2] The smaller is located in the Little Palace at Knossos (Figs. 13, 64), with three columns to a side (eight in all), surrounding a flagged court about twelve by thirteen feet (ca. 4 m. square). The Peristyle Court at Phaistos (74) has four columns to a side, and enclosed an area about twenty-five feet (nearly 8 m.) square. In each case a large hall faced south on the peristyle through the usual pier-and-door partition.

Columns add a decorative note to the standard Cretan light-wells, which occur almost entirely in the residential quarters. Light-wells with columns on two sides, or even on all four sides, are occasionally found (Figs. 17, 19, 29).

Another common use of columns is on the parapets of stairways. A single column is common in the ordinary bathrooms, at the end of the parapet between the stairs and the main room (Figs. 81, 82); its function here would seem to be purely decorative, but in larger bathrooms or "lustral chambers," where a series of columns stands on the parapet between the two rooms, as in the "Throne Room" at Knossos, these columns must have also helped to shorten the free span of the ceiling beams. Certainly the columns along the parapet of the Grand Staircase in the Palace of Minos were functional as well as decorative (Fig. 38). A single column on a parapet in the North Residential Quarter at Phaistos at the foot of the stairway opposite Room 50 allowed light to reach the stairway (Fig. 47).

A further use of the column is known from only one example in Crete, but it occurs on the façade of two "beehive" tombs at Mycenae dated about 1300 B.C. This is the use of half-columns to frame the large central door at the north end of the Central Court at Phaistos (Figs. 50, 51, 53). Their purpose here is of course entirely decorative (Ch. II, 2).

[2] Except for tiny courts or light-wells with a single pier at each corner (see Ch. IX, 2), and for a curious arrangement of pillars and columns in an early building northeast of the Palace of Phaistos, *Festòs*, I, figs. 209, 214, 215.

The form of the commonest type of Cretan column is familiar from Evans' restorations in the Palace of Minos (Figs. 39, 42, 44). Their general accuracy is assured by the representations on mural paintings (Fig. 133), and by the stone example in high relief preserved on the Lion Gate at Mycenae (Fig. 135). Columns were made of wood, never—so far as we know—of stone; their capitals consisted of a rounded bulging member topped by a square block, both resembling, in fact probably the architectural ancestors of, the echinus and abacus of the Greek Doric capital; the shafts tapered downward (Fig. 136, F). There can be no doubt of the downward taper, strange as it may seem to eyes accustomed to classical columns, for it is visible (and measurable) in the stone column of the Lion Gate relief,[3] in Minoan wall paintings, and in the carbonized remains of, and impressions left by, actual columns. Some have criticized Evans' restored columns as having too sharp a taper,[4] but those in the Hall of the Colonnades, for example, have a considerably slighter taper than that of the Lion Gate, which amounts to only one in thirty-six.

It is not likely that we shall be able to discover a logical explanation of this downward taper, to us a topsy-turvy way of doing things. Some have suggested that it arose out of a practice of setting tree trunks used as supports upside down in order to prevent the sprouting of new roots; another scarcely more likely theory is that the foot of the column would be less exposed to water dripping from the capital. At any rate it does provide the column with a slightly larger surface on which to rest the entablature, while leaving slightly more free space at floor level.

To judge from wall paintings the wooden shafts and capitals were both painted, one black and the other red (Fig. 136, E); the foot of the shaft might also be in a contrasting color, perhaps a substitute for polychrome stone bases.

[3] Dinsmoor, *Arch. Anc. Gr.*, p. 23 and note 3; Evans accepted Durm's claim that there was no taper, *Knossos*, I, p. 343, note 3.
[4] Lawrence, *Gk. Arch.*, p. 39, note 7.

Another unique feature of the Cretan columns is that frequently they were not round in cross-section but oval. For example, the two bases in the South Propylaeum at Knossos (Fig. 42), and all seven columns in the Magazine-Propylon Block at Phaistos were oval; but in only one case is the difference between the major and the minor axis (to judge from the oval bases on which they rested) greater than ten per cent. In every instance at Phaistos the major axis is parallel to the architrave, thus providing a greater bearing surface; but this is not true at Knossos.

It is obvious from the varying size of the column bases that the lower diameter, and so persumably the height, of the columns varied widely. From a few examples at Knossos where it seemed possible to estimate the height of the column fairly closely from the height of the room, Evans concluded that the column height was normally about five times its lower diameter. Nevertheless the proportions suggested by pictures of columns in mural paintings are much slenderer (Fig. 133), and, in one case at Phaistos where a fairly accurate and reliable estimate could be arrived at, the proportion was actually 1:8.[5] Indeed there must have been a considerable variation in proportions, as can be inferred from the difference in size between the oval base between 67 and 68 of the Grand Propylon at Phaistos, 4 ft. 8 in. by 4 ft. 4 in. (1.42 by 1.32 m.), and that of the three bases in front of the light-well in the same complex (69A)— 3 ft. 10 in. by 3 ft. 8 in. (1.17 by 1.12 m.) for two, and 3 ft. 3 in. by 3 ft. (0.99 by 0.91 m.) for the third—inasmuch as the height of all four columns which stood on these bases must have been approximately the same. The proportions of the column at the head of the stairs, about 4:1, were doubtless intentionally stockier than those of the other columns, which were about 5:1 or 5½:1, because of the much wider span it had to support (Fig. 48). It would not be in keeping with the spirit of Cretan architecture, which seems to delight in wilful

[5] *Festòs*, II, pp. 473-474.

irregularity, to expect Minoan columns to adhere to any rigidly fixed principles of proportion (Ch. XIII, 3); but we can at least expect that the architects would vary the size of the columns to suit the needs of the particular situation.

Like the Doric column, the Minoan column had no molded base. In fact it was often socketed into a shallow circular depression in the stone sill upon which it rested, as in the columns of the Grand Staircase (Fig. 38). Where the column was directly exposed to the weather it was commonly set for protection on a circular block of stone which might be socketed into a hole in the sill or be part of the sill itself. Sometimes this block was fairly high, a foot and a half or more, and often made of a polychrome stone (Fig. 80); usually it was lower, as little as a couple of inches, tapering slightly upward, and made of gypsum or limestone.

The shaft of the column was perhaps left plain and smooth as a rule, as Evans restored them. Yet he admitted that "there are strong indications that the originals were, in some cases at least, fluted,"[6] for in the area of the Residential Quarter he found a carbonized fragment of a wooden column, though of smaller diameter than those actually used there, with apparently twenty-four flutes or channels. Elsewhere in the palace clay impressions of two columns with twenty-eight concave flutes were discovered, and impressions of the small columns of the Little Palace "Lustral Area" indicate that they had probably fifteen convex flutes. From the Mycenaean mainland (but from no other sites in Crete) comes further evidence of fluted columns. Some of the small ivory columns recently found at Mycenae (probably decorative pieces from furniture) are fluted (Fig. 136, G, H), and so are the half-columns of the façade of the "Tomb of Clytemnestra" at the same site.[7] Yet the column of the Lion Gate is unfluted (Fig. 135). In the palace at Pylos distinct and complete impressions of concave fluting were left at several places in the cement floor in which the bottoms of the

[6] *Knossos*, I, p. 344.
[7] Mylonas, *Anc. Myc.*, fig. 30.

columns were embedded; in one case there were thirty-two flutes, in another forty-four, and in two others sixty.[8]

Spiral fluting has been found on the shafts of Cretan lamp-stands, and is represented on columns, evidently intended to be of full size, on Minoan sealings (Fig. 136, J). The half-columns of the façade of the "Treasury of Atreus" at Mycenae present an even more elaborate example, with a shaft of green stone carved with zigzags and spirals (Fig. 136, I), and it is highly likely that in this and the other examples noted the mainland was following the traditions of Minoan architecture.

We have already spoken of the "echinus" and "abacus" of the normal Cretan column. Some wall paintings show more elaborate forms with additional convex and concave moldings. In the "Treasury of Atreus" the echinus is carved with zigzags and spirals similar to those on the shaft (Fig. 136, I), and there is a leaf pattern on the concave molding below the echinus. That there may have been other elaborate forms of capitals is suggested by the capitals of some lampstands which show palm tree and other vegetable forms, clearly patterned after the contemporary Egyptian models (Fig. 140, J).

Another odd form of capital is illustrated in a few scenes associated with the bull games and with boxing, on wall paintings and on steatite vases (Fig. 136, K, L). This capital is rectangular in elevation and doubtless also in plan, and is decorated with a series of concentric rectangles and a pattern of small circles; according to the paintings the details of the capital were picked out with bright colors. The capital is set on a rather broad shaft which sometimes has an upward, but never a downward taper. The rectangular form of the capital would be more suitable for a pillar than for a column, and the association with the bull games makes it tempting to suggest that this type of capital was used on the pillars, which alternate with columns, on the east sides of the central courts of the palaces at Phaistos and Mallia. Unfortunately this suggestion cannot be proved, for no scenes

[8] *AJA*, 57 (1953), p. 60; 58 (1954), p. 29; 59 (1955), p. 32; 60 (1956), p. 99.

are at present known where the two forms of capitals, the echinus-abacus and the rectangular, alternate.[9]

2. ARCHITECTURAL DETAIL

Much of the charm of a Classical Greek building such as the Erechtheum of the Athenian Acropolis is due to the beauty of its carved decorative detail. Minoan architectural ornament was evidently much more limited, but fragments have been found at Knossos (none elsewhere in Crete) which, in excellence of carving and beauty of design, scarcely yield to the best Greek examples.[10] Yet none of these pieces has been found in its original position.

Fortunately the slightly later mainland Greek or "Mycenaean" architecture offers some help, for in its decoration it closely imitated Cretan architecture. This may be illustrated by the close resemblance between a fragment of the "triglyph half-rosette frieze" found near the northwest angle of the Palace of Minos and another from the façade of the "Tomb of Clytemnestra" at Mycenae (Fig. 136, A, B). The greater width of the rectangular element in the later frieze is a significant change, for it is clearly moving in the direction of the Classical Greek triglyph, whose form was influenced by the Mycenaean frieze.[11]

[9] The use of these capitals puzzled Evans (*Knossos*, I, pp. 688-690; III, 62-65; IV, 20-21), but he concluded that they were in some sense structural elements, with a certain symbolical, religious value as well. "They are the symbols of the Minoan 'Theatre' itself as a religious institution, just as the Doric or Ionic columns on Greek painted vases represent abbreviated indications of the Temple or Stoa" (I, p. 690). Halbherr spoke even more explicitly of these capitals "as referring to the porticoes of the courts or theatral areas (*choroi*) within which the games took place," *R. Accad. dei Lincei*, XIV (1905), p. 369 (I owe the reference to Alexiou). Recently Marinatos has declared them "perhaps standards or banners raised for festal occasions" (*C. and M.*, p. 148); but I believe this suggestion untenable. The most recent discussion is by Alexiou in his publication of an interesting new steatite rhyton fragment showing a peak sanctuary, *Kret. Chron.*, 13 (1959), pp. 347-349. He argues that they cannot be capitals, and is inclined to deny them any structural meaning; but I think we must realize that the Cretan artists used these capitals for their symbolic significance, and so with very little regard for their proper setting in an architectural context.

[10] More fragments have recently been discovered; see *JHS*, "Archaeology in Greece, 1956," p. 21, figs. 18-19.

[11] On this much discussed question see Bowen, *BSA*, 45 (1950), pp 113-125, who, in my opinion, makes the derivation certain. A simpler form of "triglyph-

Remains of a similar half-rosette frieze were found in another Mycenaean tomb, the "Treasury of Atreus," and belonged to its façade, the design of which can be approximately recovered.[12] In this the frieze formed a horizontal band running across the doorway above the top of the columns, much like the later Doric frieze. Below it ran other carved stone patterns in the form of a continuous spiral and a series of round disks, representing in wooden construction the ends of logs laid horizontally to support floors or ceilings.

Fragments of the half-rosette frieze discovered in the ruins of the Northwest Entrance of the palace at Mycenae must have been used in similar fashion.[13] But remains of the same design were found in place at the base of the walls of the main rooms, the megarons, both at Mycenae and Tiryns, showing that the frieze could also be used as a low dado, a use also paralleled by the Classical Doric frieze which is often employed around the bottom of Greek altars.[14]

Since some frieze fragments of this type were discovered at Knossos in the vicinity of one or two entrances to the palace,[15] it was natural, and perhaps correct, for Evans to suppose that they had been used as at Mycenae over doorways. But the proposal to restore a "Northwest Entrance" to the palace, of which there exists no clear architectural remains, merely on the basis of finding similar fragments in the area, cannot be regarded as convincing, especially when it disagrees with other evidence (Ch. vi, 1).[16]

The "log-ends," which appear in low relief on the façades of the Mycenaean tombs and above the column of the relief over the Lion Gate at Mycenae (Fig. 135), are also to be seen on

---

metope" arrangement is frequently found decorating the face of stone benches (see Figs. 43, 69). In Room 23 at Phaistos, e.g., the projecting member is marked with three groups of shallow vertical grooves, distinctly triglyph-like in appearance; the broader, recessed "metope" is marked with two sets of horizontal grooves (*Festòs*, II, pp. 148-149 and fig. 88).

[12] See the new restoration by Marinatos, *C. and M.*, fig. 25, and *Archaeology*, 13 (1960), p. 51, fig. 10.

[13] Mylonas, *Anc. Myc.*, p. 61.   [14] *Ibid.*, p. 52.

[15] *Knossos*, II, figs. 83, 436.   [16] *Knossos*, II, pp. 590-591.

the housefronts from the "Town Mosaic" found at Knossos (Fig. 103), and in various representations of architectural detail in the "Grandstand Fresco" and other Cretan paintings, where they appear in alternating colors (Figs. 101, 133, 136, E). These paintings also represent other designs, especially a kind of checker pattern,[17] and rows of "sacral horns" serving as a cornice for structures like the Tripartite Columnar Shrine. A simple "stepped" form of cornice for ordinary architecture is perhaps indicated by a block found in the Palace of Minos, and has been commonly used for this purpose in restorations (Fig. 44).[18]

Another feature, for which we must allow in attempting to imagine the appearance of Minoan palaces and houses, is color. Outside of the traces of red-painted stucco observed on wall blocks of the west façade at Phaistos, the evidence is largely limited to the wall paintings, whose accuracy in detail is of course uncertain. However we can feel sure that columns and decorative details were brightly painted in contrasting colors, a tradition which was perhaps transmitted to Classical Greece, and that the exterior of Cretan palaces was nearly as gay as the brilliantly painted halls within.

3. WALL DECORATION

The wall paintings of Minoan Crete undoubtedly have a more direct appeal to most people today than any other form of Cretan art. They delight us for their gaiety and charm, their color and animation, their love of nature. Yet many of the paintings reproduced time and again are a pitiful jigsaw of tiny fragments none too certainly coaxed into juxtaposition, and eked out with the twentieth century imagination of the artist-restorer. Are these idyllic little scenes of birds and flowers but subordinate elements in large scenes in which man played the predominant part? Where is this Minoan officer (?) and his squad (?) of Ne-

---

[17] *Knossos*, II, p. 600. Still valuable is Fyfe, "Painted plaster decoration at Knossos, with special reference to the architectural spheres," *Journal of the Royal Institute of British Architects*, 10 (1903), pp. 107-131, with two color plates.
[18] *Knossos*, II, pp. 814-815.

groes hastening at the double, and why? Who are the (headless) "Ladies in Blue" with their sensitively drawn hands? These are but a few of the questions which the paintings arouse, and leave unanswered.[19]

Since the viewpoint of this book is architectural we are less interested in the aesthetic aspect of the paintings (which in any event has so often been treated), or even in their composition, than in such problems as this: what rooms in the palaces and houses were adorned with figure scenes, and was there any appropriateness of scene to room? How were the paintings fitted into the scheme of the wall as a whole? What sort of wall decoration was used in rooms of lesser importance? But we shall have to be content with rather meager answers to these questions; more often than not the fragments have been tediously collected from the loose fill where frequently they have fallen from the upstairs rooms, or, in the case of more modest forms of mural decoration, the archaeologist may not have bothered to note carefully or report fully on what he has found, engrossed as he is with more spectacular discoveries.

Nevertheless we can feel reasonably sure that most of the rubble or adobe walls in the palaces and better houses were plastered, and in the more important rooms the plaster was at least given a fine finish coat of stucco and painted in some plain color. When we are specifically told that throughout the house at Vathypetro plaster fragments painted in bright colors were found in abundance, we should consider this to have been the rule rather than the exception.

A simple elaboration on the plain painted wall was to paint it in a series of horizontal bands in contrasting colors (Fig. 151). Lines lightly incised in the stucco might be used as guide lines in painting the different colors; combinations of horizontal and vertical lines might give a structural effect suggesting a wall built, for example, of squared blocks at the base either with a smooth wall above, or with narrow bands to suggest wooden tie

[19] *Knossos*, II, pls. 11 and 13; I, fig. 397.

beams throughout the rubble or adobe structure (Ch. vɪɪɪ, 2). The wall structure might be further imitated by painting bands or blocks to represent the veining of stone or the graining of wood. The lower part of the walls of the finer rooms, particularly at Knossos, Phaistos, and H. Triadha, was often lined with a dado about 4 to 6 ft. high of alabaster veneering about an inch (2½ cm.) thick and sometimes cut in panels over 6 ft. (ca. 2 m.) square (Figs. 69, 81). Above this the stucco might be treated in any way from plain color to elaborate figure designs.

The following are typical examples, proceeding from simple to more complex forms.

Walls painted with a few colored bands, and with or without incised lines, are mentioned not infrequently in the excavation reports, but precise details are rarely given and there is usually little remaining on the walls today. In the bathroom of the Mallia Residential Quarter the excavators found white stucco on the walls with a red band defined by incised lines, and on the alcove east of the bathroom in the North Residential Quarter at Phaistos three brown bands were seen on a yellowish background. Two rooms in the building at Nirou Khani (12, and the "Room of the Lamps") are said to have had colored bands; and in the small room, xxiv 1, in the palace at Mallia, there was a plain "baseboard" 16 in. (40 cm.) high, then a red band 3 in. (7.4 cm.) high, and 7 in. (18 cm.) above that four more incised lines close together.[20]

Three examples with more numerous painted bands are illustrated in Fig. 129. In the first, A, the stucco is preserved to a height of 32½ in. (82 cm.) in one corner of a room in the House of the Frescoes; here we have a low "baseboard" surmounted by a high dado divided into three white bands by two red lines; above the dado is a narrow band painted with red graining on yellow to imitate a beam of wood, followed by another narrow band painted with white on black in imitation of

[20] *Mallia*, ɪɪ, pl. 4, 2.

stone. The walls at the foot of the stairway, 71, leading to the upper state reception halls at Phaistos, have a dado nearly 3 ft. high (87 cm.) with a 10 in. (26 cm.) band of red above, edged by narrow fillets of white and red (B). Two broad zones of gray in Magazine 12 at Knossos (C) are bordered at the top by narrow bands of red.

In a corridor of the Knossos Residential Quarter, above a black baseboard, the veining of alabaster veneering is imitated in a dado at least 4 ft. (over 120 cm.) high, divided by red lines into panels about 3 ft. (nearly 1 m.) wide; the walls above the dado seem to have been decorated with an intricate labyrinth or meander pattern.[21] In the Hall of the Double-Axes, above the top edge of the alabaster veneering, a continuous spiral band is painted on the plaster, and along this band was perhaps hung a series of great figure-of-eight shields (Fig. 45). This in turn gave rise to merely painting shields against a spiral band in the porticoes of the Grand Staircase.[22]

What is known of the arrangement of figure scenes with relation to the walls of the room? Only one reasonably complete example has been recovered, the so-called Throne Room on the ground floor of the Palace of Minos (Fig. 130). On the north wall a pair of griffins guards the throne; on the west a similar pair confronts the doorway to a small cult room; the east and south sides of the room are occupied by the entrance and by the "Lustral Chamber," respectively. The griffin frieze, some 3½ ft. (over 1 m.) high, was limited above by colored bands, probably at the level of the lintels; below, a dado nearly 2 ft. high (60 cm.) was painted in imitation of veined stonework.[23]

The symmetrical arrangement of the figures certainly cannot be typical of Minoan mural decoration, but the tripartite scheme of dado, main frieze, and upper part, was probably a very common one, for it corresponds with the structure of the wall.

[21] *Knossos*, I, pp. 356-357.
[22] *Knossos*, III, pp. 301-308, 343-345.
[23] *Knossos*, IV, pp. 908-913.

The top border of the figure scene follows the line of the horizontal timbering which forms the lintel of doors and windows, while the bottom border follows that of the sill of any windows or wall openings.[24]

Another example of the tripartite division occurs in the West Porch at Knossos, where a scene of bull grappling surmounted a 16 inch (40 cm.) dado of panels painted to imitate stone veneering, and was probably separated from the ceiling by a series of colored bands or some other simple decorative treatment.[25] Certain technical peculiarities of some of the frescoes found stacked in the House of the Frescoes (see below) indicate that they were similarly arranged on the wall.

Sometimes the figure scenes were set not above a high dado but on a low baseboard, in which case the scene occupied a much larger surface of the wall. This seems to have been true of the Cat and Bird mural in the Residential Quarter at H. Triadha (Fig. 134). The lifesize figures on both walls of the Corridor of the Procession and other parts of the approach to the Piano Nobile at Knossos were arranged in two registers (Figs. 42, 131, B), the feet of the lower row of figures being appropriately only a little above floor level.[26]

Narrow, border-like friezes are also known. Around the walls of the dining pavilion (?) of the "Caravanserai" at Knossos, just below the ceiling, ran a frieze, less than a foot high, representing a row of partridges interspersed with hoopoes. Below this, painted on the white walls on three sides of the room, was a series of brownish-yellow pilasters with red bases and blue capitals.[27] A more famous frieze of this type is the Flying Fish Fresco found on the island of Melos in the Aegean, but probably shipped there, ready painted, from Crete (Fig. 132). It was about 9 in. (23 cm.) high and at least 4 ft. (120 cm.) long, and was found in a small room along with fragments of two other murals at a larger scale, one also a seascape, the other with human beings, including two men; this might indicate that

[24] *Knossos*, II, p. 460.   [25] *Knossos*, II, pp. 674-676.
[26] *Knossos*, II, p. 720.   [27] *Knossos*, II, pp. 109-116.

the Flying Fish frieze formed a high border above the main scene or scenes.[28]

The most elaborate forms of mural decoration, that is figure scenes, occur principally in the residential quarters and in the important public rooms of the palaces. Fragments of fine frescoes were found at Knossos below the rooms of the Piano Nobile west of the Central Court, and below the "Great East Hall" east of the court; figures were also painted, as we have seen, on the walls of the Corridor of the Procession and of the "Throne Room" west of the Central Court. At Knossos and H. Triadha much finer murals were found in the Queen's Hall, that is in the more private part of the residential quarter, than in the Main Hall itself. The palaces at Phaistos and Mallia have produced extremely little in the way of mural paintings either with figures or with designs, but, especially for the former palace, this must be largely the accident of destruction or preservation.[29]

Mural paintings were by no means confined to the palaces. Remains have been found at Knossos in the South House, the Southeast House, the High Priest's House, and the House of the Frescoes; also in houses at Nirou Khani, Tylissos, and even in the little hamlet on the tiny island of Pseira. In the House of the Frescoes, besides fragments found on the walls, a neatly stacked "hoard" of plaster fragments, in a pile measuring about 12 by 5 ft. (3.65 by 1.50 m.) and at least thirty-four layers deep, was found on the floor of one of the rooms. This included the Bluebird Mural, the Blue Monkeys, the Fountain, and others representing myrtle branches, crocuses, etc.[30] So slight were the remains of painted scenes in some of these houses that the fact that none was discovered in such sumptuous dwellings as the Little Palace and the Royal Villa can have no significance.

Finally, a few words about the relation of the subject matter

---

[28] *Phylakopi*, chap. III.

[29] However Miss Banti sees differences in decorative principles between Knossos and Phaistos which would account for such discrepancies, *Festòs*, II, pp. 484-485. It may also be due in part to chronological differences between the palaces.

[30] *Knossos*, II, pp. 444-460.

of the figure scenes to the rooms they were intended to decorate. In many cases there clearly was a significant relationship. For example, the heraldic griffins "guarding" the throne of the "Throne Room" evidently had a meaning and a purpose, no doubt a religious one. The figures bringing gifts to the Mother Goddess (?) in the Corridor of the Procession reflect some ceremonial procession that must have threaded its way thus into the "Labyrinth." The shields of the porticoes of the Grand Staircase would appear to represent the martial character of the last lords of Knossos, the invader kings from the Mycenaean mainland. (This is as near as the murals ever get to scenes of war.) Suitable to the rooms occupied especially by the women are the representations of a dancing girl and a seascape of dolphins at Knossos (Fig. 43), and the delightful scenes of a leaping deer, a cat stalking a bird (Fig. 134), and a lady kneeling in a bed of flowers, at H. Triadha.[31] Or we may think of the partridges in the "Caravanserai" dining pavilion (?); or the scene of the bull games in the portico at the north end of the Central Court at Knossos.

Scenes too of ladies in elaborate court dress, some sitting in "box seats" watching the bull games (?), taking part in a solemn dance amid an olive grove, or sitting on folding stools exchanging a "loving cup," clearly have a general appropriateness to the ceremonies and festivities of court life, whatever their particular meaning in the great public halls they once adorned.[32]

Of the treatment of ceilings in Cretan architecture little is known except that the Queen's Hall in the Palace of Minos was decorated with a magnificent spiral design (Fig. 43). The occurrence of similar ceilings in contemporary Egyptian tombs, and in a beautifully carved stone example on the ceiling of the side chamber of the Mycenaean tholos tomb at Orchomenos indicates their widespread popularity.

[31] *Guida*, p. 31; *Knossos*, II, fig. 201; Matz, *KMT*, pls. 48-49.
[32] *Knossos*, III, figs. 29-32, pl. 18; IV, pl. 31.

4. PAVEMENTS

A considerable variety of materials and decorative schemes were employed by the Cretans for the floors of the rooms in their palaces and houses. Cheapest and commonest was the floor of hard-packed earth, at least for the ground floors, and perhaps also for the upper storeys, for there it could be supported on a thick bedding of poles or reeds laid on the joists.

Plaster or cement floors were used for special purposes. It was the common surfacing for light-wells and small courts, for it resisted the water and could easily be sloped to a drain. In the seven magazines to the east of the Central Court at Mallia the cement floor with inset basins and a network of channels in the cement saved from loss any of the precious oil that might be spilt (Fig. 91).

Stone of various kinds was used for surfacing floors, both inside and out; slate or limestone might be employed for either, gypsum only where protected by a roof. The great central courts at Knossos and Phaistos were laid with rectangular slabs of limestone (Figs. 44, 51), and more irregular flagging was used for the outer courts of the palaces and elsewhere (Figs. 49, 128). Flagging in limestone or schist occurs also in the Main Halls and other rooms of Houses Da and Za at Mallia, and in the rooms of the Residential Quarter and the large Pillar Crypt (vii 4) of the palace at the same site. Even rooms in upper storeys sometimes had flagged floors, among them the room we have identified as a Banquet Hall north of the Central Court at Mallia. The irregular joints between the flagging were carefully filled with plaster, sometimes colored red, an attractive example being the Main Hall of House C at Tylissos (Fig. 77).

A particularly fine grade of a very hard gray-blue limestone with attractive effects of graining, called "ironstone" (*sidheropetra*) was often used in irregularly shaped blocks for flagging floors. Evans dubbed it "mosaiko." Frequently it occurs between the older *kalderim* (rough limestone) flooring and the later gypsum floor of the Palace of Minos, for it was a popular style

206

in the middle period of the palaces; it was rarely used in later times for entire floors, though it does appear in the Hall (3a) of the House of the Chancel Screen at Knossos.[32a]

The popular flooring in the late palace period, for those who could afford it, was fine white gypsum or alabaster laid in smooth rectangular slabs about 2 in. (5 cm.) thick (Fig. 64). Possibly the coldness of such a floor in winter, especially to bare feet, was relieved by mats. In the Palace of Phaistos floors paved with regular slabs of gypsum were used throughout the North and East Residential Quarters, in the large halls 93 and 25, in important smaller rooms such as 23 and 24, and even occasionally in magazines (33 and 88).

In some of the finest rooms striking effects were obtained by laying the large rectangular slabs of alabaster in regular patterns enhanced by broad joints filled with red plaster (Fig. 151). The pattern commonly consists of a series of slabs of uniform width around the walls of the rooms, followed by a rectangle framing one or more large slabs which form the center of the floor. The Main Hall, 79, of the North Residential Quarter at Phaistos is a handsome example (recently carefully restored) of this type of floor (Figs. 127, 136, N); but it may also be seen in the adjoining Queen's Hall, 81, in the Royal Villa at Knossos, and in the building at Nirou Khani (Fig. 31). In both parts of the Hall of the Double-Axes the series of slabs around the walls enclosed three long stripes of which the center is the broadest (Figs. 12, 39); the smaller part of the Main Hall at Phaistos, 77, and the large room, 25, opening on the west side of the Central Court of the same palace, are interesting variations on this theme. The pattern of the last is particularly intricate, and each of the two large transverse blocks supports one of the oval columns on the axis of the room. A unique scheme, of which only a fragment is complete, is the rhomboidal arrangement of the gypsum slabs of the floor of another large

---

[32a] This is based on Evans' conclusions, but Levi claims that this chronological sequence is not reliable; see Ch. VIII, note 8.

room at Phaistos, 93, which faces south on the Peristyle Court (Fig. 126).

A combination of a gypsum border with an ironstone center was also popular and made a very handsome floor. It is seen in the anteroom to the "Throne Room" at Knossos, in the Main Hall of the South House, in two rooms at Nirou Khani (5, 12), and in the Entrance Hall, Peristyle, and both inner and outer parts of the Main Hall of the Little Palace at Knossos. Sometimes the center was filled in with rough flagging which was then concealed with painted plaster, as in the "Throne Room" itself. Evans' restoration of this room with red plaster and white gypsum floor and the brightly colored Griffin Mural on the walls, appears as the frontispiece of volume iv ii of *The Palace of Minos* (Fig. 130).

The surface of the Minoan cement floor was sometimes studded with smooth water-worn pebbles of different colors, set in place before the cement hardened, as in the Room of the Lamps at Nirou Khani (14). Apparently the Minoans never took the further step of combining the pebbles into patterns or figure designs as was done in the Classical Greek period.[33]

Cement floors were sometimes decorated with color, for example a band of reddish-orange about 2 in. (5 cm.) wide in the vestibule to Stairway 71 at Phaistos, and red and blue spots on the floor of a room in the Residential Quarter at Mallia. A recently discovered floor in an early stage of the Phaistos palace was also painted in simple designs.[34] The most elaborately painted floor yet found in Crete is that of a small shrine of the L.M. III period (the shrine had predecessors) at H. Triadha, which represents octopuses, dolphins, and other fish, swimming on a white background decorated with blue lines to suggest waves.[35]

[33] Recent excavations at Gordion have brought to light pebble mosaics of the eighth century B.C., *Archaeology*, 9 (1956), p. 264; *Ill. Lon. News*, 229 (Nov. 17, 1956), p. 859, fig. 11.

[34] Levi, *Nuova Antologia*, 467 (1956), p. 227.

[35] It is now on display in the Herakleion Museum; a sketch of the design is given in Nilsson, *MMR²*, p. 98, fig. 23; and see Banti, *Culti di H. Triada*, p. 32, fig. 18.

On the Mycenaean mainland the floors of important rooms were often marked off by incised lines into large squares painted with a variety of patterns of lines, and at times with octopuses and dolphins.[36] Since these motives are so typically Cretan and since so many of the Mycenaean decorative schemes originated in Crete one might suspect that this type of floor also had its prototype there, but so far no exact parallels have been found. Wall dadoes painted with squares imitating marbling and very similar to the patterns on the mainland plaster floors have been found, however, in the West Porch at Knossos, and similar fragments found in the South Propylon nearby are presumed to come from a dado and not from a floor. The connecting link therefore is still missing.[37]

[36] Wace, *Mycenae,* pl. 90c; *Tiryns,* II, pl. 19.
[37] *Knossos,* II, pp. 674-676, 686, note 1.

CHAPTER XII

FURNISHINGS AND EQUIPMENT

1. FURNITURE AND FURNISHINGS

Telemachos led the way home for his travel-worn friend and brought him to the great house, where they threw down their cloaks on settles or chairs, stepped into the polished baths and washed. When the maid-servants had finished bathing them and rubbing them with oil, they gave them tunics and threw warm mantles round their shoulders, and the two left their baths and sat down on chairs. A maid came with water in a fine golden jug and poured it out over a silver basin so that they might rinse their hands. She drew up a wooden table and the staid housekeeper brought some bread and set it by them, together with a choice of dainties, helping them liberally to all she could offer. Telemachos' mother sat opposite them by a pillar of the hall, reclining in an easy-chair and spinning the delicate thread on her distaff, while they fell to on the good fare laid before them. (Odysseus returns to his palace in Ithaca with his son Telemachos, Odyssey, 17, 84-98, *Rieu translation.)*

WOULD there were some Minoan epic preserved to which we could turn to put flesh on the bare architectural bones we have so far described as vividly as this passage calls up a picture of the Mycenaean heroes and the furnishings of their palaces! Poetry failing us, what assistance can archaeology provide to fill these empty alabaster halls?

Distressingly little in some respects! The furniture itself, which was largely of wood, textiles, or other perishable materials, has vanished utterly. Wall paintings, which show us the people and their costumes, rarely depict their furnishings; and no Minoan equivalent of Tutankhamen's tomb, crammed with royal possessions, if such ever existed, has yet been discovered.

Comparing Crete with the rest of the Aegean area Marinatos remarks that "the furnishing was always rich, particularly in clay utensils; and there were many complicated devices for cooking and heating. In Gournia, Palaikastro and Chamaizi figurines, bronze gear and all sorts of implements have been excavated on a scale which cannot be matched outside Crete. Clearly the living standards of the islanders must have been much higher than they were anywhere else."[1] It is safe to say, however, that a modern would feel that even a Minoan palace was very scantily furnished. So much of the equipment of a present day house of quite modest pretensions would be entirely missing: the pianos, radios, television sets, overstuffed chairs and chesterfields, the clocks, bookcases, and writing-desks, the refrigerators, ranges, and furnaces.

Even tables were probably few and usually small. They do however appear in considerable numbers among lists of furniture on Linear B tablets from the Greek mainland,[2] so that we may surely attribute them also to the people from whom the Mycenaeans derived their civilization. But there is little to show what form these tables took except for a scene on the H. Triadha sarcophagus, which pictures a bull trussed for sacrifice, lying on a large and heavily built table with ponderous turned legs (Fig. 101, 139, E).

Mats and cushions we may suppose were used plentifully, and they may have been used to sit on or recline on as we see guests doing at Egyptian dinner parties. However Egyptians are also frequently represented as seated on chairs at social functions, and we need hardly doubt that the Cretans were also fairly well supplied with seats of various kinds. Instead of, or in addition to, movable seats, some rooms were provided with benches of stone or plastered rubble along the walls, for example the little room, 53, at the northeast entry at Phaistos, the large

[1] C. and M., p. 28.
[2] DMG, p. 339, no. 239; p. 341, no. 240; p. 342, no. 241.

Hall, 50, in the Residential Quarter of the same palace (Fig. 47), in Room 4 of the Residential Quarter at H. Triadha (Fig. 69), and again in the Queen's Hall at Knossos. They were also frequent in rooms where religious rites were performed, whether as seats or as shelves for the deposit of cult objects, such as Rooms 23 and 24 on the west side of the Central Court at Phaistos (Fig. 96), in the "Throne Room" and its anteroom at Knossos (Fig. 130), and perhaps in Room 24 of House Za at Mallia (Fig. 26).

One type of wooden chair has fortunately been preserved to us by being translated into stone in the famous throne of the "Throne Room" (Fig. 139, D). Evans, reversing the process, had replicas of this reproduced in wood and placed in the anteroom of the "Throne Room" and in the Hall of the Double-Axes.[3] Most Minoan chairs must have been less formal than this. A gold ring in Minoan style found at Tiryns (Fig. 139, H) shows a cross-legged chair with tall back as the seat for a goddess. This chair could probably be folded, and folding stools (well-known in Egypt) are clearly represented in the "Camp-Stool Fresco" from Knossos (Fig. 139, G). The flexible seat has been rendered more comfortable in this last example with a coverlet thrown over it, and the juncture of the legs is bound with a cord whose ends (mistaken by Evans for a glove)[4] hang down as they do on the Tiryns ring. Other simple forms of stools occur on rings, gems, and seal impressions, while Knossos has yielded two stone specimens of a seat only about 5 in. (13 cm.) high, shaped to fit the human form like the seat of the stone throne itself (Fig. 139, F).

The stone block on which it rested served the throne of the "Throne Room" as a footstool, but separate footstools did exist, as we learn from Linear B tablets,[5] where the ideogram shows a surprising resemblance to the footstool on the Tiryns ring (Fig. 139, H and I).

[3] *Knossos*, IV, pp. 915-919.
[4] The correction was made by Platon, *Kret. Chron.*, 5 (1951), p. 406.
[5] *DMG*, p. 345, nos. 245-246.

Egyptian tables, thrones, chairs, and footstools were often elaborately decorated with inlay in ivory, ebony, and various metals, as we know from actual specimens. The Linear B tablets indicate that the Minoan-Mycenaean culture kept pace. We read, for instance (italicized words are considered uncertain): "two tables of *yew*, of *encircled* type, *containing* box-wood, *nine-footers*, decorated with *running spirals*, inlaid with *silver*," and "one *ebony* chair with golden *back* decorated with birds; and a footstool inlaid with ivory *pomegranates*."[6]

Ivory pieces, including tiny columns, evidently preserved from wooden furniture which has otherwise disappeared, have recently been found at Mycenae (Fig. 136, G, H); and it has been suggested that two examples, strangely reminiscent of Ionic capitals, once decorated footstools (Fig. 139, B, C); both are of appropriate size, 14 in. (36 cm.) long.[7]

Beds appear to be mentioned once in the extant Linear B tablets ("*demnia*," as in Homer).[8] The fact that they were familiar both in Egypt on the one hand and in the Homeric poems on the other makes it highly probable that they were in use among the upper classes in Crete. A low plaster platform in the corner of a small room of the Residential Quarter at H. Triadha, measuring 6 ft. 8 in. by 3 ft. 2 in. (203 by 97 cm.), it has been suggested, was used as a bed by piling blankets upon it (Fig. 11); but it would have served equally well as a platform for a wooden bed, as in contemporary Egyptian houses at Amarna. Though smaller, 5 ft. by 2 ft. 8 in. (150 by 80 cm.), the platform in the room of the toilet in the Residential Quarter at Knossos may also have been so used (Fig. 12). Evans originally called this the "Room of the Plaster Couch." In general, however, bedrooms were probably on the upper floors.

Chests of many forms, and often finely decorated, were used in Egypt from early times. We may be sure that they were common also in Crete, and used for many purposes. In the

[6] *DMG*, pp. 342-343, nos. 241-242.
[7] *DMG*, p. 346, fig. 23.
[8] *DMG*, p. 349, Vn851 (under no. 251).

Odyssey "Helen went to the chests which contained her embroidered dresses, the work of her own hands, and from them, she lifted out the longest and most richly decorated robe, which had lain underneath all the rest, and now glittered like a star."[9]

Remains of wooden chests together with bronze hinges and loop handles have been found at Knossos, but never well enough preserved to give any accurate impression of their size or form. Inscribed tablets were kept in several wooden boxes in a deposit found in the Palace of Minos, and two chests containing arrows, discovered in the "Armory" northwest of the palace, had clearly been tied and sealed.[10] The Town Mosaic, Evans suggested, may have formed part of the inlay decoration of a wooden chest, and classical scholars will be reminded of the elaborate scene depicted on the Corinthian "Chest of Cypselus." The appearance of one common form of Cretan chest is almost certainly represented, translated with obvious literalness from a wooden prototype, in clay coffins of a type much used in the Late Minoan period; a handsome example is illustrated in Fig. 140, D.

Bathrooms were, as we have seen (Ch. v, 3), fairly abundant, but strangely few bathtubs have been found in the houses or palaces. The reason, perhaps, is that they were valuable, readily portable, and could be used in the next world as well as in this —the dead were often buried in them.[11] One tub found in the Palace of Minos (Fig. 140, C) was almost five feet (145 cm.) long; it compares favorably in size with our modern tubs, and is certainly more handsome. Most tubs were however considerably shorter.

A number of candlesticks of various shapes have been found in Crete, but artificial light was ordinarily supplied by lamps burning olive oil.[12] Lamps of many sizes and forms, made of clay, stone, or bronze, were in use. Shallow, open bowls of clay with a projecting nozzle for the wick, and loop or shaft handles,

[9] *Odyssey*, 15, 104-108 (Rieu translation).
[10] *Knossos*, IV, pp. 617, 836; cf. III, p. 409, and I, p. 452.
[11] Cf. *DMG*, pp. 338-339; Platon, *Guide²*, p. 121.
[12] *Knossos*, II, p. 127 and note 2.

were common (Fig. 140, B). A bronze lamp of this type with a simple incised pattern on the rim has a very long thin handle which could be thrust into a wall to support it (Fig. 140, A); wall niches were perhaps commonly used as a place to put lamps, as in the bathroom of House E at Mallia (Ch. v, 3). Stone lamps were often handsomely decorated (Fig. 140, G), and sometimes were made in one piece with a tall stand (Fig. 94, right foreground). This latter form includes the aristocrats of Minoan lamps. The stone, often of a fine purple variety, is sometimes carved in the form of a column with spreading foot, decorated shaft, and distinct capital (Fig. 140, J), clearly influenced by Egyptian column forms.

The finest known pedestaled lamp has a shaft adorned with ivy leaves and a hollow spiral groove, and was found in the Pillar Crypt of the Southeast House at Knossos.[13] Lamps have frequently been found in these dark, ground floor cult rooms, also in bathrooms (Fig. 81), and in association with stairways. A fine pedestaled lamp was found in position on a step leading to the dais in the Hall of the Royal Villa.[14]

Heat was supplied by portable clay hearths on three legs, or by small clay braziers with a handle for easy carrying (Fig. 140, E).[15] One "tripod hearth" from Knossos had a diameter of three feet (90 cm.), but this is small in comparison with the great fixed hearths in the megarons of the colder Mycenaean mainland (Fig. 150); one at Pylos measures thirteen feet across (4.02 m.). A specimen in the "Tomb of the Tripod Hearth" at Knossos still contained some of the charcoal fuel (Fig. 140, F). Fire rakes and tongs are mentioned in the Linear B tablets.[16]

No built fireplaces for cooking have been found in the service quarters of the palaces or houses (Ch. vii, 1). A common type of cooking pot, evidently to be placed directly over the fire, is

---

[13] *Knossos*, ii, p. 481, fig. 288a; Platon, *Guide*², pl. 6, 2.
[14] *Knossos*, ii, p. 404.
[15] Fixed hearths are rare; one was reported at Mallia, House Zb, *Mallia, Maisons*, ii, p. 12.
[16] *DMG*, p. 337, no. 237.

a bronze cauldron mounted on three legs. Two types are illustrated in Fig. 140, H and K. The later form, H, is the prototype of the Classical Greek tripod, often used as a prize from Homeric times on, and already known under that name by the Mycenaean Greeks, for a tablet found recently at Pylos mentions tripods several times and accompanies the text with perfectly recognizable little pictures (ideograms) of Bronze Age types of tripods (Fig. 140, I); they are further described as "of Cretan workmanship."[17] As a matter of fact the correspondence of the reading "t(i)-ri-po-de" and the ideogram on this tablet (Fig. 147), found after the decipherment had been announced, helped to prove that the language of the tablets had been correctly identified as an early form of Greek.

Clay pots in a wide assortment of shapes and sizes were provided for the cook, and many strange objects whose use is difficult to determine. Some have been ingeniously identified by excavators who have carefully noted any traces of the original contents of a vessel, or have observed similar objects still in use among modern peoples.[18] Various types of pots are shown in Fig. 141, also a funnel, an egg stand (?), a grill, and a spit support (M) for roasting those succulent morsels of lamb the Greeks today call "souflahkia." Bronze Age heroes enjoyed them too, and Homer describes the process with evident appreciation: Achilles "sliced well the meat and pierced it through with spits, and (his squire) made the fire burn high. Then when the fire was burned down and the flame waned, he scattered the embers and laid the spits thereover, resting them on the spit-racks, when he had sprinkled them with holy salt" (*Iliad*, 9, 210-214).[19]

The circular object about a foot and a half (44 cm.) high and a little less in diameter, illustrated in two views in Fig. 141, A, was obviously designed for some specific purpose. The

[17] *DMG*, p. 336, no. 236.
[18] Chapouthier, *REA*, 43 (1941), pp. 5-15.
[19] The identification and the references to modern and Homeric practice are due to Chapouthier, *idem*, pp. 12-14. A grill similar to Fig. 141, D, has recently been found in Attica, *Praktika*, 1955, p. 114, pl. 36d; it is dated E.H. III.

shallow bottom compartment was intended for the fire, no doubt of charcoal; the deep upper compartment, readily accessible through a large slot in the side, was perhaps designed for long slow cooking, somewhat like a modern "deep-well cooker."[20] The object from Palaikastro (Fig. 141, B) must have served a similar purpose.

Storage jars and vessels were abundant and varied. Characteristic examples are the two-handled "amphoras" no doubt often used for wine (Fig. 141, F); and the huge yet often handsomely decorated "pithoi" already discussed in connection with storerooms (Ch. VII, 1, and Fig. 92).

Metal vessels are rarely preserved. Typical forms of pans, bowls, pitchers, ewers, etc. are illustrated in Fig. 142. Four huge bronze cauldrons made out of large sheets of metal riveted together, and in places repaired with bronze patches, were found in one of the rooms of House A at Tylissos. Three of these were round and had diameters ranging from $2\frac{1}{2}$ to $3\frac{1}{2}$ ft. (72 to 105 cm.); the fourth was hemispherical (Fig. 142, G) with a diameter of $4\frac{1}{2}$ ft. (ca. 140 cm.) and a weight of 115 lbs. (52 kg).[21]

Pitchers, bowls, cups, and goblets in a wide range of shapes and sizes were available for eating purposes (Figs. 141, 143). The forms even in plain ware are often very pleasing; the finer ware was decorated with that Minoan eye for beauty which made it by far the handsomest pottery of its day. The earlier "Kamares" style pottery (M.M. II) was painted with a fine feeling for color, movement, and the relation of the design to the shape of the vase (Fig. 153, A). In the later Palace Period (L.M. I-II) equally attractive effects result from informally arranged motives derived from natural forms: octopus, nautilus, starfish, molluscs, and plant life from both sea and land (Fig. 153, B). To find the Cretans using graceful vases with small holes in the bottom, surely flowerpots, is therefore no great surprise (Fig. 141, J).

[20] *Mallia, Maisons*, I, pp. 91-92, pls. 39, 1 and 2; 58, 4.
[21] *Knossos*, II, pp. 569-570, fig. 355: *Ephemeris*, 1912, p. 221, fig. 29.

The looting of the palaces and the failure to locate any intact royal burials has left us with no fine examples of vessels of gold or silver found in Crete. A small silver pitcher and three bowls, one decorated with a simple spiral pattern, were excavated in the South House at Knossos;[22] and recently a gold bowl with similar design has been found in a grave.[23] A few shallow loop-handled bowls in bronze give us an idea of the perfection of design and craftsmanship to be expected, although these exhibit only simple patterns (Fig. 142, I).

The dearth of fine quality metalwork from Crete is in strange contrast to the wealth of material from the late Middle Bronze and Late Bronze Age mainland: the gold and silver vessels (we are not concerned here with the magnificent metal daggers, decorative pieces, masks, etc.) from the two Shaft Grave Circles at Mycenae (ca. 1600 B.C.),[24] the Octopus Cup from Dendra,[25] and the superb pair of Vaphio Cups from a tomb near Sparta (Fig. 143, F), to mention only a few of the finest. The Minoan style and subject matter of much of this metalwork can only mean that it was the product "of Cretan workmanship," as the Pylos Linear B tablets put it. Possibly such precious objects were acquired by the Mycenaean Greeks through legitimate trade or during the period of their occupation of Crete, but, remembering that the Homeric heroes were numbered among their descendants, it is likely that often they were the rewards of piracy or war.

No attempt has been made in our account to speak of cult objects used in the ubiquitous small shrines: altars, small idols, cult symbols, incense burners, libation vessels, and so on (Figs. 100, 101). Nor have we included small objects of personal use such as mirrors, caskets for jewelry or beauty lotions, toilet articles, razors, etc., nor the tools of craftsmen or agriculturists, found in the palaces or houses. If the reader has obtained some

[22] *Knossos*, II, p. 387, fig. 221.
[23] *BSA*, 51 (1956), pp. 87-92, fig. 5 and pl. 13.
[24] Mylonas, *Anc. Myc.*, chapters v and vi.
[25] Persson, *Royal Tombs at Dendra near Midea*, pp. 43-46, pls. 9-11.

idea of the kind of furnishings characteristically found in the living quarters, public halls, kitchens, and service rooms of upper-class dwellings, that is as much as can be hoped for even after sixty years of excavation and discovery.

2. WATER SUPPLY AND DRAINAGE

Our knowledge of how the Minoan palaces were supplied with water for drinking and other purposes is almost entirely confined to Knossos. A few cisterns have been discovered at Phaistos,[26] but no wells or springs, owing to the nature of the ground. The only drainage system of any complexity is also a feature of the Palace of Minos.

Even at Knossos the sources and methods of supplying water are only partially understood. Several wells have been discovered in the palace area, and one a little to the northwest of the Little Palace. The last, cleaned out to its original three-foot (1 m.) diameter and forty-two foot (ca. 12½ m.) depth, continues to furnish an excellent supply of drinking water.[27]

That the inhabitants at Knossos did not rely on wells alone but were supplied with running water is indicated by the discovery, beneath the palace floors, of lengths of terracotta piping. The clay pipes, made in sections about 2 to 2½ ft. long (60 to 75 cm.), were carefully flanged to fit into one another, and the joints were tightly cemented (Fig. 139, A). This would make a pressure system feasible. That the Minoans did understand and utilize the principle that water seeks its own level is further shown "by the discovery of the Minoan conduit heading towards the Palace from the pure limestone spring of Mavrokolybo and implying a descending and subsequently ascending channel."[28]

[26] The "cisterns" at the southwestern corner of the Palace of Mallia are surely granaries (in any case this is not the corner to pick for keeping water cool, though excellent for keeping grain dry)—see Ch. VII, 1, note 11. Lawrence believes that the very deep stone-lined pits ("keeps" Evans called them) at Knossos were really cisterns, *Gk. Arch.* p. 298, note 2; *JHS*, 62 (1942), pp. 84-85.

[27] *Knossos*, III, p. 254.

[28] *Knossos*, III, p. 252. R. W. Hutchinson thinks that the Knossos water-supply came from the "excellent and perennial spring on Gypsádhes," which served the Caravanserai; "an extension of this conduit could well have been carried along

The sections of clay pipe resemble those in use in Classical Greek times, though Evans claims they were more efficiently designed; each section was rather strongly tapered toward one end, with the purpose of increasing the speed of flow of the water and thus helping to flush any sediment through the pipe.[29]

The clay tubs in the Minoan bathrooms must have been filled and emptied by hand (Fig. 140, C). However, in the "Caravan-serai," a rest house on the cross-island route just south of the palace, a footbath for the weary traveler was supplied by a direct pipe, and the overflow was taken care of by another conduit; a branch of the water channel also served a drinking trough (Fig. 3). Nearby Evans excavated a Spring House con-sisting of a well-built stone chamber. Within this was a stone-lined basin, a foot and a half deep (45 cm.), through whose pebble bottom a spring welled up, and indeed still does to some degree; the stones of the basin were deeply worn by those who came there to fill their jars in the days of Minos.[30]

Rainwater from the flat roofs of the palace at Knossos was carried off by vertical pipes, one of which in the eastern wing emptied on to a stone drainhead from which a stone channel carried the flow of water.[31]

Surface water from part of the Central Court of the Palace of Minos was taken care of by a very capacious underground channel built of stone and lined with cement, which ran beneath the passage leading from the North Entrance and received several affluents from various quarters. The most fully explored portion of the palace drainage system is that which ran beneath the floors of the Residential Quarter (Fig. 12).[32] This formed a great loop with its high point under the light-well beside the Grand Staircase, and emptied via a combined channel down the slope to the east of the palace. In the area of the Hall of the Double-Axes and the Queen's Hall with its associated chambers

---

the viaduct across the bridge and so to the southern limits of the palace," *Town Planning Review*, 21 (1950), p. 212.

[29] *Knossos*, III, pp. 252-253.　　　　[30] *Knossos*, II, pp. 123-128.
[31] *Knossos*, I, pp. 378-379.　　　　[32] *Knossos*, I, pp. 226-230.

it received the drainage water from no less than five light-wells; it served a toilet on the lowest floor, and was connected with three vertical shafts which evidently received rainwater from the roof and were also probably connected with toilets on the upper floors. The drain was built of stone blocks, lined with cement, and measured about 31 by 15 in. (79 by 38 cm.) in section, quite large enough to permit men to enter it, for cleaning purposes, through manholes provided for the purpose. Airshafts at intervals also helped to ventilate the drains.

CHAPTER XIII

PROCEDURES AND PRINCIPLES

1. MEASURING AND PLANNING THE PALACES

ONE OF THE MOST intriguing yet most dangerous intellectual pastimes the archaeologist can indulge in is the attempt to determine what unit of measurement was employed in the planning and construction of the architectural remains he is studying. With a little luck and a considerable amount of ingenuity (with which he is often overly supplied) the well-meaning but incautious investigator can evoke the most astonishing results from the most unpromising set of data.

On the other hand if he is too cautious he may over hastily conclude that no unit of measurement was used at all, or one so imprecise or so laxly applied that it cannot be detected by an examination of the architectural remains. In general, the more regular and uniform the workmanship—accurate right angles and close coincidence of dimensions between similar elements in the plan, well dressed masonry laid in regular coursing, and so on—the more reasonable it will be to assume that some definite unit was actually employed in the construction, and the greater the chance of being able to detect it.

The solution may come much more quickly if a known unit with a known value or range of values is likely to have been in use in the area under investigation, for then one can test these values of the unit directly on the data being studied. This was the situation when, some years ago, I was studying for publication a series of houses of the fifth and fourth centuries B.C., excavated at the site of Olynthos in northern Greece.[1]

[1] *Olynthus*, VIII, pp. 45-51.

It was the practice of the house builders in this city to paint the upper part of the plastered wall, in the better rooms of the better houses, in a single color, usually red; and the lower part of the wall in a contrasting color, commonly white. This white dado was evidently an imitation of a course of masonry blocks supporting a wall of some other material, and it was therefore often marked off with accurately ruled horizontal and vertical lines, incised in the surface of the plaster before it had set. It was obvious that the intervals between the vertical incised lines, suggesting the individual blocks, had in some cases been carefully measured, for the same length often occurred repeatedly on the walls of the same room and, even more significantly, on the walls of rooms in different houses. Surprisingly, however, not one but two sets of measurements, each apparently incommensurate with the other, were found: one approximating 2 ft. 10¾ in. (88 cm.), the other 3 ft. 2½ in. (98 cm.). But the answer was not far to seek. Two foot-standards were in common use in Greece at this period, and both must have been current contemporaneously at Olynthos: a shorter "Ionic" foot of 11⅝ in. (29.5 cm.), and a longer "Doric" foot of 12⅞ in. (32.7 cm.). Both sets of wall blocks were therefore measured in three-foot intervals (3 × 29.5 = 88.5 cm.; 3 × 32.7 = 98.1 cm.).

This then is one type of measurement which the investigator may hope will yield a determination of the linear unit, namely comparatively short and closely measurable distances set out in *whole* numbers of that unit, and repeating frequently enough to avoid any danger of mere coincidence.

At the same site many complete blocks of identical dimensions were discovered, and such blocks, as we know from other regularly planned Greek cities, were usually laid out in round numbers of feet, such as 200 by 120. The Olynthian blocks were evidently designed to measure 300 by 120 "Ionic" feet; the width of a block, ca. 35½ m., divided by 120, yields a foot of between 29.5 and 29.6 cm. (11⅝ in.).

Here then is a second type of measurement that may be expected to assist in determining the standard of length, namely a comparatively long interval laid out in *round* numbers of the unit, recurring with sufficient frequency to rule out the possibility of coincidence.

But to return to our Bronze Age palaces—here we are forced to work almost entirely in the dark even as to the general unit likely to have been employed. The cubit is known to have been in use at this period in Egypt and the Near East with values in the neighborhood of 20 in. (ca. 50 cm.). Of the foot used as a linear standard before the Iron Age no reliable evidence has so far been presented; on the other hand, there is no good reason for believing that it may *not* have been in use in the Bronze Age.

The solution I propose was not reached as a result of a deliberate search for a linear unit, but was the by-product of a series of precise measurements made in studying the recesses of the west façades of the palaces and the related problem of windows (Ch. IX, 1). The west front of the Magazine Block at Phaistos (Fig. 48), with its symmetrical recesses, was found to repeat the same measurement very accurately four times: 3.34 m., or, on the English foot-standard, 10 ft. 11¼ in. After trying vainly to fit this to a system of cubit measures the next step was clearly to test the possibility that the Minoan builder had measured this interval as eleven feet on his scale. This would mean a foot actually much closer to the value of the modern English foot than were the Classical Greek feet mentioned above, in fact only about ⅟₁₆ in. (a little over 1 mm.) short. The near coincidence is of course of no significance, except to show that the proposed Minoan foot-length is a perfectly reasonable one.

Proof or disproof of the use by the Minoan Cretans of a foot of approximately 11¹⁵⁄₁₆ in., or 30.36 cm., can only be obtained by a systematic and intensive testing of all the available data. Here there is space to give but a few examples.[2]

On the south side of the same projecting block at Phaistos another recess measures 3.02 m. = 9 ft. 11½ in. = almost exactly 10 Minoan feet, or "10 M. ft." as we will abbreviate it. To the north of the Grand Propylon another recess and the two adjacent wall faces repeat the measurement 2.74 m. three times; 2.74 m. = 9 M. ft. (In this and in what follows we omit giving the measurement also in English feet, in order to avoid confusion.)

Further support comes from the palace at Mallia where the spacing, 3.31 m., nearly identical with the 11 M. ft. interval with which we started at Phaistos, occurs twice on the west front (Fig. 58). Just south of this the main projecting element of the façade has a broad central recess balanced by two plain units of wall on either side; the recess measures 6.06 m., the wall units, 6.03 and 6.09 m., each approximately 20 M. ft. (6.072 m.). The width of the entire element is 18.19 m. or 60 M. ft.; 60 × 30.36 cm. = 18.216 m.

As the reader will have observed, the evidence provided by the length of the recesses and the adjacent wall faces is strictly analogous to the even three-foot intervals marked on the wall plaster, which were found to be a useful guide to the foot-standard in use at Olynthos. (Actually some of the intervals between incised lines on Minoan stuccoed walls are measurable in even numbers of Minoan feet, but they are too few to avoid the possibility of coincidence.) It will be equally clear that the sixty-foot width of the projecting façade element at Mallia finds its analogy in the long intervals, expressible in round numbers of feet, found in the dimensions of the Olynthian blocks.

Nor is this likely to be mere coincidence. For the 18.19 m. = 60 M. ft. long façade element at Mallia reappears on the west

[2] For a more detailed discussion see *AJA*, 64 (1960), pp. 335-341.

façade at Gournia—18.13 m., and in the earlier palace at Phaistos—18.24 m., while at Knossos the two main projections of the façade amount to 36.23 m. = 120 M. ft., and four projecting elements amount to 60.54 m. = 200 M. ft. (Fig. 83).[2a]

If the elements of the palace west façades were laid off in round numbers of Minoan feet, the possibility suggests itself that other of the more regular parts of the palaces were similarly designed, and if so perhaps we can get some idea of the Minoan architect's procedure in planning a palace.

Of the three major palaces the most promising one with which to begin the experiment is the last palace at Phaistos, since it gives the impression of having been designed as a unified whole, or nearly so.[3] An extensive series of measurements made on the site in 1959 is the basis of the results shown in Fig. 144, and these do in fact appear to indicate that the areas of the palace to the west and immediately to the north of the Central Court, that is the most regularly planned parts of the palace, fall into a system of round numbers of Minoan feet.

It looks as if the unknown architect of the Phaistos palace had proceeded more methodically than his celebrated colleague, Daedalus, who built the Labyrinth at Knossos. Hypothetically we can trace his procedure somewhat as follows. First he laid out two base lines or axes, one running north to south, the other, exactly at right angles to this, east to west; the point of intersection, the focus or "origin" of the system of coordinates, may be termed "X." He then measured off a distance of 170 M. ft. on the north-south line south of X to mark the west edge of the west stylobate of the Central Court,[4] while on the east-west line he measured off 80 M. ft. east of X to determine the line

---

[2a] The frequency of the occurrence of 60, and once of 120, is noteworthy, and finds a parallel in numerals on Linear A tablets: "Minoan numbers follow a decimal system, and there is no doubt that the Minoans counted in hundreds. . . . That the Minoans also counted sexagesimally for some purposes is not only likely in itself, but also witnessed by a tablet from Phaistos (Ph. 2) where the account is composed of three items of sixty each," *BSA*, 55 (1960), p. 204. Cf. Palmer, *Mycenaeans and Minoans*, pp. 118-119.

[3] Cf. *Festòs*, II, pp. 13-14.

[4] *Festòs*, II, p. 8.

of façade at the north end of the Central Court, and 100 M. ft. west of X to define the south face of the north wall of the Magazine Block (Fig. 144). The east and south boundaries of the Central Court could then be determined by projecting them from the points already established.

Next the north-south width of the Magazine Block was established at 50 M. ft., and this block constructed with very thick walls because of the importance and height of the three storeys they were designed to carry (Ch. VI, 1). North of this block 45 M. ft. were assigned to the monumental stairway of approach. Parallel to and 60 M. ft. west of the north-south axis through X a line was drawn to mark 1) the west face of the great columned opening at the head of the stairway 66-67; 2) the west face of the heavy transverse wall running between 30-36 and 31-37 in the Magazine Block (probably intended to support a pier-and-door partition in the hall above); and 3) the west façade of a block of rooms to be built to the south of the Magazine Block. South of this last block another block was constructed with its west façade laid out 70 M. ft. west of the north-south axis; the combined length of the two blocks south of the Magazine Block from north to south was set at 120 M. ft.

Finally the wall lines forming the north side of the Propylon were projected eastward and returned southward to form the north and east walls of the important block of rooms north of the Central Court, in the upper storeys of which, we have suggested, the Banquet Hall or Halls were located (Ch. VI, 2).

The rest of the palace is less regularly laid out, and it would be useless to attempt to follow our architect further, except to note once again that the elements of the elaborate façade at the north end of the Central Court were carefully worked out in a symmetrical scheme in even numbers of Minoan feet (Figs. 50, 145 and Ch. II, 2).

The lines and measurements established by the architect were not always precisely adhered to by the builders, sometimes for

good practical reasons, sometimes probably through sheer care-
lessness. Thus the actual position of some of the details of the
symmetrical façade just mentioned vary somewhat from their
"predicted values," partly perhaps to improve the position of
the south window of the Banquet Hall; the west line of the
west stylobate of the Central Court veers off about one foot too
far to the east at X, possibly to allow Stairway 39 a little extra
width; and the south face of the north wall of the Magazine
Blocks works somewhat south of its true position. But the
original design is still discernible in the completed work to a
remarkable degree.

The more complicated history of partial rebuilding and repeated repair, plus modern restorations, would be sufficient to
obscure the planning of the Palace of Minos, with the exception
of the dimensioning of the west façade already spoken of. But
Mallia, as our Fig. 146 shows, seems to illustrate a process of
planning parallel to that more fully visible at Phaistos.

In closing it may be pointed out that the designing of buildings in round numbers is not only a procedure which appeals
to the reason, but for which there is good precedent. The builder
of the Great Pyramid, a millennium earlier, laid out each side
of the base to be 440 cubits, its height to be 280 cubits, and the
dimensions of the king's chamber to be 10 by 20 cubits.[5] And
about 1400 B.C. Amenhotpe III determined the dimensions of
the lake to be built for his wife as 3700 by 700 cubits.[6]

Whether the Mycenaeans used a foot with the Minoan value
is not yet clear, though the uncertainly translated description
of tables in the Linear B tablets as "six-*footers*" and "nine-
footers" may indicate that at least they did use a foot as a
linear measure.[7] It certainly would be natural to suppose that

---

[5] Badawy, *A History of Egyptian Architecture*, I (1954), p. 135. The maximum
error in the length of the four sides of the base amounts to about two-fifths of a
cubit (7.9 in.).

[6] Baldwin Smith, *Eg. Arch.*, p. 219.

[7] *DMG*, pp. 339-341, nos. 239-240. However, Emmett Bennett, a leading
authority on Linear B, has recently pointed out to me that the "feet" always occur
in multiples of three, and he therefore suspects that each leg of a three-legged

the use of the foot as a standard of measurement was inherited by the Classical Greeks from their Bronze Age predecessors, and it may not be a mere coincidence that in the Argolid, the chief center of the Mycenaean culture, the stadium at Epidauros was laid out on the basis of a foot of 30.2 cm., almost precisely the figure we have assigned to the Minoan foot.

The use of the foot as a linear standard to the present day, by those countries that have not yet had the discretion to adopt the metric system, is a tangible illustration of our architectural inheritance from the first European civilization.

2. THE ORIGINS OF MINOAN ARCHITECTURE

Before going on to consider the principles of Minoan architecture it may be wise to see whether some light can be shed on this difficult subject by a discussion of the origins of the Cretan palaces, for it is a reasonable supposition that an examination of their prototypes, if they can be found, should reveal something of the essential character of Cretan palace planning.

It has often been remarked that the Minoan palaces seem to appear with something of the sudden maturity of an Athena born full-armed from the head of Zeus. This suddenness can be explained on various hypotheses: that we have simply failed to find the earlier stages belonging to the Early Minoan period —and it must be admitted that we know almost nothing of Cretan architecture in the third millennium B.C.; that the palace type was evolved somewhere outside Crete and was imported as an almost ready-made foreign product; or that in response to certain needs the palace plan was suddenly created at, say, Knossos,[8] emerging fully formed (or nearly so) from the brain of some Cretan Daedalus, in much the same fashion as the first

---

table may have been decoratively equipped with more than one "foot"; such a table could therefore have been described as "six-foot" or "nine-foot."

[8] So Rodenwaldt suggested in a review of *Mallia*, I, published in *Gnomon*, 5 (1929), pp. 177-184 (especially p. 183), with much of which I find myself in agreement in the present section.

great complex of stone buildings was created for King Zoser by the genius of Imhotep a century earlier than the building of the Pyramids of Giza.

Against the first possibility is the fact that no considerable buildings earlier than the beginning of the Middle Minoan period have been uncovered on the sites of the three major palaces. However the recent discovery of two palaces earlier than the one known for half a century as the "First Palace" at Phaistos, in the course of exploring deeper levels at that site, warns us that more surprises of this sort are not impossible. Indeed the unsatisfactory state of our knowledge of the chronology of the palaces and of their form even in the Middle Minoan period, plus the recent doubts cast on the dating of the final stages of the Palace of Minos, has discouraged any effort to trace the evolution of palace architecture in the present study. It is essential, we believe, first to understand as completely as possible the palaces in the final forms that the excavators' spades have revealed.

The second possibility mentioned above is that the palace type originated elsewhere and was simply imported into Crete; and this indeed is what Sir Arthur Evans supposed: "We see, in fact, the more or less simultaneous introduction into the Island at various points of an already stereotyped model. That this model was derived from an Eastern source is a reasonable conclusion."[9] Sir Arthur believed that the earliest form of the Palace of Minos was a series of blocks or *insulae* built around a large court; only gradually did this coalesce into a single coherent structure which, however, continued to betray its earlier condition by a pattern of vestigial corridors. The plans of the palaces at Mallia and Phaistos fail to support the *insula* hypothesis, and few if any students of Minoan architecture still adhere to this view.

The theory that the Cretan type of palace was imported ready-made has not disappeared, however. Sir Leonard Woolley, on the basis of his recent excavations at Alalakh (Tel Atchana)

[9] *Knossos*, II, p. 269.

in Syria, has restated this view in a particularly violent form: "We are bound to believe," he tells us, "that trained experts, members of the Architects' and Painters' Guilds, were invited to travel overseas from Asia (possibly from Alalakh itself, seeing that it had its Mediterranean harbour) to build and decorate the palaces of the Cretan rulers."[10] Other British excavators, Seton Lloyd and James Mellaart, who are excavating a Bronze Age palace at Beycesultan in western Turkey (Fig. 1, inset), have been almost equally positive about the close resemblance of their palace to the Cretan.[11] Nevertheless the Alalakh and the Beycesultan palaces bear no resemblance to one another. The excavator at Mari on the Euphrates, M. Parrot, has compared his palace (Fig. 148) with the Minoan, though he gives no details. Others have followed suit. Thus Hood of the British School, in a review of *Festòs* ii, remarks that "the similarities in methods of construction, and even in details of design and decoration, between the Palace architecture of Crete and that of the contemporary Near East (e.g. the Palaces at Mari and Atchana) are in fact very striking, and might have been worth elaborating in so full a study as this" (of the last palace at Phaistos).[12] L. R. Palmer likewise uses the similarity between the Beycesultan and the Cretan palaces, claimed by the British archaeologists, as further evidence for the Luvian character of the Minoans.[12a]

That resemblances do exist between the Cretan and the Near Eastern palaces in some respects can scarcely be denied, and likewise, as Lawrence declares in his recent book on *Greek Architecture*, between Cretan and Egyptian architecture.[13]

There are resemblances of a general nature, especially be-

[10] Woolley, *A Forgotten Kingdom*, London, 1953, p. 77. The definitive publication, *Alalakh* (1955) fails to provide specific proof of the connection between the palaces of Alalakh and Crete (cf. pp. 116, 228).

[11] *Anatolian Studies*, 5 (1955), pp. 39-92; 6 (1956), pp. 101-135; 7 (1957), pp. 27-36; 10 (1960), pp. 31-41; *London Times*, Sept. 24, 1954, pp. 9-10; Aug. 1, 1955, pp. 7, 9.

[12] *Gnomon*, 26 (1954), p. 375.

[12a] *Mycenaeans and Minoans*, pp. 239-240.

[13] pp. 22, 23, 28, 34, 39, etc.; cf. *BSA*, 46 (1951), p. 83.

tween the Mari palace and the Minoan (Fig. 148): rooms are arranged around courts; different quarters of the palaces are used for specific purposes—storage, work, worship, residence, etc.; there are bathrooms with clay bathtubs, audience halls; and so on. But within the limits of this broad likeness the differences are so profound and so deep-rooted that who can positively say whether one type of palace architecture is really influencing the other to any significant degree? Certain general methods of construction are also widely spread, such as "half-timbering" and the use of orthostates; but where these arose and when and how they spread, again who can definitely say?

There are also some resemblances in detail, between, for example, the clay pipe sections at Mari and Knossos (Fig. 139, A), or between Cretan fluted column shafts and possibly some capitals (if the capitals on some Cretan stone lamps were also employed in architecture) and Egyptian columns; mural painting is also an area of contact to a limited extent.

But all this is very far from substantiating the extreme claims of the Alalakh and Beycesultan excavators. The comparisons they themselves have drawn between their palaces and the Cretan are often very forced, and even taken cumulatively are, in my opinion, practically valueless. To discuss the matter in detail would be impossible in the space available here, and, since the results would be almost entirely negative, would achieve no useful purpose.[14]

The available evidence suggests, to my mind, that when the palaces first came into being around 2000 B.C. the Cretan architects, though aware in a general way of palace architecture elsewhere, created forms suited to, and determined by, Cretan needs and the Cretan environment, and employed constructional techniques traditional to the eastern Mediterranean and with which they were already in general familiar. In the course of construc-

---

[14] The author read a paper on "The Origins of Minoan Architecture" at the "Third International Colloquium for Mycenaean Studies" held at "Wingspread" in Racine, Wisconsin, Sept. 4-8, 1961; this will be published with the other papers read at the colloquium.

tion and reconstruction in the centuries that followed, the architects, reacting to changing needs and to the experience gained from long habitation of the palaces, developed more efficient and more peculiarly local forms, forms which were in some measure affected by the architecture of their overseas neighbors, as increasing wealth and culture in Crete fostered a desire to make the structures more comfortable and more pleasing to the eye. For new decorative forms they turned especially to Egypt, as Mycenae would later draw upon Crete, and Rome in turn on Greece. The possible adoption of the Egyptian type of banquet hall when Minoan kings wished, in imitation of the pharaohs, to add this luxury feature, would fall in the same category (Ch. VI, 2).

We have thus moved to the third possibility mentioned at the beginning of this section as to the most probable explanation for the sudden appearance of the Cretan palace type in an already well developed form, namely that in its main outlines it was created by some Cretan Imhotep for his Cretan Zoser. The outside influences mentioned above do not alter the essentially native character of Cretan architecture, which seems to have arisen and developed as independently of "foreign aid" as the Cretan system of writing. The truly distinctive features of the Cretan palaces are not derived from other architectures, for example the "Cretan Hall," the pier-and-door partition, the light-well, the use of alabaster veneering, the sunken bathroom or lustral chamber, the downward tapering column, the column oval in cross-section, the porticoed central courts, the alternating pier-and-column scheme, the columned propylon, the terraced and porticoed gardens of the residential quarters, the use of monumental stairways, and the system of putting the main public rooms on the upper floors.

If our conclusions regarding the native character of Cretan palace architecture are correct we must abandon any hope of assistance from foreign archetypes in the study of the principles of Minoan architecture, the topic of our final section.

3. PRINCIPLES OF MINOAN ARCHITECTURE

To some students of Minoan architecture the title of our final section may appear highly misleading. How can Minoan architecture, they will ask, lay claim to being founded on any "principles"—an architecture which has been termed "incomprehensible, confusing, illogical, irrational, primitive"?[15] There are those who regard the development of the Minoan palaces as little more than the casual growth of groups of rooms about an open space; Zervos pictures the palace as enlarging spasmodically in much the way a city enlarges in response to increases in population, wealth, and material importance.[16] Lawrence in his recent handbook on *Greek Architecture* refers to the palaces as "confusedly planned," as an "apparently insane jigsaw," as a "senseless agglomeration," and as an "illogical disorderly growth."[17] One might infer that the tale of Daedalus building the Labyrinth to confuse the Minotaur is to be understood as a symbolic statement of the normal procedure of the Minoan architect.

That critics familiar with Classical Greek architecture should be shocked and baffled by the Minoan palaces is not surprising. The principles of design embodied in a building like the Parthenon are immediately apparent: bilateral symmetry, like a living organism; a single chamber for its divine occupant, balanced by a porch at either end; outside, from whatever point of view, a continuous circuit of columns closed above by the horizontal lines of the roof—simplicity, clarity, unity.

---

[15] *Festòs*, II, p. 475, quoting Rodenwaldt and Snijder.

[16] *L'art de la Crète*, p. 497.

[17] Lawrence, *Gk. Arch.*, pp. 34, 41, 291, and *BSA*, 46 (1951), pp. 81, 83. Yet Hugh Plommer in his recent book *Anc. and Class. Arch.*, p. 75, remarks that "Cnossus was admirably planned." Seton Lloyd has also recently written, "Cretan planning has been described by the adjective 'agglutinative,' and the familiar association of the Palace of Minos with the legend of the Labyrinth has perhaps tended to over-emphasize the complexity of its arrangement and come to suggest a haphazard and unconsidered agglomeration of miscellaneous units. That this impression is a false one has in the past frequently been shown by intelligent analyses and comparisons of the buildings concerned," *Anatolian Studies*, 6 (1956), p. 119.

It is only natural that such critics should seek for some simple unifying principle of logic and order in the architecture of the Cretan palace and, failing to find it readily, declare that the corresponding Minoan trinity must be complexity, obscurity, multiplicity.

As a preliminary move to a fresh consideration of the problem let us clear the ground by making a few general observations. In the first place we must bear in mind that the "horrifying complexity of what remains," as Lawrence puts it, is made up of little but the "basement."[18] For, though not really an excavated "cellar" in the modern sense, most of the ground floor was used for service purposes: storerooms, workrooms, small shrines, and the like. Almost the only important rooms in this storey were those composing the principal floor of the residential quarter. Secondly, it should be noted that most discussions of palace aesthetics have been based largely or entirely on the Palace of Minos, and a glance at the plans (Fig. 7) is sufficient to show how much more labyrinthine was its ground floor than that of its sister palaces. This was at least in part due to the frequent partial rebuildings to which Knossos was subjected as the result of repeated damage from earthquake or hostile attack.

Again we must remember that these palaces served a multiplicity of purposes. They were not merely the residence of the sovereign, they were storehouses for the king's wealth; factories for the production of quality goods for royal use; sanctuaries where the cult of the gods, whose chief concern was the king, was centered; administrative offices where the records of the state were kept and the daily routine of government was conducted; possibly courts where the monarch dispensed justice to his subjects;—in addition they must express the power and dignity of the king, and contain facilities for worthily receiving and entertaining important visitors from home and abroad. It is a simple matter for a one-purpose building, such as a temple or a pleasure palace like that of Akhenaton at Amarna, to be

[18] *Gk. Arch.*, p. 34.

simple, unified, and symmetrically planned (Fig. 149); sweeping generalizations on the basis of the plan of the Palace of Minos, such as the one "that the Cretan genius is asymmetric," should not be too hastily adopted.[19]

The complexity of the present remains, then, should not cause us to leap to the conclusion that the palaces were virtually unplanned. Indeed the remarkable similarity in the general design of the three major palaces as well as in detailed parts such as the residential quarter, the orientation and size of the central court, the arrangement of magazines, etc., would be difficult to explain except as the result of deliberate planning.

To attempt to discover the nature of that planning it will be best to turn first to Mallia and Phaistos, where the last state of the palaces appears to represent, by and large, a single stage of planning and construction, comparatively free from the complications met with in the Palace of Minos. They may be taken as illustrating an approximation of the "ideal" Minoan palace plan.

Let us begin with the palace at Phaistos (Fig. 4). Unfortunately its ground plan is not quite complete, for whatever rooms may have existed along the south end and the southern part of the east side of the Central Court have been lost to erosion. The remainder falls quite easily into fairly clearly marked areas or quarters: 1) guest rooms and cult rooms, west of the Central Court and south of Corridor 7; 2) magazines and entranceway, north of the same corridor; 3) service rooms, the area north and northeast of the Central Court except north of Court 48; 4) main residential quarter, north of Court 48; 5) secondary residential quarter, east of the Central Court; 6) the Central Court, 40. Above 2), part of 3), and possibly above 1), were the main public rooms.

---

[19] An instructive example is provided by the "Palace of the Rulers" at Eshnunna in Mesopotamia, built about 2000 B.C., which exhibits no symmetry of design, yet the two contiguous and contemporaneous temples on either side present almost perfect illustrations of bilateral symmetry about a medial axis, Frankfort, *op.cit.*, fig. 19.

The ground plan of the Mallia palace is well preserved (Figs. 5, 6): 1) cult rooms, vi and vii, west of the Central Court; 2) storerooms, i, viii, xx, along the west façade; 3) guest rooms (?), xviii, at the southwest corner of the palace; 4) storerooms, x-xii, east of the Central Court; 5) residential quarter, iii, at the northwest corner of the palace; 6) storerooms and workrooms, xxi, xxii, xxiv-xxviii, at the north end of the palace; 7) the Central Court. Above i, viii, and ix, were the main public rooms.

Even at Knossos a similar arrangement in quarters can be discerned (Fig. 2): storerooms along the west side; cult rooms west of the Central Court; the northeast quarter given over to workrooms and storerooms; and the southeast to the Residential Quarter. The public rooms were mostly above the rooms west of the Central Court.

It therefore seems evident that considerable deliberate planning must have preceded the actual construction of these buildings. It also seems evident that the focal point of the plan was the central court, and around this and facing on it most of the quarters were built. Further groups of rooms built beyond these were served by corridors or by smaller courts.

Support for the view that the palace was planned in units radiating from the central court has been presented in the first section of this chapter. It was suggested there that in the palace at Phaistos a pair of straight lines crossing one another at right angles was first laid out to mark the west and north boundaries of the Central Court, and that from these as base lines the most important quarters were planned in round numbers of Minoan feet (Fig. 144). The available evidence at Mallia indicates a comparable procedure of planning (Fig. 146), and something of the same sort at least can be made out for Knossos on the basis of the scantier data. Deliberate planning in detail, accompanied by definite dimensioning, can also be followed, and has already been described (Ch. 11, 2), in the laying out of the symmetrical façade of the north end of the Central Court at Phaistos (Figs. 50, 145).

However, the guiding principle in this planning of the quarters about the central court was not aesthetic—there is no attempt to arrange them symmetrically, for example—but practical. The efficient arrangement of these quarters in a well coordinated whole evidently took precedence over any theoretically conceived architectural scheme; and whether the modern eye censures the results as untidy and illogical, or praises them for their variety and interest, is strictly irrelevant.

Another conspicuous feature of the palace plans which seems to violate normal principles of design, and which has therefore frequently provoked the surprised comments of critics is the bizarre irregularity of the "trace" or outline of the exterior walls, particularly along the west façade; the clearest illustration of this is the palace at Mallia (Fig. 6). In lack of symmetry Near Eastern palaces resemble the Minoan, but in this respect they differ, for they are normally firmly bounded by a more or less regular, often rectangular, enclosing outline (Fig. 148). Lawrence's explanation of the indentations along the west façade as either aesthetic, showing "an architectural sense," or structural—"long stretches of wall were avoided, probably because the builders distrusted their stability"—are not satisfying.[20] The explanation given by Evans and others, that the projections were a vestigial architectural legacy from times when the walls were fronted by defensive towers, is no longer in favor; indeed it was due to the very fact that the Minoan palaces were not fortified, that they were under no compulsion to assume the compact form and tight-drawn outline seen in Near Eastern palaces like that at Mari.

The correct explanation of the "indented trace" is surely the one already clearly enunciated by the French excavators at Mallia: "The indented line of the outer wall is easily explained if it was desired to place around the central court quarters of different importance; it is not, in fact, toward the exterior that the apartments face; the true façade gives on an interior court, on the large or the small court (that is, the Central and North

[20] *BSA*, 46 (1951), p. 81.

Service Courts at Mallia). The exterior wall marks only the rear of the building; each quarter—often conceived, if isolated, as a complete rectangle—projects to a greater or less degree in accordance with its own depth."[21]

This indented outline or uneven projection into horizontal space, so characteristic of the Cretan palaces, was repeated in a vertical sense; in other words the roof levels were far from uniform over the whole building. For it is quite clear that the number of storeys (and the height of the individual storeys) varied considerably, for purely practical reasons, in the different quarters, from one storey (probably) along the whole south end of the palace at Mallia (Fig. 58), for example, and perhaps east of the Central Court at Phaistos (Fig. 55), to three or four storeys east and west of the Central Court at Knossos (Fig. 44). Exaggerating this differential in elevation the palaces were built on a succession of terraces, partly from necessity, partly it would seem from deliberate choice. The excavators reckon the number of terraces at Phaistos and H. Triadha at seven and eight respectively.[22]

The irregularity of outline in plan and the disparity in the roof levels in Minoan architecture was encouraged by the apparently universal Cretan practice of flat roofs. In these features, as in others, Cretan palaces and houses bear a strong resemblance to the type of houses still common in many of the Greek islands, including Crete,[23] though in a more regularized and sophisticated form, and, in the case of the palaces, with the addition of inner courts. Such houses, or agglomerations of houses, are often veritable labyrinths of small rooms, the flat roofs of the inner rooms being built higher in order to be lighted, clerestory

[21] *Mallia*, III, pp. 71-72. This is not quite exact for the indented line of the west façade at Mallia and Knossos. There the irregularity is caused by the difference in size among the great halls of the Piano Nobile (Ch. VI, 1), and these front not on the central court but on the long north-south corridor of the magazines. Nor can the west façade be described as the "rear" of the building.

[22] *Festòs*, II, p. 478.

[23] E. Heinrich has recently studied this "Inselarchitektur" and has noted examples extending from the 4th millennium B.C. in the Near East to modern towns in Greece and Italy; it is not clear that all these are actually related, *AA*, 73 (1958), cols. 89-133.

fashion (Fig. 152); indeed this clerestory principle may have been used as a supplementary device for lighting the great halls of the Piano Nobile, as represented in our restoration of the Palace of Mallia (Fig. 58).

A few examples of clusters of rooms similar, at least in plan, to the modern "Island-architecture," and dated to the pre-palatial period (third millennium B.C.), have been found in Crete (Fig. 33); Lawrence refers to the "interminable chaotic rambling" plan of one of these and suggests them as prototypes of the palaces.[24] A kind of embryonic survival of this primitive "agglutinative" principle might help to explain the existence of such a maze of small rooms as that at the south end of the palace at Mallia, or to the west of the Central Court at Knossos. But the planning of the last Palace of Phaistos, for example, had surely reached a far more advanced level of architectural design.

So far in our search for principles determining the form of the Cretan palaces in their final stages we seem to have found them to be mainly functional rather than aesthetic in character; but, although practical considerations may have dominated the Minoan architect, aesthetic considerations were also bound to claim his attention. For one thing, the living quarters of the royal family must be commodious and, in a civilization as advanced as the Minoan, pleasing to the eye. As a matter of fact there was not a little "keeping up with the Joneses" even in those days; kings kept their eye on the palaces built by their brother monarchs and strove to rival or surpass them in magnificence. For example we read in an ancient text that the king of Ugarit in Syria sent his son, about 1700 B.C., to see the palace of Zimrilim, king of Mari, and bring back some ideas which he could apply for the improvement of his own residence.[25]

So successful was the Cretan architect in beautifying the residential quarter that some have seen in the main room of these apartments—the "Minoan Hall," as we have called it (at

[24] *Gk. Arch.*, p. 22.
[25] *Syria*, 18 (1937), pp. 74-75.

Knossos it was the Hall of the Double-Axes)—or in this Hall together with the associated sequence of rooms, the dominant aesthetic principle of Minoan palatial architecture. However exaggerated we may consider a view which suggests that so small a tail should wag so large a dog, we must grant that the aesthetic effect of these apartments must have been very striking, and not only for the rich decoration in gleaming alabaster and the painted stucco surfaces of floor, walls, and ceiling. A far more original feature is the ability to open at will entire walls, composed of rows of double doors, in order to reveal views of terraced gardens and distant landscapes. Complex patterns of light and shade were created by series of such pier-and-door partitions, by light-wells, windows, corridors, porticoes, etc. (Fig. 151). Schweitzer suggests that "these spatial shadings developed into a very finely felt instrument on which, as on a light-organ, the architect could compose fugues as he liked."[26] Whether the Minoan was in fact consciously sensitive to "photo-fugues" we have no way of knowing, but it would be dangerous to elevate this to the level of a determining principle guiding the Cretan designer in his architectural compositions.

The desire to impress the king's power and magnificence upon visitors, native or foreign, introduced another stimulus to aesthetic treatment in palace design.

The principal exterior façade of all the major palaces was the west. Along this side, in the Piano Nobile, were the state reception halls, and here was located the main entrance to the palace, except in the less pretentious palace at Mallia. The comparatively lofty walls rising above the heavy orthostate course must have been impressive, and their massiveness would have been increased by the strong contrasts of light and shadow created by boldly projecting room forms and by the shallower recess in the face of each façade element (Figs. 55, 58).

The west entrance at Knossos was further dignified by a broad porch with a single central column, at the rear of which

[26] *Die Antike*, 2 (1926), p. 305.

opened the Corridor of the Procession (Fig. 128). After two right-angle turns this corridor reached a formal Propylon (Fig. 42); at the rear of this a broad stairway led to the Piano Nobile, which was approached by still another fine stairway opening directly from the west side of the Central Court (Fig. 44).

Far more monumental is the approach to the state apartments at Phaistos. At the northeast corner of the West Court a great forty-five foot broad stairway of a dozen steps leads up to a grandiosely proportioned portal, and all this is balanced by the adjacent massive three-storeyed block to the south (Fig. 48).

Impressive and effective as these stairways and others, such as the Grand Staircase to the Residential Quarter at Knossos, must have been, it is unrealistic to elevate them, as Rodenwaldt suggested doing, into a dominant principle of palace composition.[27] They do constitute an important element, but the palaces were certainly not planned around a series of grand stairways.

Nor must we neglect, in estimating the aesthetic effect of the Cretan palaces, to take account of the central courts, which were certainly designed with appearance as well as usefulness in mind. Long porticoes with columned galleries above not only conveniently accommodated the spectators of the various sports and ceremonies which took place there (Ch. iv), but relieved the otherwise long monotonous walls with a variegated pattern of light and shade. On the west side the columned and pillared façades of the Tripartite Shrine at Knossos (Fig. 44), of Room 25 at Phaistos, and of Room vi 1 at Mallia, plus the broad stairways to the Piano Nobile at Knossos and Mallia, further enhanced the central courts; the handsome symmetrical north façade of the court at Phaistos, with its axial doorway flanked by half-columns, also added a decorative element (Figs. 50, 51).

It is clear that many features contribute elements of beauty to the Cretan palaces: the Halls of the residential quarters, the alabaster-lined bathrooms, the long porticoes of the central courts, the monumental stairways, the columned entranceways.

[27] *Gnomon*, 11 (1935), p. 331.

In fact it is commonly recognized that much of the aesthetic appeal of these buildings lies in details such as these. It is in general organization that their architectural design appears weak to us: in a well balanced relationship between the parts, in a proper subordination of lesser features to more important ones. The richly detailed diminutive shrine on the west side of the Central Court at Knossos, set in a framework of comparatively massive porticoes and a monumental stairway to the Piano Nobile, is a good illustration of architectural inappropriateness, at least to modern feeling (Fig. 44).[28] The narrow, winding Corridor of the Procession, forming, in spite of its richly decorated walls, an inadequate approach to the South Propylon at Knossos, and the reverse situation at Phaistos of a grandiose Propylon leading up to an area whose only exit consisted of three moderate-sized doorways, are further examples of architectural inexperience and naïveté.

We are reminded of the analytic approach of all early drawing and low relief, including the Minoan. Each detail may be done correctly enough, but the synthesis, the combination of the parts to form the whole, is awkwardly managed: full-front eyes in profile heads (Figs. 131, A, B), full-front bodies on side-view legs; even, in Egypt, left hands on right arms or right feet on left legs.

Yet it may be that this loose, uncoordinated architectural syntax, this imbalance of the component parts, was in part, at least, deliberate, "wilful irregularity." "Surely," says Snijder in his penetrating study of Cretan art, "*if he* (the Minoan designer) *had wanted to*, if the disciplined, centralizing architectural-style of the Orient had impressed him as something essential, important, unqualifiedly necessary, he would have succeeded. He had evidently not so wished, and therefore we must probably conclude from this fact that 'the power to create plastically unified compositions out of which all later European architecture grew' was foreign to him and remained so."[29]

[28] Karo, *Greifen am Thron*, p. 26.
[29] *Kretische Kunst*, p. 81.

Although this fact is rarely noticed, the Cretan architect certainly did understand the principles of formal balance and symmetry, and occasionally used them in details of his composition, yet he never thought of forcing his whole plan into such a rigid system. Instances readily come to mind, such as the recesses in the west façades at Mallia, and the double recessed Magazine Block at Phaistos (Fig. 48); even, to a degree, the recesses at Knossos. The symmetrical arrangement of important entrances, particularly the one at Phaistos with its single central column, its two portals, and the three columns of the light-well behind, is another example; symmetrical also is the front of Room 25 in the same palace, with its central column and pairs of pillars on either side (Fig. 50). But the most conspicuous instance is the nearby north façade of the Central Court; the formal balance here has been carefully thought out: axial door, half-columns, niches, and recesses. If the execution was not precise in its measurements this was not the fault of the designer, and the discrepancies would not have been readily apparent to the observer.

Symmetrical designs appear in other Cretan arts, such as the pottery both of the Middle and the Late Minoan periods. But the informality and asymmetry which were, it seems, particularly congenial to the Minoan temperament, may be best brought out by comparing the Minoan with the Mycenaean Greek treatment of the same theme. On a Cretan vase of the L.M. II period the octopus swims slantwise with writhing tentacles amid a litter of marine vegetation (Fig. 153, B); the contemporary mainland version sets the octopus firmly upon the axis of the vessel, combs out the tentacles into an ordered symmetry, and arranges the seaweed particles in forms carefully calculated to fill the vacant spaces (Fig. 153, C).[30] The Cretan genius delights in life and movement, in a baroque feeling for variety and unexpected effects; the Greek, whether Mycenaean or Hellenic, prefers balance and order, symmetry and formal pattern.

[30] Cf. Furumark, *Op. Arch.*, 6 (1950), pp. 157-159, fig. 3.

In Minoan architecture too the unexpected prevails. Doors tend to be placed near corners, not on the axis; columns alternate with piers in long porticoes; corridors bend in "dog's-leg" forms (Evans); the straightness of column shafts may be denied by spiral fluting; stairways wind and twist from storey to storey; rooflines rise and fall in constant oscillation; façades sway in and out in a shimmering mass of lights and shadows; and even more kaleidoscopic patterns are set adancing through the labyrinths of door openings, windows, pillared porticoes, and light-wells reflecting on the polished alabaster surfaces of floors and walls—all creating an atmosphere of restless movement, or in the architectural philosopher's language, "a motor-optical experience of spatiality."[31] Masses are broken up by the interplay of light and color. The very outlines of the buildings are loosely drawn; flickering forms advance and retreat both outwards into the surroundings and upwards into the sky. The general effect is pictorial rather than plastic (Figs. 55, 58).

Miss Banti sees this pictorial tendency particularly strong in the Phaistos palace, and finds in it a unifying principle which raises it from a merely clever work of construction to the level of a work of art. "The architect has made clear in his work and infused into it his essentially pictorial spirit, which is revealed in this center of southern Crete better and more clearly than elsewhere, and gives artistic unity to the vast complex." The construction of the palace in a series of terraces contributes to the effect, "the lines, surfaces, volumes join together to lend variety, movement—to take away from the mass all excessive heaviness. It is the modern architectonic conception in opposition to the classic. . . . The Minoan architects reveal here (at Phaistos) a technical ability and resource that is truly remarkable. It is wrong in reference to them to speak of empiricism, of primitiveness: they exhibit remarkable experience which, though it does not coincide with classical experience, is not inferior to that of any other people of antiquity."[32]

[31] *ibid.*, p. 87, "ein motorisch-optisches Erleben der Räumlichkeit."
[32] *Festòs*, II, pp. 480, 478, 479.

Snijder concludes his analysis of Minoan architecture some-what as follows: "Such an art of building makes sport of all our architectural conceptions, and defeats all attempts to force it into a logical, rational system. Yet it captivates even modern man and delights him with its charm. The Palace of Knossos is to the adult an adventure in the grand style, while it reminds him of his youth when as a child he reconnoitered the old-fashioned house of a friend and kept discovering it full of charms, new rooms, secret nooks, unexpected cupboards and passages, without his coming to understand the arrangement as a whole. So the modern investigator is charmed and delighted —until he remembers that it must yield some design; that he must discover the logical thread of Ariadne. Then he begins his researches and forgets that it is the irrational in these dwell-ings that constitutes their excellence and charm. Inevitably these logical attempts come to nought, and the investigator takes refuge in a world of dreams and fairytales, a gay world of change and movement far from restrictions of logic and reality."[33]

It is easy to romanticize the impressions that Cretan art makes on us, and in the absence of any written record of their own thought and feelings we shall never know how sensitive the Minoans actually were to such effects and to what extent they intentionally expressed them in their art. We must not forget that the voices that speak to us are but those of the stones them-selves, not those of the people who built with them.

We have confined our discussion of Minoan architectural principles to the palaces, but much would apply likewise to house architecture: the division into "quarters," the irregularity of outline (with occasional exceptions such as Mallia Za, Fig. 25), the variations in the height of the flat roofs, and the light-ing effects in the "Cretan Hall." In many ways the house is the palace on a small scale—the resemblance of the living quar-ters to those of the palaces is a striking illustration of this (Ch.

[33] *op.cit.*, pp. 89-90.

v, 1)—though the absence of a court in all but a few of the largest houses is a significant point of distinction. The Cretan house was of course far less complex than the palace. Its unpretentious, unsymmetrical design is to be expected; so even in Classical Greece, where monumental architecture represents the epitome of formalism, houses preserve a non-axial plan.[34]

The sensitive, volatile Gallic temperament has, we may fancy, not a little in common with the ancient Minoan. It is fitting then to close our account of the palaces of Crete by quoting the discriminating sentiments of M. Gustav Glotz in his account of *The Aegean Civilization* (p. 119).

"To estimate the level reached by Cretan architecture and to enjoy its charm one must first forget those intellectual qualities of order, symmetry, and balance which give Greek buildings their incomparable beauty. The Cretan architect made no effort to offer to the gods temples worthy of them. He wanted to build comfortable houses and mansions and magnificent palaces, in which the master could conveniently accommodate his whole family, an army of servants, and the offices of a complicated administrative system, and display his wealth by brilliant entertainments. The great artistic skill with which all crafts combined their resources at the call of the Cretan architect is clearly shown not so much in the majesty of the general effect or even in the splendour of the external decoration as in the perfect adaptation to climatic conditions, happy distribution of light and shade, and intelligent ventilation and drainage, in the ease of communication between the countless rooms, the arrangements made to satisfy quite modern notions of comfort, and the harmonious opulence of detail, and finally in a sure sense of the spectacular and picturesque which indulges in monumental entrances, the elegant ordering of terrace upon terrace and vistas of noble landscapes on every side."

[34] *Olynthus*, VIII, p. 147.

BIBLIOGRAPHY

BRIEF LIST OF RECENT BOOKS
AND ARTICLES

Cottrell, Leonard, *The Bull of Minos*, London, 1953.

Dinsmoor, *Architecture of Ancient Greece*, 3rd ed., London, 1950.

Graham, J. W., "The Phaistos 'Piano Nobile,'" *AJA*, 60 (1956), pp. 151-157.

————, "The Central Court as the Minoan Bull-Ring," *AJA*, 61 (1957), pp. 255-262.

————, "The Residential Quarter of the Minoan Palace," *AJA*, 63 (1959), pp. 47-52.

————, "Windows, Recesses, and the Piano Nobile in the Minoan Palaces," *AJA*, 64 (1960), pp. 329-333.

————, "The Minoan Unit of Length and Minoan Palace Planning," *AJA*, 64 (1960), pp. 335-341.

————, "The Minoan Banquet Hall," *AJA*, 65 (1961), pp. 165-172.

————, "Mycenaean Architecture," *Archaeology*, 13 (1960), pp. 46-54.

Hutchinson, R. W., "Prehistoric Town Planning in Crete," *Town Planning Review*, 21 (1950), pp. 199-220.

*Karo, Georg, *Greifen am Thron, Erinnerungen an Knossos*, Baden-Baden, 1959.

Lawrence, A. W., *Greek Architecture*, Penguin Books, 1957.

————, "Alleged Minoan Fortifications," *JHS*, 80 (1942), pp. 84-85.

————, "The Ancestry of the Minoan Palace," *BSA*, 46 (1951), pp. 81-85.

**Marinatos, Spyridon, and Hirmer, Max, *Crete and Mycenae*, New York, 1960.

Matton, Raymond, *La Crète au cours des siècles*, Athens, 1957.

*Matz, Friedrich, *Kreta, Mykene, Troja*, Stuttgart, 1957.

Palmer, L. R., *Mycenaeans and Minoans, Aegean Prehistory in the Light of the Linear B Tablets* (London, 1961).

Pendlebury, J. D. S., *Archaeology of Crete*, London, 1939.

————, *A Handbook to the Palace of Minos*, 2nd ed., 1954.

Pernier, Luigi, and Luisa Banti, *Guida degli scavi italiani in Creta*, Rome, 1947.
**Piggott, Stuart (ed.), *The Dawn of Civilization* (ch. VII, M. S. F. Hood, "The Home of the Heroes, the Aegean before the Greeks"), London, 1961.
Plommer, Hugh, *Ancient and Classical Architecture*, London, 1956.
Press, Ludwika, "Les maisons et les palais de Crète à l'époque du néolithe et du bronze," *Archeologia*, 9 (1957), pp. 1-31 (in Polish, with French summary, pp. 33-34).
————, "Les sites et les villes de la Crète aux IIIe et IIe millénaires avant notre ère," *Archeologia*, 10 (1958), pp. 28-58 (in Polish, with French summary, pp. 60-61).
*Rau, Heimo, *Kretische Paläste, Mykenische Burgen*, Stuttgart, 1957.
Renault, Mary, *The King Must Die*, New York, 1958.
Snijder, G. A. S., *Kretische Kunst*, Berlin, 1936.
*Zervos, C., *L'Art de la Crète*, Paris, 1956.

* The items marked with an asterisk are particularly valuable for their illustrations; a double asterisk indicates color as well as black and white illustrations.

BIBLIOGRAPHY OF MINOR SITES

The following brief bibliography mentions some of the later notices, from which earlier accounts may be traced.

ACHLADIA (Siteia): *To Ergon*, 1959, pp. 142-147; *BCH*, 84 (1960), pp. 822-826.

APODHOULOU: Platon, *Guide²*, p. 23.

ARKHANES: *Knossos*, II, pp. 64-67; *Kret. Chron.*, 10 (1956), p. 409.

KANLI KASTELLI (LYKASTOS?): Society for the Promotion of Hellenic Studies, *Archaeological Reports for 1957*, p. 30; *Fasti Archaeologici*, 12 (1959), no. 243 (includes Arkhanes).

KEPHALA (Khondrou Viannou): *To Ergon*, 1959, pp. 134-139.

KATSAMBA: *Kret. Chron.*, 9 (1955), pp. 558-559; *Praktika*, 1954, pp. 369-376; *Praktika*, 1955, pp. 311-320.

MONASTERAKI: Matz (ed.), *Forschungen auf Kreta*, Berlin, 1942, pp. 35-37.

PRASA: *Praktika*, 1951, pp. 246-257.

PSEIRA: Seager, *Excavations in the Island of Pseira, Crete*, Univ. of Pennsylvania, Anthrop. Publ. III, 1 (1910).

SITEIA and ZOU: *Kret. Chron.*, 9 (1955), p. 562; *Praktika*, 1954, pp. 361-368; *Praktika*, 1955, pp. 288-297.

ZAKROS: BSA, 7 (1900-1901), pp. 121-149.

Madame Wroncka has commenced an exhaustive listing of Minoan sites in Crete, *BCH*, 83 (1959), pp. 523-542 (eparchy of Siteia, with a detailed map).

ABBREVIATIONS

PERIODICALS

AA	*Archäologischer Anzeiger*
AJA	*American Journal of Archaeology*
Annuario	*Annuario della R. Scuola Archeologica di Atene*
Ath. Mitt.	*Athenische Mitteilungen*
BCH	*Bulletin de correspondence hellénique*
BSA	*Annual of the British School of Archaeology at Athens*
Ephemeris	Ἀρχαιολογικὴ Ἐφημερίς
JHS	*Journal of Hellenic Studies*
Kret. Chron.	Κρητικὰ Χρονικά
Mon. Piot	*Monuments et Mémoires Piot*
Op. Arch.	*Opuscula Archaeologica*
PdP	*Parola del Passato*
Praktika	Πρακτικὰ τῆς Ἀρχαιολογικῆς Ἑταιρείας
RA	*Revue archéologique*
REA	*Revue des études anciennes*
To Ergon	Τὸ Ἔργον τῆς Ἀρχαιολογικῆς Ἑταιρείας

MISCELLANEOUS

A. of C.	Pendlebury, J. D. S., *Archaeology of Crete*, London, 1939.
C. and M.	Marinatos and Hirmer, *Crete and Mycenae*, New York, 1960.
DMG	Ventris and Chadwick, *Documents in Mycenaean Greek*, Cambridge, 1956.
Guida	Pernier and Banti, *Guida degli scavi italiani in Creta*, Rome, 1947.
Guide[2]	Platon, *A Guide to the Archaeological Museum of Heraclion*, 2nd ed., Heraclion, 1957.
KMT	Matz, *Kreta, Mykene, Troja*, Stuttgart, 1957.
Minoica	Grumach, editor, *Minoica, Festschrift zum 80. Geburtstag von Johannes Sundwall*, Berlin, 1958.
MMR[2]	Nilsson, *Minoan-Mycenaean Religion*, 2nd ed., Lund, 1950.

PRINCIPAL SITES

Alalakh	Woolley, *Alalakh*, Oxford, 1955.
Festòs, I	Pernier, *Il Palazzo Minoico di Festòs*, I, Roma, 1935.
Festòs, II	Pernier and Banti, *Il Palazzo Minoico di Festòs*, II, Roma, 1951.
Gournia	Hawes, and others, *Gournia*, Philadelphia, 1908.
Knossos, I-IV	Evans, *The Palace of Minos at Knossos*, vols. I-IV (in six) and Index volume, London, 1921-1936.
Mallia, I	Chapouthier and Charbonneaux, *Fouilles exécutées à Mallia, premier rapport (1922-1924)*, Paris, 1928.
Mallia, II	Chapouthier and Joly, *Fouilles*, etc., *deuxième rapport, exploration du palais (1925-1926)*, Paris, 1936.
Mallia, III	Chapouthier and Demargne, *Fouilles*, etc., *troisième rapport, exploration du palais bordures orientale et septentrionale (1927, 1928, 1931, 1932)*, Paris, 1942.
Mallia, Maisons, I	Demargne and Santerre, *Fouilles*, etc., *exploration des maisons et quartiers d'habitation (1921-1948), premier fascicule*, Paris, 1953.
Mallia, Maisons, II	Deshayes and Dessenne, *Fouilles*, etc., *Exploration des maisons et quartiers d'habitation (1948-1954), deuxième fascicule*, Paris, 1960.
Mari, II	Parrot, *Mission archéologique de Mari*, II, *Le Palais*, Paris, 1958.
Mochlos	Seager, *Explorations in the Island of Mochlos*, Boston and New York, 1912.
Olynthus, VIII	Robinson and Graham, *Excavations at Olynthus*, VIII, *The Hellenic House*, Baltimore, 1938.
Palaikastro	British School at Athens, Supplementary Paper No. 1, *The Unpublished Objects from the Palaikastro Excavations 1902-1906*, Part I, London, 1923.
Phylakopi	Society for the Promotion of Hellenic Studies, Supplementary Paper No. 4, *Excavations at Phylakopi in Melos*, London, 1904.
Tylissos	Hazzidakis, *Les Villas minoennes de Tylissos*, Paris, 1934.

ILLUSTRATIONS:

SOURCES, CREDITS, DIMENSIONS

1. Drawn for *Palaces of Crete* by W. S. Schoonhoven.
2. *Knossos*, IV, p. xxvi; by permission Macmillan & Co.
3. Drawn by JWG.
4. Drawn by JWG, after *Festòs, Tavole*, pl. 2.
5. Drawn by JWG.
6. Drawn by JWG, after Chapouthier, *Deux épées d'apparat*, Paris, 1938, fig. 1.
7. Combination of Figs. 2, 4, 6.
8, 9. *Gournia*, plan, and fig. 10.
10. *Festòs*, I, fig. 8, by permission.
11. Drawn by JWG, detail after *Festòs*, I, fig. 8.
12. Drawn by JWG, after *Knossos*, I, fig. 239.
13. *Knossos*, II, fig. 318; by permission.
14. *Knossos*, II, fig. 227; by permission.
15. *Knossos*, II, fig. 208; by permission.
16. *Knossos*, II, fig. 224; by permission.
17. *Knossos*, I, fig. 306; by permission.
18. *Knossos*, II, fig. 251; by permission.
19, 20. *Tylissos*, pls. 6, 11.
21. Drawn for *Palaces of Crete* by Frances Brittain.
22. *Mallia, Maisons*, I, pl. 63; by permission.
23. Drawn by JWG, after *Mallia, Maisons*, II, plan 7.
24. *Mallia, Maisons*, II, plan 1; by permission.
25. *Mallia, Maisons*, I, pl. 66; by permission.
26. Drawn by JWG, detail of preceding.
27. *Mallia, Maisons*, II, plan 3; by permission.
28. *BSA, Supplement* I, pl. 1.
29. *BSA*, 8 (1901-1902), pl. 20.
30. Drawn by JWG, after *BSA*, 20 (1913-1914), pl. I.
31. *Knossos*, II, fig. 167; by permission.
32. Drawn by JWG, after *Ephemeris*, 1939-1941, p. 71, fig. 4.
33. Drawn by JWG, after Pendlebury, *A. of C.*, fig. 5.
34-42. Photos by JWG.

43. Mural in Royal Ontario Museum, by Sylvia Hahn, after *Knossos*, III, frontispiece; by permission R.O.M.
44, 45. Water-colors in Herakleion Museum; by permission of Piet de Jong and Nikolaos Platon.
46, 47. Photos by JWG.
48. Drawn by Frances Brittain for *Palaces of Crete*; after drawing by JWG, *AJA*, 60 (1956), pl. 59.
49. Photo by JWG.
50. Drawn by JWG, figures by Sylvia Hahn.
51–53. Photos by JWG.
54. *Knossos*, III, fig. 129; by permission.
55. Drawn by Prof. Hugo-Brunt for *Palaces of Crete*.
56, 57. Photos by JWG.
58. Drawn by Frances Brittain for *Palaces of Crete*, after a perspective by JWG.
59–80. Photos by JWG.
81. *Knossos*, III, fig. 255; by permission.
82. Photo by JWG.
83–90. Drawn by JWG; Fig. 86 after *Knossos*, II, plan C.
91. *Mallia*, III, pl. 1; by permission.
92. *Mallia*, III, pl. 14; by permission.
93. Photo by JWG.
94. Marinatos and Hirmer, *C. and M.*, fig. 62; by permission.
95, 96. Photos by JWG.
97. *Knossos*, II, fig. 235; by permission.
98, 99. Photos by JWG.
100, 101. *DMG*, fig. 15.
102. Photo by JWG.
103. Drawn by JWG, after *Knossos*, I, fig. 226, A, B.
104. Drawn by JWG, after: A) *Mallia*, II, fig. 12 B) *Festòs*, II, fig. 32 C) *Alalakh*, p. 118, fig. 48. Dimensions: A) 16 cm. diam. B) 11 cm. diam. C) not given.
105–107. Drawn by JWG.
108–111. Drawn by M. Hugo-Brunt.
112. Photos and model by JWG.
113A. Drawn by JWG, after *Knossos*, II, fig. 214.
   B. Drawn by JWG.
   C. Drawn by JWG, after Pendlebury, *Handbook*, plan 8.
114. Drawn by JWG.
115–128. Photos by JWG.
129. Drawn by JWG.
130. *Knossos*, IV, Part II, frontispiece; by permission.

131A. *Knossos*, I, fig. 311; by permission.
    B. *Knossos*, II, pl. 12; by permission.
132. *Knossos*, I, fig. 393; by permission.
133. *Knossos*, III, pl. 16; by permission.
134. *Knossos*, I, fig. 391; by permission.
135. Photo by JWG.
136. Drawn by JWG. A) Tomb of Clytemnestra, Bossert, *The Art of Ancient Crete*, fig. 24. B) From *Knossos*, II, fig. 368. C) From *Knossos*, III, fig. 35. D) From *Knossos*, I, fig. 226, I. EFK) From Grandstand Fresco, see Fig. 133. GH) *Archaeology*, 7 (1954), p. 152. I) Wace, *Mycenae*, figs. 49-51. J) *Knossos*, III, fig. 209. L) H. Triadha Boxer Vase, *Knossos*, I, fig. 508.
137, 138. Photos by JWG.
139. Drawn by JWG. A) From *Knossos*, III, fig. 173. BC) From *DMG*, fig. 23. D) *Knossos*, IV, fig. 890. E) See Fig. 101. F) *Knossos*, IV, fig. 899. G) *Knossos*, IV, pl. 31. H) *C. and M.*, fig. 207; *Knossos*, IV, fig. 329. I) *DMG*, p. 234. Dimensions: A) Length of each section, 70 cm. BC) Each 36 cm. long. D) Total ht. 1.38 m. F) Length 55 cm., ht. 13 cm.
140. Drawn by JWG. A) *Knossos*, II, fig. 401. B) *BSA, Suppl.* I, pl. 28F, fig. 112, 1. C) *Knossos*, I, fig. 424. D) *Archaeologia*, 9 (1905), p. 398, fig. 3b. E) *ibid.*, p. 439, fig. 46. F) *Knossos*, II, fig. 398, a. G) *Mallia, Maisons*, II, pl. 17, 2. H) *Knossos*, II, fig. 398. I) *DMG*, fig. 16. J) *Knossos*, III, fig. 14. K) *Knossos*, II, fig. 392. Dimensions (where available): B) Length ca. 13 cm. C) Length 1.45 m. D) Similar one 95 cm. long. E) Ht. 15 cm. G) Diam. 19.3 cm. K) Ht. 19.3 cm.
141. Drawn by JWG. A) *Mallia, Maisons*, I, pl. 39, 1, 2. B) *BSA*, 9 (1902-1903), p. 325, fig. 25. C) *Knossos*, II, fig. 178. D) *BSA, Suppl.* I, p. 73, fig. 58c. E) *Festòs*, II, fig. 232. F) *Knossos*, II, fig. 176, A. G) *Gournia*, pl. 2, no. 70. H) *Mallia, Maisons*, I, pl. 30, fig. 5. I) *ibid.*, pl. 30, fig. 2. J) *Knossos*, III, fig. 186. K) *BSA, Suppl.* I, p. 73, fig. 58. L) *Mallia, Maisons*, I, pl. 30, fig. 2. M) *Mallia*, III, fig. 28. Dimensions (where available): A) Ht. 44 cm., top diam. 40 cm. B) Ht. ca. 24 cm. C) Diam. 25 cm. D) Length 37.5 cm. G) Diam. ca. 24 cm. H) Ht. ca. 16 cm. I) Ht. ca. 13 cm. J) Ht. ca. 18 cm. K) Ht. 12.5 cm. L) Ht. ca. 18 cm. M) Ht. 15 cm.
142. A–H drawn by JWG; I) from *Knossos*, II, fig. 403, by permis-

sion. A) *AJA*, 13 (1909), p. 287, fig. 10. B) *Knossos*, II,
fig. 394. C) *Knossos*, II, fig. 396. DE) *Knossos*, II, fig. 398.
F) *Knossos*, II, fig. 400. G) *Knossos*, II, fig. 355. H) *Knossos*,
II, fig. 398. Dimensions (where available): A) Diam. 31 cm.
B) Diam. ca. 45 cm. C) Diam. ca. 18 cm. G) Diam. 1.40 m.;
wt. 52.564 kg. I) Diam. ca. 39 cm.

143. Drawn by JWG. A) *Festòs*, II, fig. 171. B) *Knossos*, II,
fig. 398, n. C) *Knossos*, IV, pl. 31. D) *Mochlos*, fig. 31. E)
Knossos, I, fig. 435. F) *C. and M.*, fig. 178-185. G) *Festòs*,
II, fig. 46. H) *Mallia*, III, fig. 24. Dimensions (where available):
D) Diam. 11.5 cm. F) Ht. ca. 8 cm. G) Ht. 43 cm. H) Diam.
ca. 55 cm.

144-146. Drawn by JWG.

147. *Archaeology*, 7 (1954), p. 18 fig. 3; by permission.

148. Parrot, *Mari* (Paris, 1953), plan 3; by permission.

149. Smith, E. B., *Eg. Arch.*, pl. 71; by permission.

150. Drawn by JWG.

151. Photos and model by JWG, scale of model 1 : 40; figure by
Sylvia Hahn.

152. Photo by JWG.

153ABC. Drawn by JWG.

154. Photo by JWG.

Special acknowledgements should be made to the following: to M.
Georges Daux, Director of the French School of Archaeology at Athens
for kind permission to reproduce Figs. 22, 24, 25, 27, 91, and 92 from
the *Mallia* publications; to Nikolaos Platon and Piet de Jong for Figs. 44
and 45 (drawn by the latter under the supervision of the former); to
M. André Parrot and the Librairie Orientaliste Paul Geuthner, Paris,
for permission to reproduce Fig. 148; and to the Istituto Poligrafico
dello Stato, Libreria dello Stato, Roma, for permission to reproduce Fig.
8 from *Palazzo Minoico di Festòs*, vol. I (riproduzione autorizzata dall'-
Istituto Nazionale di Archeologia e Storia dell'Arte, Roma); to Hirmer
Verlag, Munich, for permission to reproduce Fig. 94; to the Cambridge
University Press for permission to reproduce Figs. 100, 101; and to
Macmillan & Co. Ltd. for permission to reproduce Figs. 2, 13-18, 31,
54, 81, 97, 130, 131A, 131B, and 132-134. The following figures
have appeared in my articles in the *AJA* and by kind permission are here
reproduced, some in somewhat altered form, and two redrawn (Figs.
48, 50): Fig. 4, *AJA* 64 (1960), pl. 96, fig. 10; Fig. 11, *AJA* 63
(1959), pl. 16, fig. 3; Fig. 12, *AJA* 63 (1959), pl. 16, fig. 2; Fig.

48, *AJA* 60 (1956), pl. 59, fig. 4; Fig. 50, *AJA* 61 (1957), pl. 79, fig. 14; Fig. 52, *AJA* 61 (1957), pl. 79, fig. 10; Fig. 83, *AJA* 64 (1960), pl. 93, fig. 3; Fig. 84, *AJA* 64 (1960), pl. 94, fig. 5; Fig. 85, *AJA* 64 (1960), pl. 97, fig. 12; Fig. 86, *AJA* 64 (1960), pl. 97, fig. 13; Fig. 87, *AJA* 65 (1961), pl. 62, fig. 4; Fig. 88, *AJA* 65 (1961), pls. 62, 63, figs. 6, 8; Fig. 89, *AJA* 65 (1961), pl. 63, fig. 7; Fig. 90, *AJA* 65 (1961), pl. 61, fig. 3; Fig. 99, *AJA* 65 (1961), pl. 64, fig. 11; Fig. 144, *AJA* 64 (1960), pl. 95, fig. 7; Fig. 145, *AJA* 64 (1960), pl. 95, fig. 8; Fig. 146, *AJA* 64 (1960), pl. 96, fig. 9.

INDEX

Bold-faced type is used for principal discussions where the references are numerous.

PLATES

LIST OF SITES

1. APODHOULOU
2. H. TRIADHA
3. PHAISTOS
4. GORTYN
5. KAMARES CAVE
6. SKLAVOKAMBOS

7. TYLISSOS
8. PRASA, KATSAMBA
9. KNOSSOS
10. ARKHANES
11. VATHYPETRO
12. KANLI KASTELLI
13. AMNISOS

14. NIROU KHANI
15. MALLIA
16. PLATI
17. KEPHALA
18. GOURNIA
19. VASILIKI
20. PSEIRA

21. MOCHLOS
22. SITEIA
23. ZOU
24. PALAIKASTRO
25. ZAKROS
26. MONASTIRAKI

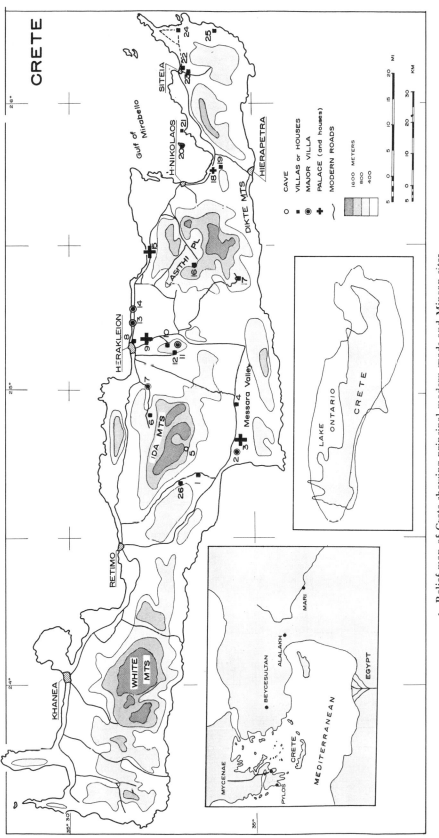

1. Relief map of Crete showing principal modern roads and Minoan sites

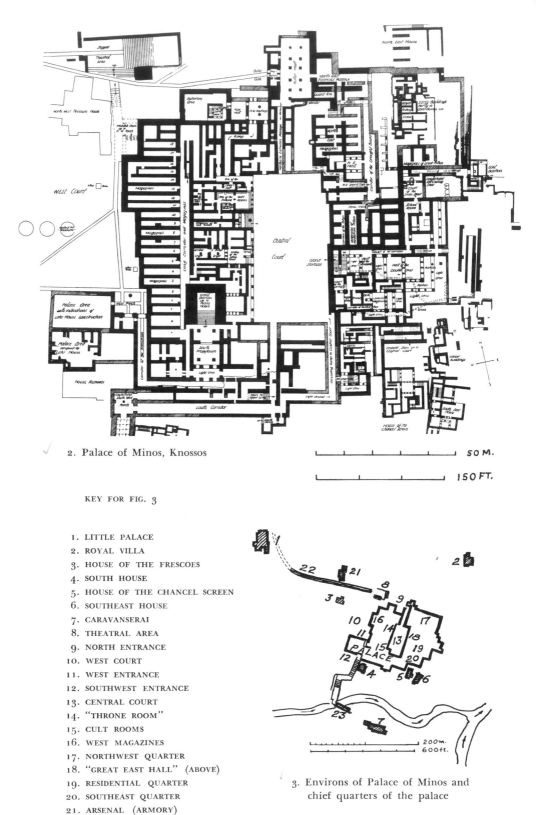

2. Palace of Minos, Knossos

50 M.

150 FT.

KEY FOR FIG. 3

1. LITTLE PALACE
2. ROYAL VILLA
3. HOUSE OF THE FRESCOES
4. SOUTH HOUSE
5. HOUSE OF THE CHANCEL SCREEN
6. SOUTHEAST HOUSE
7. CARAVANSERAI
8. THEATRAL AREA
9. NORTH ENTRANCE
10. WEST COURT
11. WEST ENTRANCE
12. SOUTHWEST ENTRANCE
13. CENTRAL COURT
14. "THRONE ROOM"
15. CULT ROOMS
16. WEST MAGAZINES
17. NORTHWEST QUARTER
18. "GREAT EAST HALL" (ABOVE)
19. RESIDENTIAL QUARTER
20. SOUTHEAST QUARTER
21. ARSENAL (ARMORY)
22. "ROYAL ROAD"
23. VIADUCT

3. Environs of Palace of Minos and chief quarters of the palace

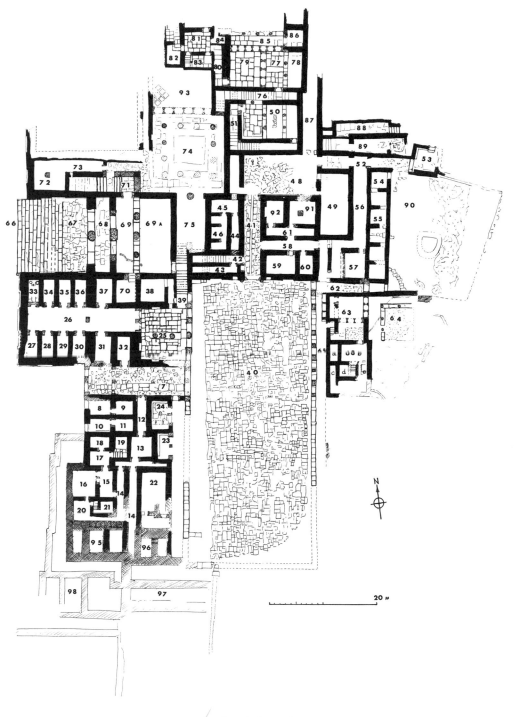

4. Last Palace of Phaistos

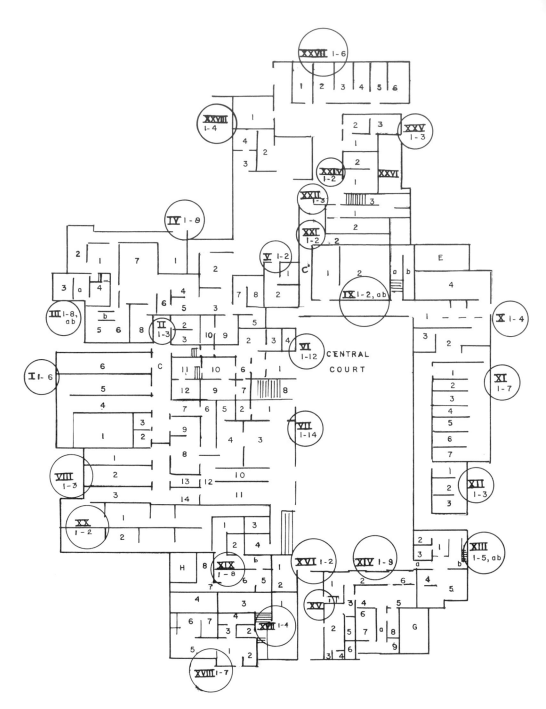

5. Key to plan of Palace of Mallia

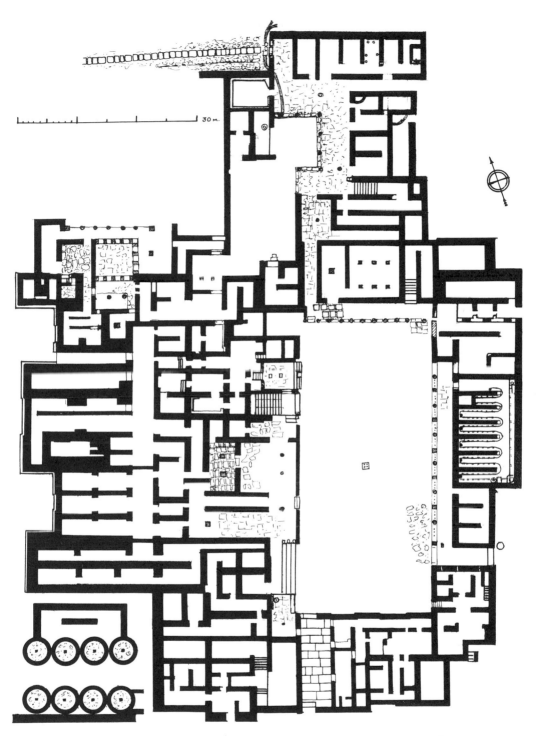

√6. Palace of Mallia

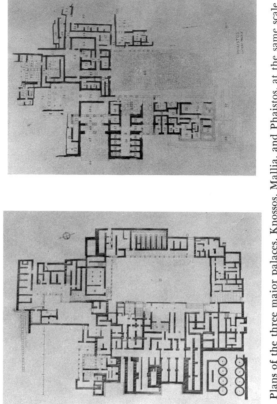

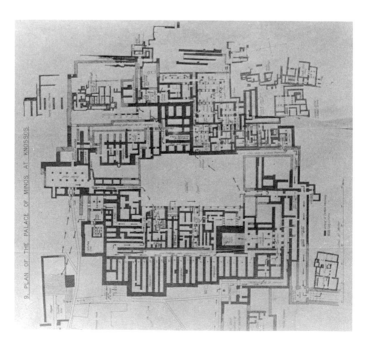

7. Plans of the three major palaces, Knossos, Mallia, and Phaistos, at the same scale
(See Figs. 2, 6, 4, for enlargements)

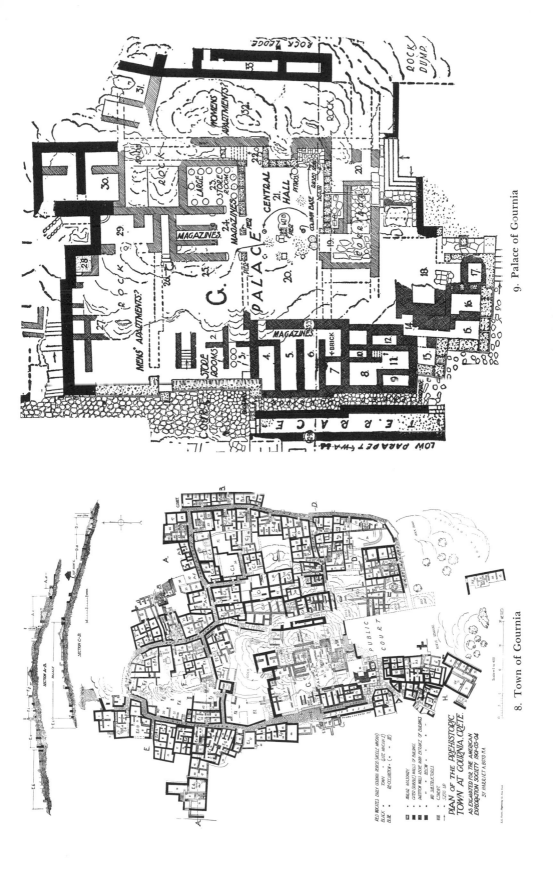

9. Palace of Gournia

8. Town of Gournia

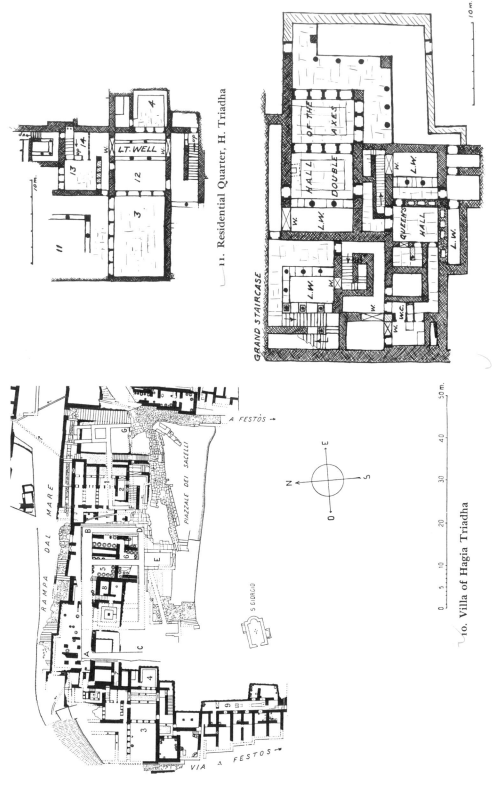

11. Residential Quarter, H. Triadha

12. Residential Quarter, Palace of Minos. North at top

10. Villa of Hagia Triadha

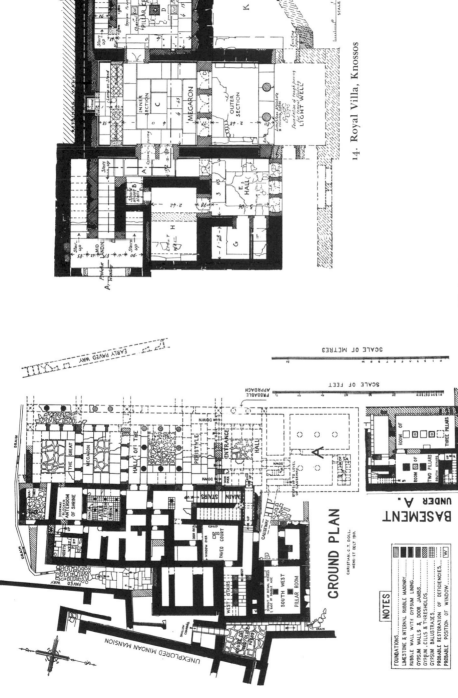

14. Royal Villa, Knossos

13. Little Palace, Knossos

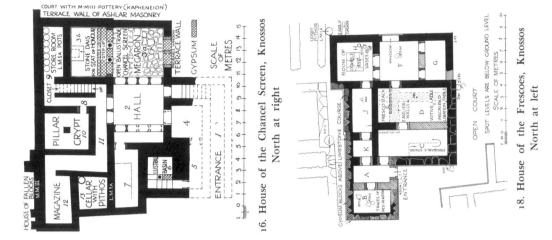

16. House of the Chancel Screen, Knossos
North at right

18. House of the Frescoes, Knossos
North at left

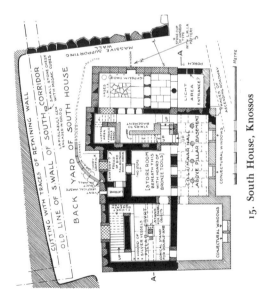

15. South House, Knossos

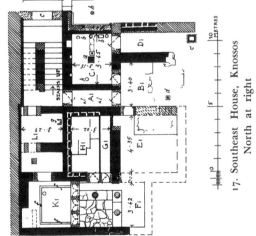

17. Southeast House, Knossos
North at right

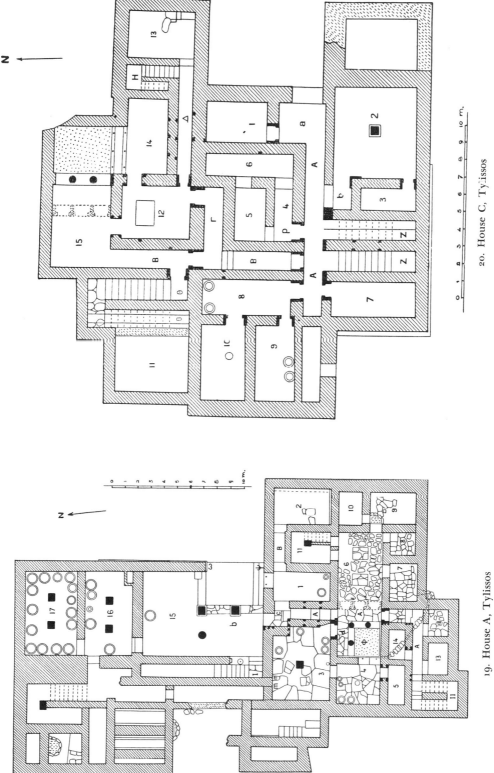

20. House C, Ty·issos

19. House A, Tylissos

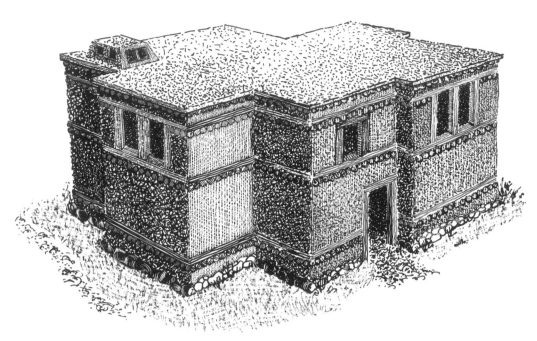

21. Restoration of House Da, Mallia, from northwest

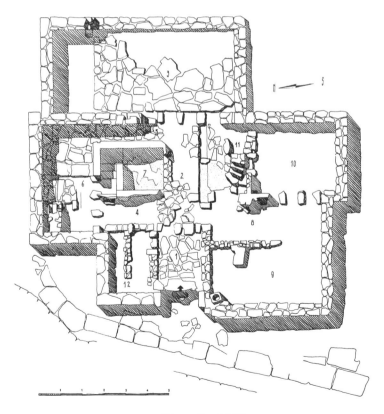

22. House Da, Mallia

23. House E, Mallia (simplified plan)

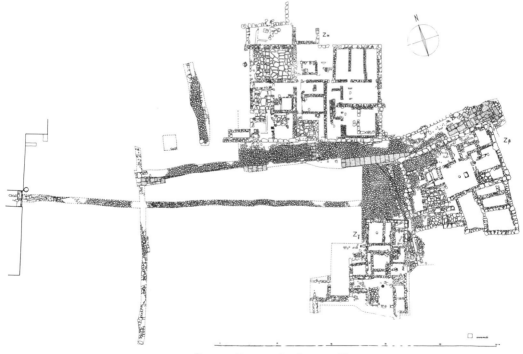

24. Quarter Z, east of palace, Mallia

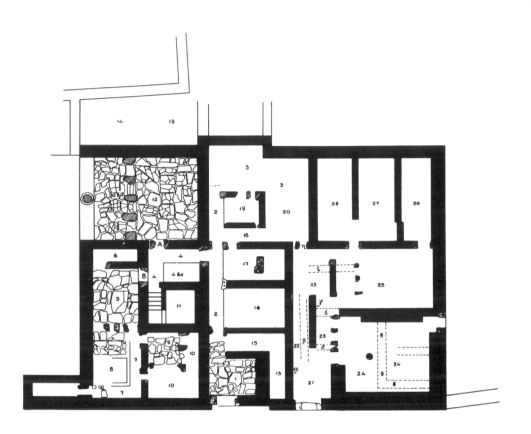

25. House Za, Mallia

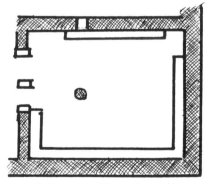

26. Room 24, House Za, Mallia

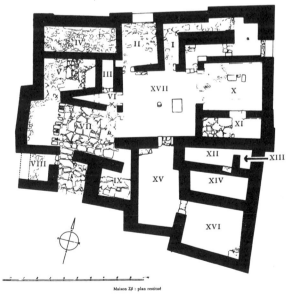

Maison Zβ : plan restitué

27. House Zb, Mallia

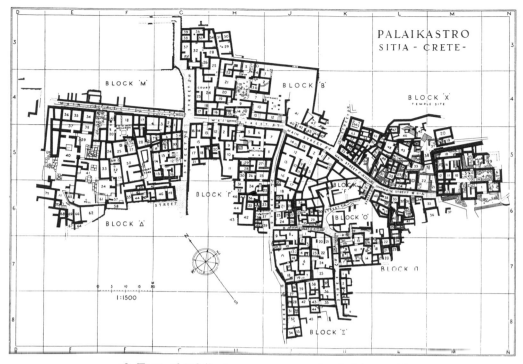

28. Town of Palaikastro; squares 20 m. (ca. 65 ft.) to a side

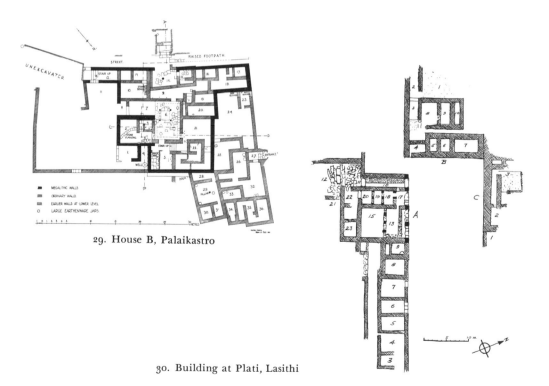

29. House B, Palaikastro

30. Building at Plati, Lasithi

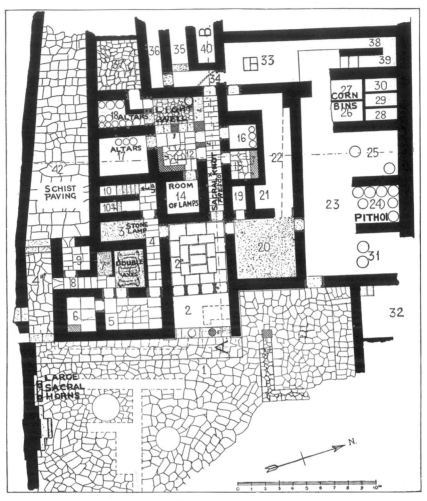

31. House at Nirou Khani

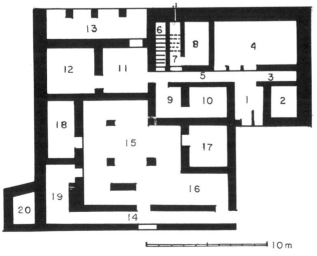

32. House at Sklavokambos. North at top

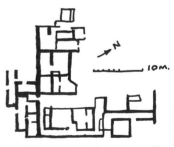

33. House of Early Minoan II
period, Vasiliki

34. White Mountains and river in west Crete

35. Mountains and Gulf of Mirabello west of Gournia

36. View from hill east of Knossos: a) Palace of Minos b) Royal Villa
c) Little Palace d) New Hospital e) Herakleion

37. Palace of Minos from hill to east (telephoto)

38. Grand Staircase of Residential Quarter, Knossos

39. Hall of Double-axes from light-well, Knossos

40. North Pillar Hall, Knossos, from southwest

41. Theatral Area, Knossos, from northwest

42. Restored South Propylon, Knossos, from southeast

43. Queen's Hall in Palace of Minos, painting in Royal Ontario Museum

44. Restoration of west side of Central Court, Knossos,
by Piet de Jong under supervision of Nikolaos Platon

45. Restoration of east end of Hall of the Double-axes,
by Piet de Jong under supervision of Nikolaos Platon

46. Palace of Phaistos and Messara Valley from northwest

47. North Residential Quarter, Phaistos, from southeast

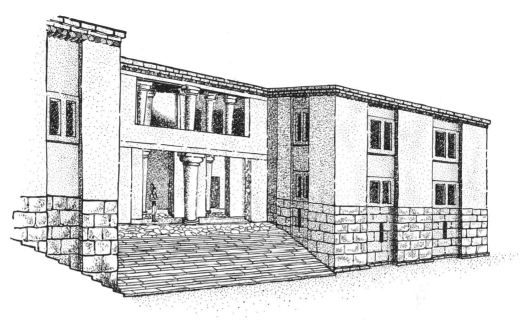

48. Restoration of Grand Propylon, Phaistos, from northwest

49. West Court and main entrance of Palace of Phaistos, from the west

50. Restoration of north end of Central Court, Phaistos, from southeast

51. Central Court and range of Ida from south, Phaistos

53. Niche and half-column west of Corridor 41, Phaistos

54. Minoan gem with scene from bull games

52. Northwest corner of Central Court, Phaistos

55. Palace of Phaistos from southwest, axonometric restoration

56. Site of Mallia from south (telephoto): palace in middle ground, Chrysolakkos necropolis near sea

57. Central Court of Palace of Mallia from northwest; modern shed over East Magazines at left

58. Palace of Mallia from northwest, perspective restoration

60. Stairs xxii 2 from west, Palace of Mallia

62. Granary at southwest corner of Palace of Mallia

59. Rooms ix 1 and 2 from northwest, Palace of Mallia

61. Circular stone with cups at southwest corner of
Central Court, Palace of Mallia

63. Site of Gournia and Mirabello Bay from southeast

64. Little Palace, Knossos, from southwest

65. H. Triadha and view toward Ida, from south

66. Villa of H. Triadha from northeast

67. South wall of Room 3, H. Triadha

68. Queen's Hall from southeast, H. Triadha

69. Room 4 from west, H. Triadha

70. Light-well and window, Room 12, from northwest, H. Triadha

71. South House from southwest, Knossos

72. East half of South House from north, Knossos

73. Staircase of Royal Villa from south, Knossos

74. Balustrade in Hall (C) of Royal Villa, Knossos

75. Main Hall (2) from east, Nirou Khani

76. Villa of the Lilies from west, Amnisos

77. Hall with light-well and window from northwest,
House C, Tylissos

78. Exterior wall west of Hall, House C, Tylissos

79. Drain from toilet, House C, Tylissos

80. Southeast House from southeast, Knossos

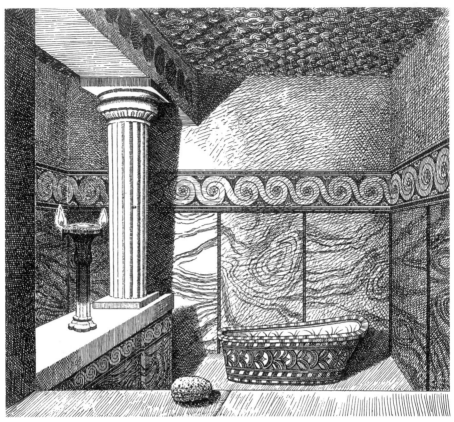

81. Restoration of bathroom in Residential Quarter, Knossos

82. Bathroom and Queen's Hall in North Residential Quarter from south, Phaistos

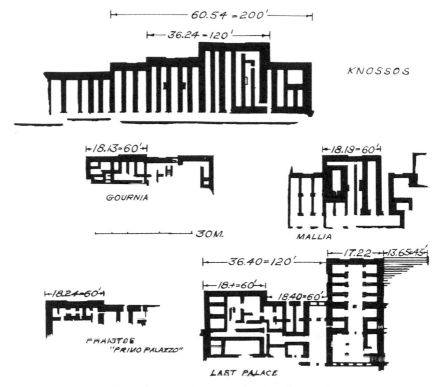

83. Plans of rooms along west façades of five palaces

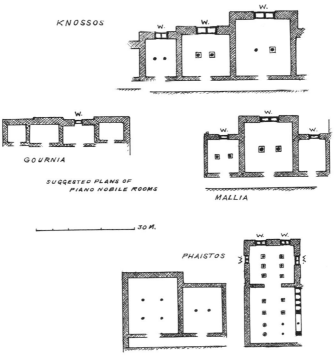

84. Conjectural plans of second floor rooms along west façades of four palaces

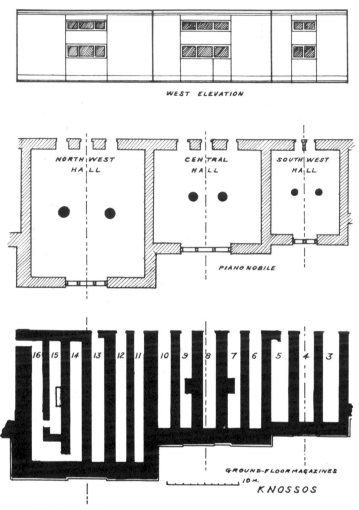

WEST ELEVATION

NORTH WEST HALL · CENTRAL HALL · SOUTH WEST HALL

PIANO NOBILE

16 15 14 13 12 11 10 9 8 7 6 5 4 3

GROUND-FLOOR MAGAZINES
10 M.
KNOSSOS

85. Ground floor, conjectural plan of second floor, and restored elevation of part of west façade, Knossos

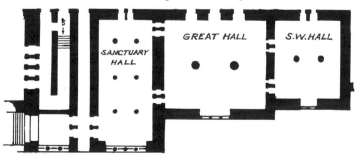

SANCTUARY HALL · GREAT HALL · S.W. HALL

86. Evans' conjectural plan of second floor of same area

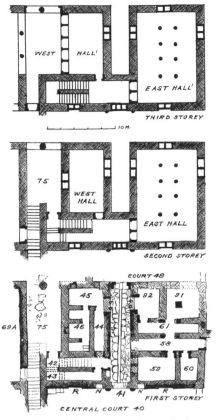

WEST HALL'

EAST HALL'

THIRD STOREY

10 M.

75

WEST HALL

EAST HALL

SECOND STOREY

COURT 48

69A   75   45   92   91

46   44   61

58

42   59   60

43

R   N   41   N   R   FIRST STOREY

CENTRAL COURT 40

87. Ground floor and conjectural plans
of upper floors north of
Central Court, Phaistos

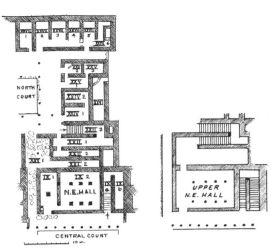

1 2 3 4 5 6

XII

NORTH
COURT

XX

XXIV 2

XIX

XVIII 1

XXII 3

XXIII 1

XVII 2

XVI

XXI 1

XV

IX 1   IX 2   IX
N.E. HALL   a   b

CENTRAL COURT
10 m.

UPPER
N.E. HALL

88. Ground floor and conjectural plan of upper
floor north of Central Court, Mallia

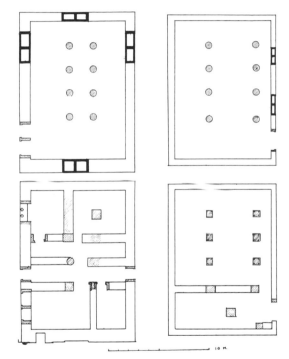

89. Conjectural plans of Banquet Halls at Phaistos
(left) and Mallia (right) at same scale

10 M.

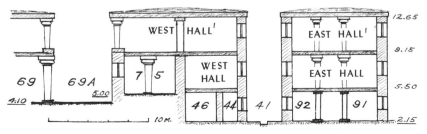

WEST HALL'   EAST HALL'   12.65

9.15

WEST
HALL   EAST HALL   5.50

69   69A   7 5

4.10   5.00   46   44   41   92   91   2.15

10 M.

90. Conjectural east-west section north of Central Court, Phaistos

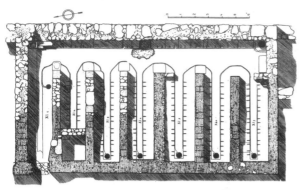

91. East Magazines, Palace of Mallia

92. Pithos from Mallia

93. West Magazines, Palace of Minos

94. Wine press, Vathypetro

95. Pillar Crypt (vii 4) from southeast, Mallia

96. Room 23 from southeast, Phaistos

97. Pillar Crypt of Royal Villa, Knossos, restored
view from northeast

98. South pillar in vii 4 from
northeast, Mallia

100. Scene from H. Triadha Sarcophagus: offerings

102. Figurine of bull in terracotta from Pseira

99. Niche in wall of Room 46. Phaistos

101. Scene from H. Triadha Sarcophagus: bull sacrifice

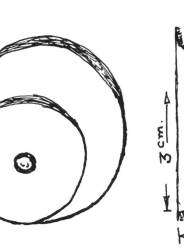

104. Three door-pivot caps: A. from Mallia
B. from Phaistos C. from Alalakh, Syria

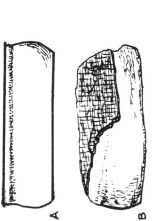

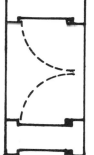

106. Threshold in Hall of
Double-axes, Knossos

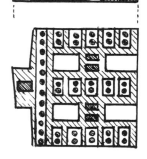

103. Two houses from Town Mosaic, Knossos

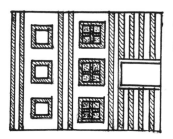

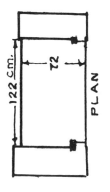

105. Threshold of Room 22,
Phaistos

107. Pivot-hole in threshold of
Room iv 3, Palace of Mallia

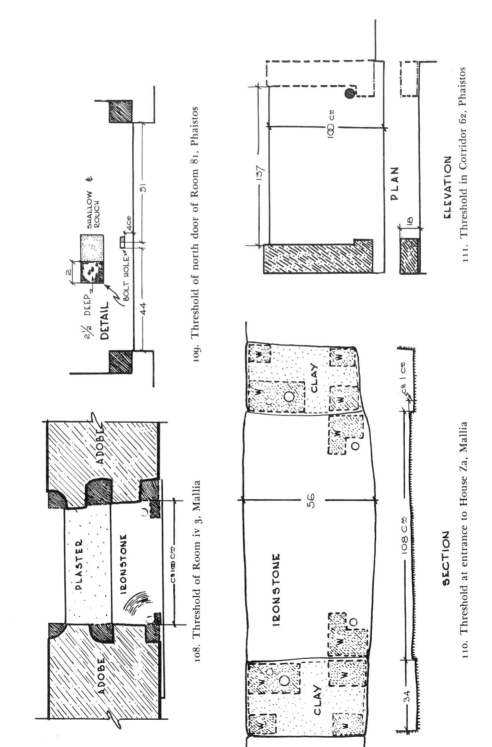

109. Threshold of north door of Room 81, Phaistos

111. Threshold in Corridor 62, Phaistos

108. Threshold of Room iv 3, Mallia

110. Threshold at entrance to House Za, Mallia

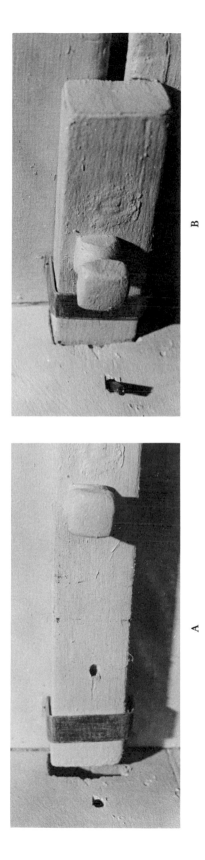

B

A

D

C

112. Four views of model of lock to basement room, South House, Knossos

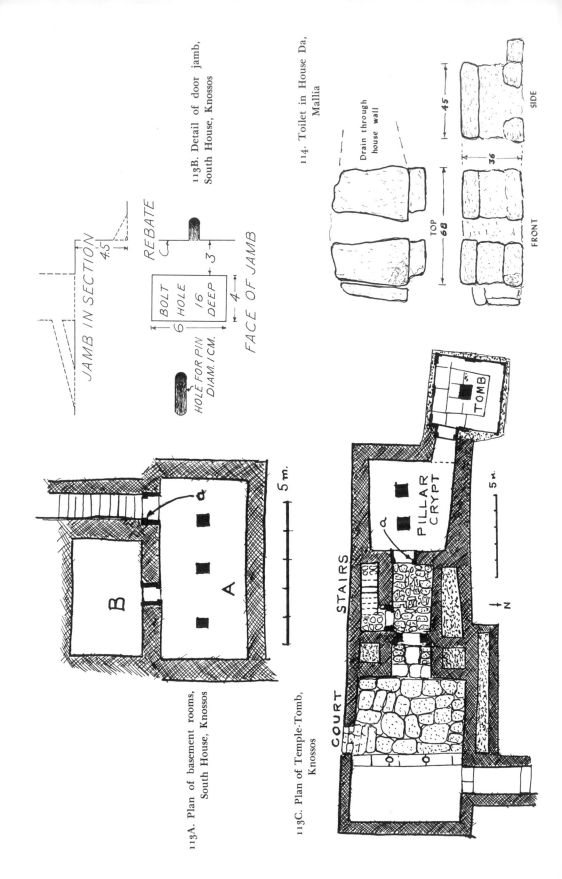

REBATE

JAMB IN SECTION

4.5

BOLT HOLE 16 DEEP

6

4

3

HOLE FOR PIN
DIAM. I CM.

FACE OF JAMB

113B. Detail of door jamb,
South House, Knossos

114. Toilet in House Da,
Mallia

Drain through
house wall

45

SIDE

68

TOP

36

FRONT

B

A

α

5 m.

113A. Plan of basement rooms,
South House, Knossos

TOMB

PILLAR
CRYPT

α

STAIRS

COURT

N

5 m.

113C. Plan of Temple-Tomb,
Knossos

115. Base in Magazine 15 from west, Palace of Minos

116. Restored Central Hall from southeast, Palace of Minos

117. Eroded gypsum base, Southeast House, Knossos

18. Construction of west orthostate wall, Palace of Minos

119. Tiny mason's mark, Phaistos

120. Chisel strokes on wall block, Phaistos

121. Stuccoing of wall blocks, Phaistos

122. Recess in north façade of Central Court, Phaistos

124. Present day house in Delphi, Greece

126. Room 93 and Peristyle 74 from northwest, Phaistos

123. Bases with mortises, H. Triadha

125. Gypsum quarry near H. Triadha

127. Alabaster floor of Room 79, Phaistos

128. Flagged West Court from north, Knossos

129. Diagrams of wall decoration:
A. House of Frescoes, Knossos
B. Room 71, Phaistos
C. Magazine 12, Knossos

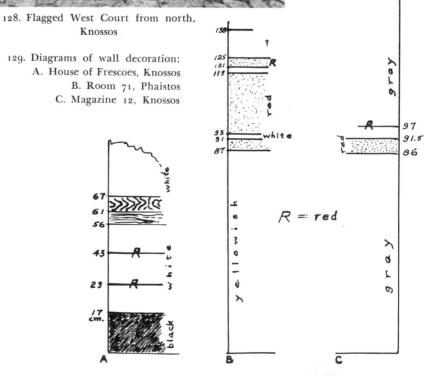

130. Restored Throne Room, Knossos

131A. "La petite Parisienne," Palace of Minos

131B. The Cupbearer, Palace of Minos

132. Flying Fish Fresco, Melos

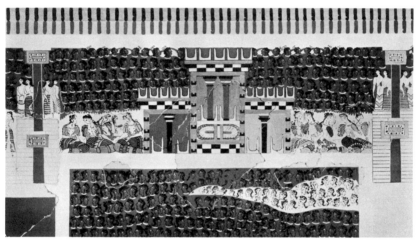

133. Grandstand Fresco, Knossos

134. Cat and Bird Fresco,
H. Triadha

135. Detail of Lion Gate, Mycenae

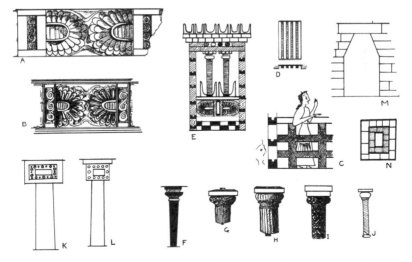

136. VARIOUS ARCHITECTURAL DETAILS: A. Half-rosette frieze, Mycenae   B. Half-rosette frieze, Knossos   C. Fresco fragment, Knossos   D. Door, Town Mosaic detail   E. Detail of Tripartite Shrine, Grandstand Fresco   F. Column from same   GH. Ivory column fragments, Mycenae   I. Treasury of Atreus half-column, detail   J. Spiral column, gem   KL. Rectangular capitals from Grandstand Fresco and Boxer Cup   M. Tomb doorway, Knossos   N. Floor pattern, Room 79, Phaistos

137. Horizontal curvature in Stairway 66, Phaistos, from west

138. Stairways 66 and 6 from south, Phaistos

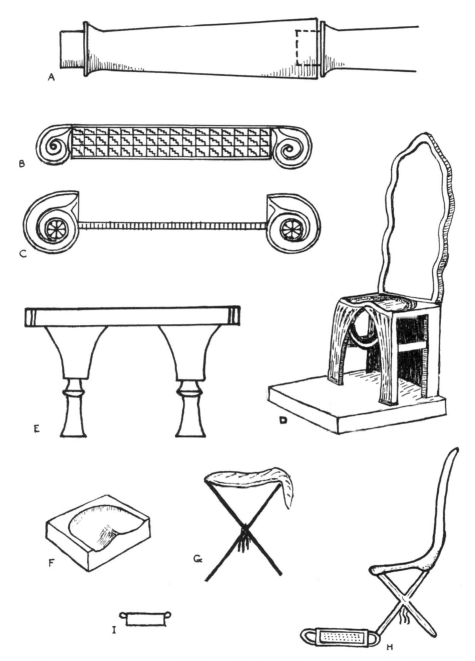

139. MINOAN PIPE AND FURNITURE: A. Terracotta pipe sections BC. Ivory appliqué for footstools (?) D. Wooden throne, based on Knossos stone throne E. Table from H. Triadha
Sarcophagus F. Stone seat, Knossos G. Folding stool, fresco detail, Knossos H. Chair and
footstool, gem I. Footstool, Linear B ideogram

140. VARIOUS FURNISHINGS: A. Bronze lamp B. Clay lamp C. Clay bathtub D. Clay sarcophagus in form of wooden chest E. Portable clay charcoal burner F. Clay tripod hearth
GJ. Stone lamps HK. Bronze tripods I. Linear B tripod ideograms

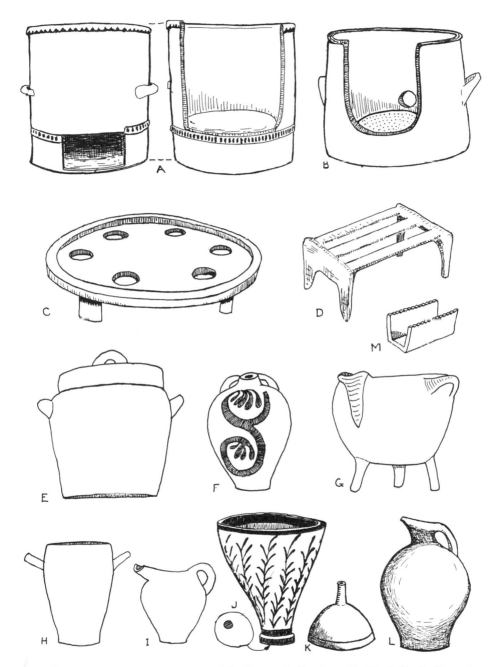

141. CLAY OBJECTS FOR COOKING, ETC.: AB. Ovens C. Egg tray (?) D. Grill E. Stewpot
F. Amphora G. Spouted tripod pot H. Two-handled jar IL. Pitchers J. Flower-pot
K. Funnel M. Spit support

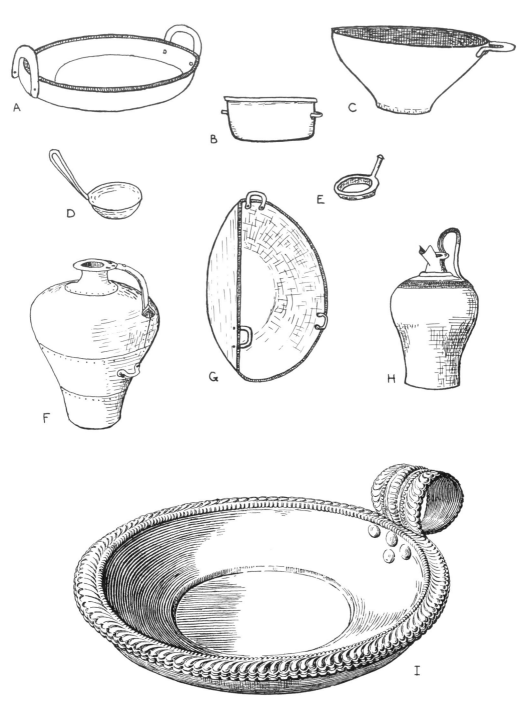

142. MINOAN BRONZE VESSELS: D. Ladle FH. Pitchers G. Large cauldron
I. Cup with fine cast detail

143. CLAY AND METAL OBJECTS: AE. Clay cups   BD. Bronze cups   C. Cup from Campstool
Fresco   F. Gold cup from Vaphio, near Sparta   G. Clay stool   H. Oil separator (clay)

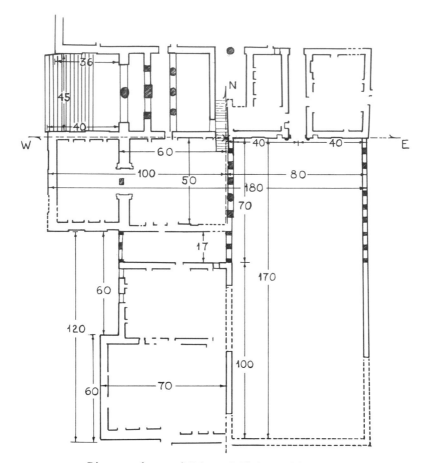

144. Diagram of part of Palace of Phaistos with dimensions
in round numbers of Minoan feet

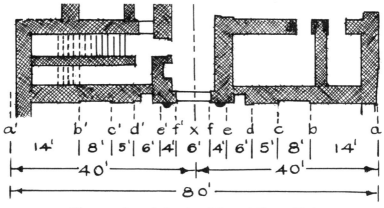

145. Diagram of north façade of Central Court, Phaistos,
with dimensions in Minoan feet

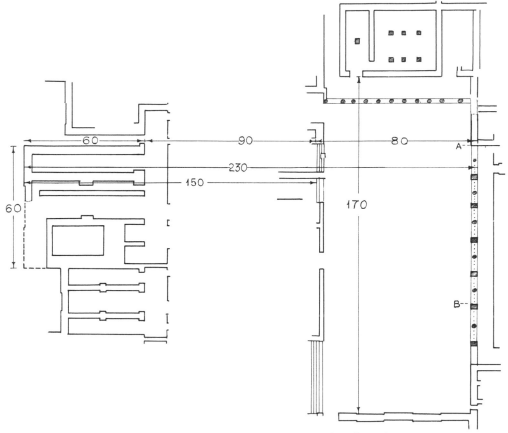

146. Diagram of part of Palace of Mallia with dimensions
in round numbers of Minoan feet

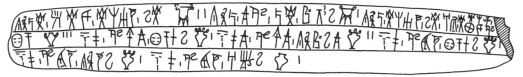

147. Linear B "Tripod Tablet" from Pylos

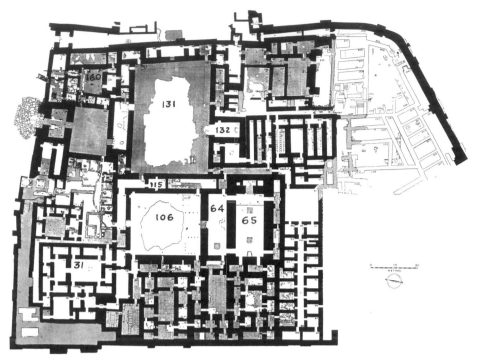

148. Palace of Mari on the Euphrates

149. North Palace at Amarna, Egypt

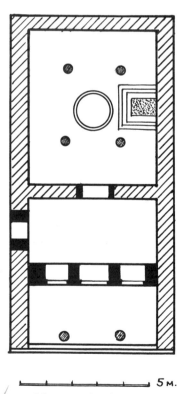

5 M.

150. Megaron of Palace of Tiryns, Greece

151. Four views of a model of a suite of rooms (3, 12, 4) in
Residential Quarter, H. Triadha. See Figs. 11, 69, and 70

152. Present day town in the Greek islands

154. Doorway in Residential Quarter, H. Triadha

A

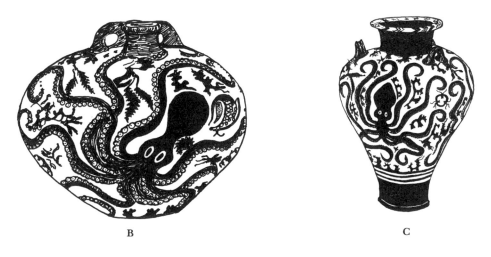

B   C

153. DECORATED POTTERY: A. Kamares vase, Middle Minoan II B. Stirrup jar from Gournia, Late Minoan Ib C. Amphora from Greek mainland, Late Helladic II